TO: Tom

James Kees Baughman

MW01047289

issued on northwest florida's magnificent emerald coast

an epic chronicle of america's

Civil War

Co. A, 73rd Indiana Volunteer Infantry Regiment

THE BOYS FROM
LAKE COUNTY

JAMES KEIR BAUGHMAN

The Boys From Lake County

(Soft Bound Edition)
ISBN: 0-9790443-5-9
ISBN-13: 978-0-9790443-5-9

(Hard Bound Edition)
ISBN: 0-9790443-4-0
ISBN-13: 978-0-9790443-4-2

Cover Painting
"Union Standard Bearer"
by Don Troiani
www.historicalartprints.com

Cover Layout & Design
Ashley Spears
AES Graphics

Contents

James Wilson Baughman Circa 1926

Dedication

I went to see what the years had wrought
'pon land that was home to me,
I went to see, and stood and thought
'bout the way things used to be.

Gone was the willow we loved so well
and so the aged cherry tree,
Gone were the chickens and goats and
ducks that had kept us company.

One timeworn henhouse unsteadily stood
where six had served us well,
No more were banks of the Union fort
where Richmond's road was held.

There was nothin' to mark a little dog's grave
long sheltered by weeping bough,
Tho' the cottage we called the 'little house' still
was in field seldom turn'd by the plow.

Grandfather's house stood firm and strong
fifty years upon the land,
evidence that man's devoted work
Ofttimes outlives the man.

I've often remembered the tall green corn,
the gentle curve of the lane,
and runnin' 'neath the summer sun,
the cool fresh'nin' rain.

I ponder'd long haired friends by name
and thousands of chickens fed,
pictured starlight and a cold black sky
'bove a warm winter bed.

I recall'd the smell of the mailman's car
the feel of bare feet on the ground,
and harken'd again to the whisper of trees
when wind came sighin' around.

Back then I flew the woodshed roof,
bailed out from henhouse eaves,
and sailed the shop on victorious jaunts
'cross fanciful World War seas.

I mused on silence that still'd the earth
when snow whiten'd the land,
and thawin' a frozen back porch pump
with mittened, freezin' hands.

I traced again the mile I'd walked
a thousand times before,
attendin' school or errand bound
to Varina's country store.

I went and found one thing unchang'd
in the midst of things that were gone,
with twenty-five years of bein' away
there still was the feel of home.

James Keir Baughman
Summer 1970

This book is dedicated to my Grandfather, James Wilson Baughman. He was born in Lowell, Indiana on July 10, 1871... the second child, the second son, of Private Wilson Shannon Baughman, Company A, 73rd Indiana Volunteer Infantry Regiment, and his wife Sarah Jane Corkings (Caulkins) Baughman.

When research was begun for this powerful story more than 20 years ago, I did not even know my Great-Grandfather's first name. Though a big, raw-boned outdoorsman, 6'2", 212 pounds, my grandfather was quite taciturn about many things... speaking little of his father or of his own growing years. In fact, it was surprising to learn from research sources that his father fought in America's Civil War.

James Wilson Baughman left home from Rothville, Missouri in 1888 when he was just 17, riding the famed transcontinental railroad - it had been in existence only 19 years then - to the Imperial Valley of California. Apparently, though he never said, he went to visit his mother's sister, his aunt, Catherine "Kate" Wilson Parks.

"I didn't stay out there too long, though," he said.

"Why...?" I asked.

"Well..." he pondered it a bit, "there was this widow. She was older than I was. Had four children, and she wanted me to marry her."

On his way back across our Nation, he stopped in Denver, Colorado. There, they were building a big conduit to bring fresh, mountain water into the city.

"I got a job driving a four mule team and wagon to haul Dynamite up into blasting sites in the mountains," he said, "but I didn't stay there too long either."

"Why...?" I asked.

"Well, Dynamite wasn't always very stabile then," he replied. "One day coming back down out of the mountains with that wagon and team, I got to thinking about what would happen if a load of Dynamite blew up. I just drove those mules with the wagon down into the depot, walked into the boss's shack..., and quit."

In 1917, thinking of retirement, James Wilson Baughman bought the 60 acre farm described in the verses above. The land lay in a community called Varina, 7 miles southeast of Richmond, Virginia. Varina is where the Indian maiden Pocohontas lived with her husband John Rolfe in the very early years of our Nation. It is also the community in which Thomas Jefferson's daughter Martha lived with her husband Thomas Mann Randolph, Jr on his 950 acre plantation soon after the formation of the United States of America. The history of our Country is such a major part of Richmond, Varina, and Virginia itself.

In an odd coincidence, there remained on the Baughman farm earthen banks and trenches of a Civil War Union fort built for one of the many battles against the Confederate capital city. In fact, a number of skirmishes as well as major battles of America's Civil War occurred within five miles of our farm. The road on which our land fronted is the old Williamsburg highway between that early capitol city and Richmond. I often wondered how many of our Nation's founders, in those beginning years, had passed by the land where we lived.

In 1922, inside the enclosure of that Union fort my Grandfather built the main house for the farm. Born in 1932, I grew up in a small, elderly, cottage already on the farm, amid five acres of fields abutting the fort.

When I was near 12, long after grandfather had gone to Florida, where most of his immediate folks lived by then, our family moved into the "big" house inside the fort to care for grandmother in her latter years. So..., at least in the emotional sense, my link to America's Civil War is a palpable one. When we were children, my sister Jean and I often found Civil War bullets (Minie Balls) on the ground inside the Fort.

My grandfather's forebears seem to have been largely farmers... for generations. James Wilson Baughman chose a different course. At some point, relatively soon after leaving home, he became a millwright...a builder of sawmills. Following that profession all his working years, he developed the skills to become a Sawmill Engineer...selling sawmill equipment, contracting to boss the job of building the huge mills, installing heavy, steam powered, sawmill machinery.

In this work, he must have been a potent, if un-famed, force in building the America we know today. How much lumber those many sawmills must have cut to construct the homes, factories, and businesses that prospered our great Nation. In doing so he lived in, worked in, or passed through every one of the, then, 48 States as well as Canada.

For years he lived in Milwaukee, Wisconsin, working as a chief field operative with Filer-Stowell & Co., a leading sawmill machinery manufacturer. The company was begun about Civil War years, continuing far into the late 1900's.

In 1938, when I was six, my father and grandfather set about improving our small cottage. My father hand-built a water system and kitchen cabinets for the house, and had a much needed bathroom put in. Grandfather installed a small sawmill behind his house, run by a long belt from the power take-off on our big, iron wheeled, Fordson tractor. The two of them began building. It didn't cost much, except for nails and hardware. We owned about 50 acres of forest. The two of them provided the labor.

Trees were cut down with a two man cross cut saw. (If one yearns to learn about team work...there's no better place than pushing and pulling together in perfect unison with wooden hand holds on both ends of that big handsaw.) Then they snaked logs out of the forest with the tractor, rolled them onto the carriage of the bantam mill with hand held log rollers. The screaming saw blade, about 4' high, spewed out boards at a surprising rate.

Within a year or two they had built a big, two car, garage and work shop with high pitched roof containing a roomy, upstairs, storage loft. They also built a dozen or so chicken houses. So you see, grandfather's sawmill skills gave my father a back-up income in those lean times after the Great Depression. When civil engineering jobs ran out, we would simply turn to raising fryer chickens, and eggs. If you think I'm not an expert on feeding and watering chickens, cleaning chicken houses, and handling loads of chicken manure... think again.

James Wilson Baughman loved the big mountains and wide open spaces of America's west. In long sawmill management years with Filer-Stowell, he spent many of them in big sky country with, huffing, narrow gauge, steam railroads. He loved railroading just as well, and he clearly knew how to run the small railroad engines that were the workhorses of sawmill camps. When I was a child, he told me of personally running an engine up a nearby mountain in winter to rescue an inbound train and passengers stuck in a high mountain snowdrift.

In 1906 my grandfather built a sawmill in a village named El Vado, in the mountains of northern New Mexico. In 1998 when our brother Jeff found it, the little community of buildings had been under the waters of El Vado Lake since 1935. When the lake is drawn down, though, the top of a huge boiler, likely from the hundred year old sawmill, can still be seen.

In those years, grandfather said, Indians would come down out of the mountains and sit on the steps of his house, whittling with large knives on pieces of wood. Sometimes when the family was eating they would step up onto the porch, press noses against glass windows and watch. Emphasizing a wild west atmosphere we little understand today, he said the Indians played a macabre game. Two braves, astride horses, one holding a live chicken by one leg, would gallop toward each other. The purpose was for the facing Brave to grab the other leg, ripping the live chicken in two as horses galloped past each other.

In the early 1950's James Arness played the television role of fictional, western sheriff Matt Dillon, supposedly patterned after famous Sheriff Bat Masterson. Matt Dillon wore a big white Stetson hat, was very tall, had a fast draw, with long barreled pistols slung in holsters on both hips.

"Don't believe everything you see on TV," grandfather said. "I saw Sheriff Bat Masterson in Dodge City, Kansas. He was a good bit shorter, pot bellied, often unshaven, scruffy looking... and carried a shotgun."

From years in the outdoors of those rough sawmill camps, James Wilson Baughman was a man who lived close to the earth...in eloquent simplicity. When he was hatching eggs into chicks, the brooder, about the size of a small, short, refrigerator sat in his tiny bedroom, near his bed under watchful, 24 hour a day, care. It takes 21 days to hatch chicks.

His small house, painted a soothing shade of darker green, was sided with un-planed lumber, the living room inside never fully finished. On a pine tree outside hung a small round mirror with a minute table and wash basin underneath. Grandfather often shaved out there, in the open air of morning, when weather was mellow, a soft carpet of brown pine needles under his feet.

He walked across farm fields to our well for water. I can still watch him, in my minds eye, coming across a path in the fields, head down, two empty buckets swinging, his figure tall, big boned, lean, robust..., his hair gray, shaggy.

When I was near eight, there came an evening when the living room door in our cottage was perversely closed, the sound of loud, arguing voices, James Wilson Baughman and his son.

My father did not explain, until I was old enough to understand. It seems, though, that grandmother, still living in the "big" house inside the Civil War fort , had been pressing him for alimony. It was untenable. He was retired with little income. At the divorce she had gotten all the money, furnishings, and the house. He had given the rest of the farm to my father, except for the small plot where he built his own little house. Where would additional money have come from in those lean years?

Grandfather did not say goodbye. When morning came, we just found him gone...back to be near his siblings in St. Petersburg.

For many years Jean and I played in his small, empty house...rocked in the big rocking chair next to his bed...smelled the lingering scent of kerosene at his two burner cook stove ...touched oil cloth on the rough, home made, table where he had eaten meals. It was a place that kept his presence at the forefront of our minds.

With severe gas rationing during the four years of World War II, we did not make a trip to St. Petersburg to see Grandfather until I was about 14. The tiny home he built in that palm tree city was even more elemental. I never knew whether he planted the two grapefruit trees in his small front yard, or whether they had been in a grove subdivided for homes.

His life, though, was just as uncomplicated, natural. He drove, or rode a city bus, to the famous old downtown St. Petersburg pier and fished. His talk was of Florida, of that sunny city he had come to love, of Tallahassee, Senator Claude Pepper, his own siblings..and still of the great American west. In 1951, when we also came to Florida, we were able to visit more often with him, share the wild west travel and adventures of his life.

His business and building success, his accomplishments, his broad travels across America in frontier and railroad days lasted 38 years , from the time he was 17, until he chose to retire at 55.

James Wilson Baughman was blessed, then, with 30 years of retirement, by far most of it in robust health. In that wonderful span of time, he endured limited financial resources ...mainly because he had given most everything he owned to his ex-wife and son. A greater truth is, though, that few of us expected monetary wealth in that era.

In our time he would have been called a "suit"...an exec. And from the few photographs that remain, when he worked in Filer-Stowell's office in Milwaukee he did, indeed, wear three piece, vested, suits.

But he was the kind of field manager, much like the officers who led his father into battle, who worked side by side with his men , one who could swing a sledge hammer with the best of them. In retirement years, he continued the rough attire of a working man...although I remember seeing him often in natty looking pinstripe shirts with the cuffs turned back , collar open, casual.

In times of excellent pay, business leadership, family, good homes, wide ranging rail travel, ownership of new, exciting, horseless carriages...and equally in those years of much less, his outlook remained as the pioneers who built our great Nation...quietly determined, steady, content, self sufficient. What seemed meaningful was to enjoy each place in which he found himself, to treasure the experiences of each day, especially the day itself, to accept life as it was, to live it as best he could.

Can any of us do more?

*Elba Altdoerffer Baughman (son of James Wilson Baughman) and
Iris Keir Armour Baughman at about the time of their wedding Circa 1931*

Prologue

The years of man are measured by gyrations of Earth...the willful orbit that bears the unfailing rise and setting of our Sun. In the light of that bright and glowing star, it is not surprising that American Indians called the day a Sun. Their month they declared a Moon, it's slow, steady, wax and wane pacing thirty or so Suns of the Moon course.

In the Moon of April, in the year 2006, we live in an age in which countables are measured in numbers so vast they're near unimaginable. Yet, if we could roll back the Suns, not billions or trillions, but a mere 51,450 times or so, we'd find ourselves a few yesterdays ago, in a time, a terrible conflict, that opened our great nation to even greater freedom and prosperity, to the world leadership we know today.

For, it is just that relatively meager number of days, sunrise upon sunset, since a small brigade of men in Union blue set out on a fearsome mission. The tale of their raid, alone, unaided, deep in enemy territory is well spoken in local lore, yet little known in the national annals of America's Civil War. It's courage, perhaps far more than it's triumph, has a vital place in history. It speaks for so many unremembered young gallants, so many small attacks and defenses that might never, otherwise, be honored.

For the Confederate folk of Northern Alabama where Yankee boys from Lake County, Indiana intruded, the sounds of gun and saber, creaking wagon, plodding hoof, blasting cannon, whistling Minie-Ball still echo, albeit softly now, in the small towns and forest hills and muddy roads through which they passed.

It was 135 years - to the Sunday - after their bold trespass that my wife Sandee and I, and our tiny pup, Dobry, set out to follow their trail...to see the mountains and valley streams of Confederate land they touched. We were aided mightily by the writings of Rucker Agee, a painstaking local historian who traced their path in the years 1948 to1958, four decades before us, 95 years after the incursion. Following his carefully penned lead, and descriptions written in 1864 by Col. Abel D. Streight, commander of the Union brigade, we were astonished at how much of the 124.5 mile route we could still find, how many of the places and points of battle we could touch. To our surprise, we found roadside memorials depicting battle sites, and a stone monument at the site of their capture 21 miles from Rome, Georgia.

More than twenty years of research, the discovery of 233 pages of Private Wilson Shannon Baughman's Civil War pension records, our travels over the route of their raid, and a trip to the National Archives in Washington, D.C. to read for ourselves the age-yellowed, hand written records of the 73rd Indiana Volunteer Infantry Regiment brought us to the day when this powerful story can be told.

In our brilliant age of technology it's surprising to learn that our great grandfathers fought the first truly modern war 140 years ago. There were railroads far faster than foot or hoof, steamships, and instant telegraph communications where lines were strung. As the war advanced, day by deadly day, there came repeating rifles, cameras, surveillance balloons, and - late in the war - Gatling machine guns which could spew out death in impetuous streams of whining bullets.

In seven days of arduous, exhausting, running battles, neither the Union boys from Lake County nor their wily Confederate pursuers would possess such advantages. It was little more than their own hands and feet, their physical toughness, the horses and army mules they rode, the rifles and bayonets each carried, their own proud determination, courage, and devotion to duty which would sustain their purpose.

In mind and heart, as we search back toward those terrible years we cannot help but feel the presence of those who bought, with blood and fear and courage, the America we know today. Wading upstream in time's torrent, we might hope for one last glimpse, to feel, to breathe, perhaps to share with them those hours. We'll hurry past forgotten sunsets, peer into dark corners of old nights, give sunrise another chance at the joy of morning..., relive - even as we know it - their hope in a new day.

Along the way, we cannot help but pass the long silent, dusty bones of those who preceded us in boldness, and in faith, who charted the course of a great Nation. They fought our battles, bled our blood, gave our grandfathers breath to bring us the life we know.

In searching back...not so far from our own Millennium, we'll glance toward the explosions of Iraq and Afghanistan and Desert Storm...then the smaller engagements of Granada and Panama. A quarter century before we'll find the confusing violence of Vietnam. Before that, Korea, the raging conflagration of World War II, the muddy trenches of World War I, parades to the Spanish-American War in 1898. Even so, the dusty heroes of our Indian Wars, the lonely courage of those who waggoned toward sunset to settle the great American West.

None, in their time, amassed the awful suffering or loss counted by American soldiers of both the North and South..., so many proud, eager Volunteers..., in the awful devastation of America's Civil War.

It is exactly there that we'll finally come upon...the Boys From Lake County.

Chapter One

In The Beginning

We sense a slackening in the pace of our ardent search, the backward roll of earth-time easing, slowing, as an aged train pulling into the station. Sunrise has rushed in reverse to its previous sunset, hurrying upwards to the former dawn, day after flashing day.

Moons, fleeting against earth's time-tide, have flickered in gushing stream, swimming, like salmon leaping homeward, against their 30 day course, then monthly, yearly. The full glory of the Moon's silvery disc wanes quickly to the slimmest of crescents, then on to brilliant star points in black night, month by month, year by year. It has been so throughout our brief, backward journey...reclaiming sunrise and sunset, just near 51,450 times.

Time traveling, back-reaching hurriedly, we've barely glimpsed the agony of America's other, latter day, wars. Just so, we've seen only brief flourishes of joy and happiness, the pain and suffering, success, failure, faith and peace of our fathers and mothers, generations between that time and our own.

The backward rush of day and night slows more noticeably, shudders to a halt, stabilizes, firming a grip on the one we've been seeking... then beginning second by second, minute by minute, to creep forward again toward the 140 years we've spanned so swiftly.

We find ourselves near a wee city in the far northwestern corner of the State of Alabama. It is indeed modest in size, perhaps 1200 or so souls in residence, nestled in the Tennessee River Valley in foothills of the Appalachian Mountains. Far from unusual, in this troubled Year of Our Lord, a great many American towns are of such dimension.

This one lies in land that Chickasaw Indians had called home for eons...their "land of many waters." Despite it's limited community, the little town is already more than four decades old, first incorporated on October 4,1819, just 71 days before Alabama entered the Union as America's 22nd state. It's history, though, far predates even that span of years.

In 1780, during the upheaval of America's founding, a French Colony from the Wabash River of Indiana established an Indian trading post at the juncture of Spring Creek - which traverses from the town - and the Tennessee River.

In the spring of 1815 Michael Dickson, his wife Sene, and sons Michael, Hugh, Lewis, and Joseph escaped the Reynoldsburg, Tennessee tragedy known as "Johnson's Massacre." The family put all their earthly possessions into a keel-boat, traveled down the Tennessee River to that same Spring Creek. Boating their belongings the mere two miles up the creek to its source, they found an enormous outflow from deep in the earth...one that pours out 35 million gallons of cold, fresh, water every day. Simply enough, it is called Big Spring.

At that garden spot the Dickson family found a Chickasaw Indian town on a hill overlooking the spring. It was not a nomadic encampment of tepees, but a year-round village of wooden homes. And they were greeted by its Chief, Tushka-Ambi (the Warrior Who Kills). Soon trade was begun with the tribe, and the Dicksons negotiated a purchase of all land reaching from the mountains on the south, then northward to the shores of the Tennessee River. In the spirit of Manhattan, they paid the sum of one five dollar gold piece and two pole axes for that immense territory, and built their own log cabins on another hill over looking the spring, about a quarter mile east of the Chickasaw village.

The Dicksons found an abundance of game, good water, and rich farmland that attracted many more settlers from the east. Within two years there were three homes, a mill, and one merchant near the spring. By that same year, 1817, General Andrew Jackson's troopers had built a Military Road from

2

Nashville, Tennessee to Columbus, Mississippi cutting through the area... while General Coffee had surveyed and laid off a city, settings its limits 1 ½ miles east and west and 1 mile north and south.

First called Occocopoosa (Cold Water), then Big Spring, in 1822 it was re-named in honor of the Indian Chief Tushka-Ambi.

The city soon became the community center for one of the best agricultural areas in northern Alabama, with a variety of goods, services, and businesses available to serve a rush of settlers. Just two years later, the growing town could boast nearly a thousand residents, a dozen merchants, and four new hotels... Tuscumbia Inn, Challen House, the Franklin, and the Jackson Hotel. There were also Farnsworth Tin Manufacturing, Finley's Blacksmith Shop, and Pinkard & Massey's Cabinet Makers... along with a tailor, milliner, watchmaker, jeweler, silversmith, cobbler, harness maker, and both a male and female academy. Commercial lots on Main Street were selling for as much as $2,000 each.

Early on, merchants had no choice but to ferry farm products across the Tennessee to docking facilities in Florence, Alabama on the big river's north side. In the year 1824, though, enterprising citizens built a dock at the mouth of Spring Creek so steamboats could load and unload trade goods..., especially burgeoning cotton production..., on the south side of the river. That was a prosperously wise, though innately obvious, move since the Tennessee River was navigable only to that area. From there to Decatur, Alabama were 43 miles of rocky shoals in the river, impassable to the big, paddlewheel, river steamers.

In 1832, only three years after the advent of railroads in America, progressive citizens inaugurated the first railroad on what was then America's frontier. The line was short, covering only two miles from the dock on the river into warehouses of the town. But then quickly came of the idea of expanding the Tuscumbia Railway Company to form the Tuscumbia, Courtland and Decatur Railroad carrying freight across the 43

3

miles of river shoals to deeper waters past Decatur. As a result, the economy of all the shoals area boomed, and the little city became its agricultural and commerce center with two rows of brick warehouses and prosperous, expansive wholesale businesses. The town's Post Office grew into a mail distributing center...likely the largest and most vital one between Nashville and New Orleans.

By the time of America's Civil War, Isaac Young's Carriage Factory and Tuscumbia Shops and Foundry were prosperous businesses among large warehouses at the river landing and in the downtown area. Besides, by then, the town was on the main line of the Memphis and Charleston Railroad, the longest railroad in the world in its day. As War approached, the small town had grown into a vibrant, well-heeled little city.

Although perhaps far more prosperous than many, the history of the town reflects the vibrancy, progress, and dimension of so many communities as America spiraled into it's awful Civil War years. As such, it gives us a fateful glimpse into daily life in the towns through which our Union and Confederate soldiers passed... the villages in which they were born and reared...the homes to which so many returned to make their own peaceful contribution to the continuation of life itself, and the development of our great Nation.

Sadly, during Civil War years, because of her business vitality, and strategic location on navigable river and major railroad, the affluent little city found herself caught squarely in the path of both Union and Confederate armies. She paid dearly for her business wisdom and progressiveness. Blocks of fine, brick commercial buildings, and many private homes, were left in wreckage, or in ashes... with store shelves barren of goods, and about thirty of her young men killed during the years of combat. After battles of the Civil War had ceased, she sat shocked, faded, declining... for nearly twenty years before wounds healed and she began to flower, grow, prosper again.

The State of Alabama lists 336 military engagements during the four years of America's Civil War. Although not major battles, more than a dozen of them will devastate this one little city. And the events of this night will be one of it's worst.

Indeed, it is a Sunday..., April 26, 1863 that we find ourselves near Tuscumbia, Alabama... far, far late in the evening of the day. In fact, it is biting close to the hour in which this day passes into the quiet of earth's history.

Surrounding, enveloping us, the pungent scent of wet horse flesh, horse dung, of damp creaking leather, woolen uniforms, oil that preserves military rifles, rain soaked canvas assails our nostrils, mingling with the smell of moist earth and sprouting Spring greenery in Northern Alabama's Tennessee River Valley.

The aroma of the equine is strange now to those of our time. But to the 100 or so we join, those of Company A, 73rd Indiana Volunteer Infantry Regiment... the Boys From Lake County... the scent and feel of horseflesh is yet a vibrant part of daily life. To be sure horses and mules were to them as automobiles are in our day,... a mode of daily transport, production, commerce, recreation. City boys..., clerks, lawyers, bankers, newspaper men were as familiar with horses as they were with their homes. Even so their women folk. Country lads, farmers, earned their daily bread toiling side by side with the powerful animals. Infantrymen could be transformed into horse soldiers, cavalry, perhaps not perfectly at once, but much more facilely than one might imagine today.

The feel of living outdoors, wet, chilled, in a rainy season remains a common experience shared by soldiers of all the ages.

As we glance around in wonder at what we've found, hundreds of horses and army mules stand quiet, patient, tails idly flicking Alabama Spring flies off wet haunches. Others snort, shift nervously, perhaps a hoof stomping mushy earth, muscles rippling a fly away. Blue uniformed infantrymen stand beside the great animals, knapsacks packed behind Army saddles. Outdated 1842 Springfield smooth bore .69 caliber muskets are sheathed. Many men hold reins, gentling, calming the animals, waiting now for the order. Others, tired of standing, of the waiting, have stepped into stirrups, swung up onto saddles, up out of the muddy road ...biding the dwindling time in a bit more comfort. Murmurs among them seem soft, hushed, muffled by rain slickers and the occasional downpour.

The Boys From Lake County, soldiers of Company A, are already stationed in line of march, commonly four horses abreast, along with their fellows of the 73rd Indiana Volunteer Infantry Regiment.

How many in all? Records indicate that there were 450 in the ranks of the 73rd that night. Of the individual Companies, records are silent, melded into Regimental rosters. So we can only assume that there were something near the 100 who originally enrolled. We certainly cannot count them in damp dark relieved only by the occasional kerosene lantern here and there. Some had already been lost in previous battle, and some to sickness or discharge for one reason or another.

A Regiment of those years might be comprised of four Companies, 400 men. Or it may have eventually borne eight or ten companies, 800 or 1,000 men. Indiana's 73rd varied between those assemblies, Companies A through K, throughout America's Civil War.

Counted as a matter of historical record, on Sunday April 26th 1863, the total in that gallant gathering were about 1500 in all, a column of sturdy young humanity and war steeds, stretching well over half a mile long.

Company A, The Boys From Lake County, and their fellow Union soldiers of the 73 Indiana were commanded by Col. Gilbert Hathaway. With them were men of the 51st Indiana Volunteer Regiment commanded by Col. Abel D. Streight. The 3rd Ohio Volunteer Infantry Regiment was commanded by Col. Orris A. Lawson. Lt. Col Andrew F. Rogers commanded the 80th Illinois Volunteers. Though enrolled as infantry, foot soldiers, all were mounted on horses or army mules as they readied to move out that night. Or, to put it more accurately, most of them were mounted.

Also among the 1500 were two units actually trained as fast moving horse soldiers, Companies D and E of the First Middle Tennessee Cavalry commanded by Captain D. D. Smith.

The 1500 men of the combined units are bearing an extra designation this night. Officially labeled an "Independent Provisional Brigade for Special Secret Service," it became far better known as Streight's Brigade, named for the commander of the 51st Indiana, who was chosen to lead. And so..., the strenuous mission on which they are about to embark can be found, quiescently secluded among so many others, as Streight's Raid, in annals of America's Civil War.

A few days before there had been 1700 assigned to the newly assembled force. Officers, clearly, were keenly aware of the physical stresses that awaited Streight's Brigade in the days to come.

"We arrived at Tuscumbia at about 5:00 p.m. on April 24th" reported Col. Streight. "I ordered my surgeon to carefully examine my command," he said, "and send back... all men who were not fit for the arduous duties before us." That lowered the number of Streight's multitude to the 1500 who actually started out. 200, ill and left behind, will be sorely missed in days to come.

As we watch it becomes clear that rain has been overweening, intermittent... drizzle, then calm, often heavy showers, for the past three days or so. It will be remembered as just one more intense hardship in a grievous series of them. For this military adventure will be noted, not only for the skill, determination, and bravery of its men, but for it's misfortune. In fact, everything that could go wrong, did so...except, perhaps, one!

Ahead of the 1500 stands an Army of 8,000 Union Blue commanded by Brigadier General Grenville M. Dodge. Their order is not extended in line of march, of travel, like the men of

Streight's Brigade. Their ranks are stretched wide, side-by-side, rank upon rank, in line of battle.

Slowly, heads turning, listening, men around us become aware that the powerful force ahead is moving forward. Many more in Streight's Brigade and the Boys From Lake County lift a foot into stirrups, swing legs up and over, slide into saddles, expectant. Just as surely, before many minutes escape, a distant sound of skirmish, the hollow boom of cannon, rattle of rifle fire echoes back from the front.

Col. Abel D. Streight passes the order to mount up down the long column. Col. Hathaway repeats that "move out" to Captain Alfred Fry, his First Sergeant, and he to the Boys From Lake County and their fellow Union soldiers of the 73rd Indiana. Streight and his new Brigade begin to move forward as though a part of the 8,000 advancing through Tuscumbia toward the smaller village of Town Creek, Alabama.

It is now 11:00 p.m.

The long column plods, gropes, along the muddy road in deep darkness, soaked by the continuing, on again-off again rain. Reaching a cross road in Tuscumbia, Streight clandestinely bears the long column to the right, heading his Brigade south, away from the town and the rattle of gunfire..., into the wet, pitch dark, night. Behind 1200 mounted riders are 150 more that have no mounts, slipping, sliding afoot in oozing mud of the road. 150 more are afoot, as well, because their steeds are too poor to carry anything heavier than saddles and gear.

In this fretful way, Streightht's Brigade sets out on one of the most combative small-scale missions of America's Civil War.

Chapter Two

Days of Preparation

In early battles of the Civil War, it became increasingly clear that the North would, in general, be the aggressor with Southerners in posture of defense. There were, of course, engagements in which Southerners undertook powerful offensive assaults. General Robert E. Lee's advance deep into Northern territory, the attack on Gettysburg with horrific battle losses on both sides, is a prime example. And of course Southern commanders often took the offensive in individual combat with galvanizing success.

Confederate General Joseph E. Johnston's assault on Union forces at tiny Shiloh Church in Tennessee was one which turned out badly for Southern strategy. Worse, with it's combined North and South battle losses totaling more than 24,000 men, Shiloh was not only a disastrous engagement...but an early wake up call to both sides that the War would not be quick, easy..., nor painless.

Still, in the overall thrust of Civil War strategy, the North attacked and the South defended. In the final analysis, by far, most battles and civilian property damage fell on Confederate states.

Even in very early months of the War, military strategists of the North perceived that the large, prosperous state of Tennessee must be the source of a main thrust into vitals of the Rebel South. The broad, lengthy, highly navigable waters of the Tennessee and Cumberland Rivers, spearing from the state deep into Rebel heartland, were of central interest in that perspective.

As Civil War loomed, Tennessee was a state at forefront of the American scene, its population second greatest in the

South. It already had been the home of two presidents, and was lauded as the "Volunteer State" for national loyalty in the tradition of Andrew Jackson himself.

By the end of hostilities Tennessee had provided more soldiers for the Rebel cause than any state except Virginia. Evincing a sharp political divide among its citizens, Tennessee, at the same time, enrolled more Union soldiers than all other Southern states combined.

In fact, Tennessee at first refused to secede in a February referendum. Then in June 1861 it became the last state to join the Confederacy. President Abraham Lincoln believed Tennessee "winnable" in the political sense, and endeavored to extend the North's support to large numbers of Unionists who remained in eastern parts of the state.

At the time of the 1860 census, Tennessee found itself at the acme of America's farm production, so much so, it was deemed by many as the "breadbasket" for the deeper South.

In parallel importance, the state held an equally vital portion of the South's manufacturing capability...copper mines, ironworks, gunpowder mills, munitions factories. Furthermore, the South's main east-west railways operated through Tennessee, as well as the north-south railroad of western Confederacy.

Though invented in Europe, America's initial steam railroad first began operations about 1829. However, development of powerful steam engines for marine use predated that vitalizing event. In Alabama, the first steamboat was built in 1818 at St. Stephens. On October 22, 1820 the steamboat "Harriet" completed a ten day trip from Mobile to Montgomery, opening river trade between the cities.

In parallel transport innovation, Alabama's first steam train, the Tuscumbia Railroad began operations on June 12, 1832, running a brief two miles from Tuscumbia Landing on the Tennessee River into the town of Tuscumbia.

Between that era and the opening salvos of America's Civil War in 1861, there were three decades in which development of both systems of transport were rapidly progressing, expanding. By the time of the Civil War's early battles, major navigable rivers, and railroads in major population centers east of the Mississippi, had become - like super highways of today - modes of relatively fast personal and cargo transport. And as combat neared, steam ships and river boats were converted to heavily armed war vessels, some of them even iron clad for protection against rifle bullets or cannon balls.

All things considered, there was no doubt in the minds of military strategists on both sides that Tennessee, heart of commerce and trade in the upper South, contained massive strategic economic resources.

In early to mid February 1862, the battles and capture of earthen Confederate Forts Henry and Haimen on the Tennessee river, and larger, stronger, log built, Fort Donelson on the Cumberland River were leading major assaults into the heart of Tennessee. Those two warily planned, cool headed, sieges were led by then virtually unknown Brig. Gen Ulysses S. Grant. In fact, the efficiency, aggressiveness, and success of those engagements brought him to the forefront of national attention, later the command of the entire Union Army, eventually the Presidency of the United States of America.

The siege and defeat of those major Confederate river defenses in the first year of the War are especially notable here..., for three reasons.

First, they provided a resounding lesson in the combined deployment of massive Infantry forces catching an enemy in a pincer between land assault and bombardment by river gunboats. River warships, the New Uncle Sam, Carondelet, Lousiville, St. Louis, Pittsburgh, and Agamemnon, composed a fleet commanded by Flag-Officer A. H. Foote. Particularly the battle for the larger Fort Donelson on the Cumberland River was a massive, hard fought one with near 17,000 Confederates defending the fort, more than 14,000 Union troops squeezing them against the river and Foote's gunboat fleet.

11

Second, the loss by the South of the three, vital, river defenses led soon after to the capture and occupation of Clarksville and Nashville, Tennessee by Union forces. Thereby, early in the Civil War, Nashville became headquarters for the North's massive Army of the Cumberland... and remained so throughout the war despite a major assault in 1864 to recapture the city by Confederate Gen. Joseph E. Johnston who had been it's previous Rebel commander.

Third, and surely more important to us here, after those Union successes... and on Thursday, April 7th, 1863, it is the reason why Union soldiers of the North, the Boys From Lake County and compatriots of their 73rd Indiana Volunteer Infantry Regiment, found themselves bound to Nashville, the capital city of a vastly important Southern state.

For it was the day that Col. Abel D. Streight received a verbal order that set in motion days of preparation. At the moment his Regiment, the 51st Indiana, was stationed near Chattanooga. The Boys From Lake County and others of the 73rd Indiana had been left for several months to guard the city of Murphreesborough after it's famed engagement, and their part in it, since hallowed as the Battle of Stones River. The orders were for all units to proceed to Nashville to ready for an "expedition."

Written confirmation followed the next day, Friday, April 8th, 1863.

A massive volume of 128 books entitled "THE WAR OF THE REBELLION...A Compilation Of The Official Records of the Union and Confederate Armies" was begun at the end of the Civil War in 1865. It took almost 35 years to assemble the thousands upon thousands of records and data, and the work was not completed and published until the year 1899. It's hundred year old records are found today mostly in large libraries, often those of universities. However it is still possible to compile a list from its extensive indexes and follow every station, battle, assignment, and exact copies of the written orders for every regiment of both Armies of the Civil War.

Needless to say, definitive records from "The War of the Rebellion" are a major guide for, at least, part of our history of the "Boys From Lake County." The order received that day by Col. Abel D. Streight is perfectly remembered in its pages.

We won't often burden you with full renditions of such, simply touching upon them or excerpting occasionally for historical detail. We're going to include this order in it's entirety, however, since it offers such a vital portrayal of the purpose and design of Streight's Raid, as well as glimpses into the gentleman-like integrity with which the Civil War was commanded... in spite of its intensity and horrendous losses.

Streight's order actually was directed by the Commanding Officer of the Army of the Cumberland, Major-General William S. Rosecrans. However it was transmitted by Rosecrans' Chief of Staff, Brigadier-General J.A. Garfield.

HEADQUARTERS DEPARTMENT OF THE CUMBERLAND
Murphreesborough, Tenn., April 8, 1863

Col. A. D. Streight
51st Indiana Volunteers

Colonel: By Special Field Orders, No 94, Paragraph VIII, you have been assigned to the command of an independent provisional brigade for temporary purposes. After fitting out your command with equipment and supplies as you have already been directed in the verbal instructions of the general commanding this department, you will proceed by a route, of which you will be advised by telegraph, to some good steamboat landing on the Tennessee River not far above Fort Henry, where you will embark your command and proceed up the river.

At Hamburg you will communicate with Brigadier-General Dodge, who will probably have a messenger there awaiting your arrival. If it should then appear unsafe to move further up the river, you will debark at Hamburg, and without delay join the force of General Dodge, which will then be en route for Iuka, Miss. If, however, it should be deemed safe, you will land at Eastport and form a junction with General Dodge.

From that point you will then march, in conjunction with him, to menace Tuscumbia, but you will not wait to join in the attack unless it should be necessary for the safety of General Dodge's command or your own, or unless some considerable advantage can be gained over the enemy without interfering with the general object of the expedition.

After having marched long enough with General Dodge to create a general impression that you are a part of his expedition, you will push to the southward, and reach Russellville or Moulton. From thence your route will be governed by circumstances, but you will, with all reasonable dispatch, push on to western Georgia, and cut the railroads which supply the rebel army by way of Chattanooga. To accomplish this is the chief objective of your expedition, and you must not allow collateral and incidental schemes, even though promising great results, to delay you so as to endanger your return. Your quartermaster has been furnished with funds sufficient for the necessary expenses of your command. You will draw your supplies and keep your command well mounted from the country through which you pass. For all property taken for the legitimate use of your command you will make cash payments in full to men of undoubted loyalty; give the usual conditional receipts to men whose loyalty is doubtful, but to rebels nothing.

You are particularly commanded to restrain your command from pillage and marauding. You will destroy all depots of supplies of the rebel army, all manufactories of guns, ammunition, equipments, and clothing for their use, which you can without delaying you so as to endanger your return.

That you may not be trammeled with minute instructions, nothing further will be ordered than this general outline of policy and operation.

In intrusting this highly important and somewhat perilous expedition to your charge, the general commanding places great reliance upon your prudence, energy, and valor, and the well-attested bravery and endurance of the officers and men under your command.

Whenever it is possible and reasonably safe, send us word of your progress. You may return by way of Northern Alabama or Northern Georgia. Should you be surrounded by rebel forces and your retreat cut off, defend yourself as long as possible, and make the surrender of your command cost the enemy as many times your number as possible.

A copy of the general order from the War Department in regard to paroling prisoners, together with necessary blanks, are herewith furnished you.

You are authorized to enlist all able-bodied men who desire to join the Army of the Union.

You must return as soon as the main objects of your expedition are accomplished.

Very respectfully, your obedient servant.

J. A. Garfield,
Brigadier-General and Chief of Staff

Military records often omit humble details of daily operations, focusing on the major. In our own time, we still overlook recorded mention of that which seems the norm, usual, unremarkable. We may glean, perhaps even surmise, such routines from other more personal sources, or from painstaking reconstruction of median daily life and movement in those years. The locations of three of the Regiments were not recorded in his report. But with Streight and his 51st Indiana Regiment in Chattanooga, The Boys From Lake County and their fellow soldiers of the 73rd Indiana Volunteer Regiment still at Murphreesborough...travel of the various units to Nashville from scattered assignment was clearly accomplished hastily. It was not described by Streight, but given the very brief time allotted it is certain most of the men, on their trip to main camp at Nashville, were "riding the cars" as they described the huffing steam trains of the Civil War era.

Without any direct reference to the short time for preparation, Streight described it simply. "On April 7, 1863," he said, "I received orders from General Rosecrans to proceed with the Provisional Brigade - about 1,700 Officers and men - to Nashville to fit out as speedily as possible for an expedition..."

In fact, many in the newly assigned Brigade were proceeding... back... to Nashville where they had been encamped before being ordered to Murphreesborough, into the famed "Battle of Stones River." And, as it turned out, they would have a mere three days to complete their return trip, as well as the process of "fitting out."

But, there is another central fact not mentioned in Brig. Gen. Garfield's order to Col Streight...one which demonstrates the vital importance of military field officers who are enterprising, innovative, daring in their pursuit of duty. To be sure, without such battlefront commanders an army is rendered listless, prone to defeat. Within the language of Garfield's order one would easily assume that the idea for this foray had come from the highest ranks within the giant Army of the Cumberland. And Col. Streight's report, in the customary pattern of deference to military rank, said nothing of it.

It was left to Streight's Brigade aide-de-camp Lt. A.C. Roach to give credit where such is due. After the War, Lt. Roach wrote a book about the events of 1863. Furthermore his information was confirmed by historian Rucker Agee of Alabama 95 years later. The idea for this brilliant military incursion came, not from higher command, but from Streight himself. Here's how Lt. Roach described it...

> The spring of 1863 opened with the prospect of being a season of inactivity for the Army of the Cumberland. The rebel General Bragg, with a large and well equipped army, occupied near Tullahoma, Tennessee, a strong natural position, improved by all the ingenuity known to military science, until it was almost impregnable. Consequently it was not in the programme of the cautious and sagacious Rosecrans, then commanding the Army of the Cumberland, to make an advance movement until his command was in a condition of health, numbers, and equipments, that certain and decisive victory would be inevitable. These important military items it was not expected could be brought about before, perhaps, the middle of the approaching summer.
> To the mind of Col. A. D. Streight, of the Fifty-First Indiana Volunteer Infantry, (also Roach's home Regiment) this term of inaction was a period of ennui, and afforded the enemy in his stronghold at Tullahoma a rest and feeling of security, that his restless spirit could not contemplate. He therefore made application to the commanding General for an independent mounted brigade, a command of this description necessarily affording an opportunity for constant and active service; and would, if directed in the proper manner, draw from the banks of the Cumberland and Ohio the guerila bands of Forrest, Morgan and other noted chieftains in the rebel service, and give them employment in their own boasted land of "Dixie."

Historian Rucker Agee, himself, added further enlightenment. "In the spring of 1863, most people of the Sand Mountain Plateau (Confederate territory through which the raid would pass) had become strongly Union in sympathy. When Streight was stationed at Decatur (Alabama) after the Battle of Shiloh the year before he had recruited these mountaineers for the Union Army and two such companies accompanied him on this expedition." From this it is clear that Col. Streight was already familiar with the area in which he suggested the Brigade's effort.

Upon arrival at Nashville, Colonel Streight at once selected staff leaders of the new Brigade, not just from his own regiment, but from among several of the others. Capt. D.L. Wright of the 51st Indiana Volunteers became acting assistant adjutant-general. Maj. W.L. Peck of the 3rd Ohio was Brigade surgeon. Lieut. J.G. Doughty, regimental quartermaster of the 51st Indiana became acting assistant quartermaster for the new Brigade. Capt. Driscoll of the 3rd Ohio was appointed acting assistant inspector-general. Lieut. J. W. Pavey of the 80th Illinois became ordnance officer. And Lieut. A.C. Roach of Streight's own 51st Indiana, whom we have already mentioned, was named aide-de-camp at the Brigade level.

With 1,700 men busily at work a great deal could be, and clearly was, accomplished in that short time. In such a readying, appropriate clothing must be carried for days under nothing but sun, moon, stars, rain, the cool air of Spring. Garments must be selected, washed, packed into knapsacks, along with items for cleanliness and such creature comfort as may be had "on the march."

In knapsacks or pockets, there will be personal mementos, small remaining links that tie a combat soldier to a home and family he fears he may never see again. Rifles and pistols must be carefully checked, cleaned, oiled. In combat, a soldier's life will hang on the condition of his weapon. The new unit also had cannon, two 12 pound mountain howitizers, which had to be readied. Ammunition for each weapon must be gathered, packed. Food for 1,700 men to last for days properly stored for portage.

In camp, soldiers of the Civil War often lived in big, teepee-like, Sibley tents that would accommodate up to eighteen men. On the march, shelter was far more crude. Tents, if there was time to use them, were small two man affairs...half carried in the knapsack by each man.

In this special instance, there was another vital preparation, one that would turn out to be the most severe of hindrances for the expedition...perhaps it's fateful flaw. Since, in the moment, infantry soldiers were to be converted to cavalry, horses or army mules, their saddles, bridles, reins, and bits must be provided, assigned to them from Cavalry equipment depots.

"I was instructed to draw about half the number of mules necessary to mount my command, at Nashville," said Streight. On the day the Brigade left Nashville, "...it was late in the evening before the mules were brought to the landing for shipment," he lamented. "I was temporarily absent at the time, attending to some business affairs preparatory to starting; consequently did not see them."

The oddest thing, perhaps, in an era when most men knew horseflesh intimately, is that no one else...no other officer, no soldier... noted - or reported to his commander - anything unusual about those mules.

Chapter Three

Farewell...Again...to Nashville

In fact, it was on the afternoon of Friday, April 10th, 1863 that Col. Abel D. Streight received final orders from General Garfield. He, along with The Boys From Lake County, their 73rd Indiana Regiment, and other units of Streight's Brigade, was to embark "at once" aboard a fleet of eight river steamers waiting at a Nashville landing. "General Ellet's Marine Brigade and two gunboats accompanied the fleet to Fort Henry," Streight reported, "and informed me that they were ordered to proceed with me as far as Eastport, Mississippi."

Streight was referring to Brigadier General Alfred Washington Ellet whose Civil War fame has faded, more than many others perhaps, into the mists of history. Yet, he was a well noted, accomplished leader in Civil War years and descended from a family famed for participation in America's Revolutionary War as well as in vital developments of the Civil War itself. His brother Charles, a successful engineer, who, in 1842 built the first important suspension railroad bridge in the United States, had already achieved the attention of Secretary of War Edwin Stanton and President Abraham Lincoln.

Charles, while traveling in Europe during the Crimean War had urged Russia to use his idea of iron clad "ram boats," though he found neither Russia, France, nor England interested. Back in the United States he urged the Secretary of the Navy to build them. Again he was ignored until 1862 when the famed iron clad "Merrimac" proved the efficiency of his idea. Two weeks later he was actively preparing a ram fleet to fight on the Mississippi River, commissioned a Colonel under the sole direction of Secretary of War Stanton himself, with the concurrence of President Abraham Lincoln. Union generals had expressed disdain, but Ellet's idea of iron clad "ram boats" caught the attention of Lincoln and Stanton with subsequent great effect for the Union's Civil War effort.

Ram boats were often old heavy wooden steamboats reinforced with iron, the deck lined with cotton bales for added protection. Usually unarmed, they were used only for ramming and transporting troops and supplies. The Confederates had ram boats too, and had already used them with great effectiveness. But the ram was not their primary weapon, and their boats were slower than Ellet's. It was in the second year of the Civil War, March 1862, that Charles began work on his Mississippi River Fleet, remodeling nine boats.

On June 6, 1862 he and his fleet sank four Confederate boats at the Battle of Memphis, receiving the surrender of that city. Sadly Col. Charles Ellet was the only Union man injured in that engagement. He died as his boat touched shore at Cairo, Illinois on June 21st and was honored with burial from Independence Hall in Philadelphia.

When Charles had been given his ram boat commission he had asked that Secretary of War Stanton appoint his brother Capt. Alfred Washington Ellet of the 59th Illinois Infantry Regiment, as his second in command. At his brother's death, A.W. Ellet was promoted to Lt. Col and assumed command of the fleet. Within three weeks he had been so instrumental in river successes at the early siege of Vicksburg, Secretary of War Stanton promoted him to Brigadier General.

Nashville's 687 mile long Cumberland River rises in east Kentucky, winds generally southwest through Kentucky and Tennessee, then in a long loop northwest past Nashville. Farther down river, it touches briefly into the Ohio River near Paducah, Kentucky, then connects westward to the mighty Tennessee River.

In fact, it would have been much easier for The Boys From Lake County and the entire Brigade to simply remain aboard the river steamer fleet and ride the complete river loop northward on the Cumberland, a bit west on the Ohio, then south down the Tennessee to their destination in Rebel country.

But we must remember that Col Streit's orders were to draw half his mounts at Nashville, then pick up the other half from farms along his march. For this reason an extra march was planned beginning at the town of Palmyra, Tennessee. It seems clear that Palmyra was chosen for three reasons.

First, it had either excellent, or at least reasonable, accessibility to bring the steamers to dock or shore and unload the animals and men. Steamboat landings in the Civil War era might consist of either extensive, solidly built, wooden docking piers…or an area with a long, low, shoreline in which the shallow draft paddle wheel steamers could simply nose onto shore, lower a gang way, and load or unload.

Second, though Palmyra was a very small town in those years, it served a fine farming area. Notably hilly, the route of the march contained many farms in the hollows between the hills… with a much larger area of more level farming country closer to town. There was no doubt in the mind's of Col Streight and his commanders that there would be many good work horses in a farming region such as this. It seems clear they, collectively, felt sure he could pick up all the additional horses he needed in that agricultural countryside before boarding the steamers again.

Third, Palmyra was just a few miles below Fort Donelson on the Cumberland with passable (unpaved, of course) roads connecting across the isthmus between the rivers to Fort Henry on the Tennessee which had good docking facilities for the steamers.

"I received orders from General Garfield," in Col Streight's explicit words, "to embark at once on steamers then at the landing and proceed down the river to Palmyra, land my command there, and march across the country to Fort Henry, and to seize all the horses and mules I could find. Everything was speedily put on board. As soon as everything was ready we proceeded down the river…."

To a great extent Col. Streight's rather dry reporting might make it seem the Boys From Lake County and the rest of the Brigade simply rushed down to the steamboat landing... with 1700 men, 700 animals, and all the rifles, cannon, ammunition, food and supplies to outfit such an army... jumped aboard the vessels, and shoved off down river on the afternoon of April 10th.

Lt. Roache's equally brief description of this expansive effort..., necessarily including hundred's of individual mundane chores... put the leave taking into a more living, realistic, perspective. In one terse sentence he enveloped that busy, clattering, dusty, mule braying time into a far more understandable number of hours. For it was actually not until "...the morning of the 11th..." he said, "...we took a farewell view of the Capitol of Old Tennessee."

"We arrived at Palmyra," Col. Streight related, " on the evening of the 11th, and disembarked at once." He sent the fleet, including all eight of the river steamers, up around the river loop and down the Tennessee to Fort Henry, under command of Col. Lawson of the 3rd Ohio Regiment. Lawson was sent with four companies of Streight's own 51st Indiana Volunteers as a very substantial force of rifled guards. He had orders to stop at the river town of Smithland and take on board the steamers a quantity of rations (food for the soldiers) and forage (animal feed, usually hay) for General Dodge's command.

As soon as it was daylight on the morning of Sunday, April 12th, The Boys From Lake County with all remaining troops, except the four companies of the 51st Indiana sent with the steamers, were set to work to catch and saddle the mules. It was at this moment, this dawning, that the new Brigade commander discovered the first awful obstacle to hope of success in the perilous mission.

"I then for the first time discovered," Col. Streight says, " that the mules were nothing but poor, wild, and unbroken colts, many of them but two years old, and that a large number of them had the horse distemper; some 40 or 50 of the lot were too near dead to travel, and had to be left at the landing; 10 or 12 died before we started, and such of them as could be rode at all were... wild and unmanageable..."

As suggested previously, it is intensely puzzling that a situation so bad - 40 or 50 animals with a major, usually fatal, equine disease and obviously near death...10 or 12 more already dead before the steamers were boarded - had not been communicated to the commander of the Brigade. After all the horses and mules were obviously ordered as the Boys From Lake County and their fellow infantry men's ride right into the teeth of some sort of potential battle action. There's no doubt, by then, everyone knew that.

It is also equally unquestioned that large numbers - likely far more than half - of the troopers in the volunteer regiments were farmers, as most American citizens in Civil War years were. Even small town "city" slickers like store clerks, office workers, tradesmen, lawyers and doctors rode horses and drove carriages and wagons as modes of personal and provisional transport. The more affluent had horse stalls and carriage sheds behind their city houses. They were, therefore, intensely familiar with horseflesh and it's ailments. Rest assured, a good many of the Boys From Lake County knew. That certainly included Wilson Shannon Baughman, and others who were farmers.

Horse distemper was one of the most feared of equine ailments, especially among those who owned them as vehicles used in producing daily bread. It was a disease virtually incurable...and also an ailment well known to spread disastrously and quickly through a herd, if sick animals were not hurriedly separated from others. Even that was far from a guarantee of preventing further spread of infection.

Why? Why was Col. Streight not told of this disastrous, unfolding, situation by one of the Boys From Lake County or others of their fellow Brigade regiments before the steamers left Nashville...while there was time to obtain replacements? Yes, we know now that time for preparation was short... and rushed. But...total silence on such a potentially deathly issue?

Likely, we're seeing the result of very young men quickly enrolled from civilian life into a totally unfamiliar military environment, rushed through basic training, still awed with the relationship, awkward with the propriety, of communication between an officer and a soldier. It is a fact of history that the Boys From Lake County, and their fellows of the 73rd Indiana, were headed toward combat within two weeks after their induction on August 16, 1862. And, in fact, over centuries of the human conduct of war, officers are (perhaps necessarily) thought to be more than a bit infallible...soldiers (just as necessarily) required to silently do what they're ordered to do, even - or especially - at the point of combat death. In other words, officers are supposed to know, and not be questioned about, what the hell they're doing. That, of course, does not mean that rank and file soldiers will not quietly grumble and wonder among themselves about the peril of such an unexpected, devastating, event.

"It took us all that day and a part of the next," Col. Streight continues, "to catch and break them before we could move out across the country; but in the meantime I had sent out several parties to gather in horses and mules, and they had been successful in getting about 150 very good animals, but mostly barefooted (without iron horseshoes)." Lt. Roach expanded the picture of that effort, "We had scoured the country as far south as it was safe on the account of the proximity of a large force of the enemy in that direction under Woodward."

Again, it is left to Lt. Roach in his postwar book, "The Prisoner of War and How Treated," to breathe a sense of life into this time. In his words we can more surely be there, stand nearby, watch and hear the clatter of hooves and boots down the gangplank of the steamers, soft gurgles of flowing river water past their sides, the unfurling of tent halves, erection of the tent encampment near Palmyra, the bright glow of campfires reflecting on sturdy young faces, the smell of frying meat and bread or bubbling stew, the smell of wood smoke from hundreds of campfires permeating the air. And the next morning the harsh braying of big, wrathful, muscular animals, the rush of stomping steeds, the swirl of dust created by flying hooves and boots.

His further explanation reaches out to us, spanning nearly 140 years, still gripping the intenseness of reality: "Landing at Palmyra. At this place our command disembarked and bivouacked for the night. We remained at Palmyra one day and a half, during which time every member of the command was actively employed - those to whom the animals were issued that were furnished us at Nashville, breaking their mules, the remainder scouring the country through in every direction, in quest of animals to put through the same interesting ceremony, during the performance of which the long-eared and stubborn quadruped before mentioned would tax his ingenuity and muscular power to the utmost, to divest himself of his unwelcome rider. And as our boys were 'foot soldiers' they were at first very easily dismounted, frequently in a most undignified and unceremonious manner."

From the lack of individual company records in America's Civil War, we cannot tell whether the Boys From Lake County were being bucked off their steeds or out scouring the countryside for more of them. If they were among the ones who brought back the 150 new animals they may have been doing both. It is likely, though, that farm boys, like Wilson Shannon Baughman, were having a better go at "breaking" their animals than the "city" boys.

Of additional specific interest, Lt. Roach also thoroughly answers another question left hanging in Col. Streight's description of the raid's preparations...that is, why the Brigade was not furnished with a sufficient number of good animals before leaving Nashville.

"For the very good reason," Roach explains, " that the grand object of the expedition was to cripple the enemy as much as possible; and one very effectual way of doing this, was to seize the animals whose labor furnished subsistence for the rebel armies and roving bands of guerillas, whose dastardly and fiendish deeds have cursed the fairest portions of Kentucky, Tennessee and other border States. General Rosecrans therefore gave orders to Colonel Streight to mount his command in the above manner; and which could very easily have been done, had there been one-third as much stock in the country as we expected to find; and had there been one-tenth the number General Morgan found in the course of his expedition through Indiana and Ohio, we could have marched to the coast of Florida and back in safety, but on the contrary the line of our expedition afforded but a very few animals, and those of an inferior quality."

Chapter Four

Down the Mighty Tennessee

After a day and a half of intense effort by troops of the Streight's Brigade to solve the problem with their war steeds, the men broke camp. It was on Monday morning the 13th of April, 1863 that the Boys From Lake County and their fellow soldiers packed up tents, supplies, and personal items, mounted up onto their Army saddles...those of them who had horses or mules...and headed out in a southwesterly direction. In fact, Fort Henry lay northwesterly from Palmyra, but It was necessary to take a more westerly aim at first to stay south of a sharp bend in the Cumberland River.

"We marched about fifteen miles," Streight relates, "and encamped on Yellow Creek. In that era of America's growing pioneer development, creeks were important reference landmarks, especially in yet unpopulated areas where there were no intersecting roads to the (usually mapped) main road traveled. Named creeks crossing the road (and also mapped), gave an assured point of reference. It became precise location information dispatched by fast horsemen...often telegraphed in more populated areas... back to those who were monitoring a military advance. Even more important, creeks were vital stopping points because of the water afforded for animal and human alike. In many, if not most, small villages in pre-Civil War America, extended areas of town were often identified by named creeks.

In our modern day, fast moving automobiles, a fifteen mile trip may easily be a brief joy ride of fifteen or twenty minutes. In the time of Col. Streight's Brigade, with 1700 men, more than 400 of them still afoot, it was a long, hard, grueling day's travel. "This was, " Lt. Roach pointed out, "our first day's march as mounted

29

infantry." Likely, there was many a sore behind among the Regimental young men. Even the many farmers, closely familiar with the big work animals, were often far more accustomed to walking behind them... guiding a plow in the furrows of a field, or riding behind them in a wagon, rather than sitting in a hard, rolling, pitching Army saddle.

During that day they continued to try to seize new horses from farms in the countryside. "The scouting parties" Col. Streight lamented, " did not succeed in finding many good horses or mules. The people had got warning of our movements and the stock was mostly run off."

But then, there was the setting up of tents again, hundreds of campfires, the pungent scent of wood smoke, hot coffee, meat, bread...and a good night's rest at Yellow Creek.

"Early the next morning," said Streight," we resumed our march, and arrived at Fort Henry about noon on the 15th." It was a mid April Wednesday, 1863, by then. If the Brigade moved at the pace of Monday the distance from Yellow Creek to Fort Henry, taking all of Tuesday and half of Wednesday, must have been twenty-three miles or so. "We had scoured the country as far south as it was safe on account of the proximity of a large force of the enemy under Woodward." It seems apparent, though he does not explain it further, that Streight is referring to Confederate units led by Lt. Col. T.G. Woodward, commander of the 1st Kentucky Cavalry.

Clearly there continued to be acute problems with the horses and mules issued in Nashville. "Although about 100 of the mules gave out and had to be left behind on our march," Streight explained, "yet when we reached Fort Henry our animals numbered about 1,250. Those that we had collected in the country were mostly in good condition, but were nearly all barefooted." In the rocky, mountainous Rebel land through which the route of their raid lay, animals without iron horseshoes would present another daily stress.

When the Brigade arrived at Fort Henry on the Tennessee River, it was not long before Col. Streight confronted yet another trouble. "Contrary to my expectations," he said, "the boats had not arrived, nor did they reach there until the evening of the 16th, having been delayed in getting the rations and forage." To be sure, it is not surprising that it might it take longer than hoped to secure, deliver, and load aboard river steamers the quantity of supplies needed for General Dodge's 8,000 man army. Nevertheless, the Brigade command suffered a further delay and the troops had another day and a half to struggle with their new mounts, as well as to rest up for the hard days ahead.

As we know, General Ellet's Marine Brigade, with two gunboats, guarded the fleet to Fort Henry. "They informed me that they were ordered to proceed with me," Streight said, "to Eastport, Mississippi." That certainly must have been highly welcome news, for the ships would be moving, daily, deeper into the nearness of enemy territory. "General Ellet," Streight said, "assumed command of the fleet, and we embarked as soon as possible." But, once again, "as soon as possible" was not immediately, far from as rapidly as Streight had planned. "The pilots declared," Streight explained further, "that at the existing low stage of the water it would be unsafe to run at nights."

So... in an interesting sidebar of history... we now know that on Thursday, Friday, Saturday, and Sunday, April 16th, 17th,18th, and 19th 1863, waters of the Tennessee River were at low level...likely because of a lack of rain for many days or weeks... and perhaps because of a lack of snow throughout winter months just passed.

"Hence we did not start until the morning of the 17th when we steamed up the river," Streight grumbled, "but, despite all my efforts to urge the fleet ahead as fast as possible, we did not reach Eastport until the afternoon of the 19th.

Three days steaming, and two nights at anchor, or tied to trees along the riverbank, cannot have been the most comfortable of times for the Boys From Lake County. The small steamer fleet was packed with 1700 men, about 1250 horses and mules, as well as the human rations and horse feed loaded aboard for General Dodge's 8,000 men waiting ahead. Still, it was a time of riding the smooth river instead of walking, or in the hard leather

31

of a saddle. And it was likely a time to wangle a few feet of space and catch a nap, to talk, perhaps engage in the horseplay of youth, to write letters and share thoughts of home...activities so common to soldiers of all generations before the din and anguish of battle. But, at least, we know exactly where the Boys From Lake County were and a bit of what their life was like on these mid-April days of 1863.

We also know it was a Sunday afternoon, April 19, 1863 that the river steamers docked on the Tennessee River near Eastport, Mississippi. With no information of threatening Rebel forces the steamers were not required to shorten their course, but were able to continue on to the originally planned destination near Eastport. It meant just that much less marching in saddle, or on foot, for the Boys From Lake County and their fellow soldiers of Streight's Brigade.

"As soon as we arrived," Streight says, "I left Colonel Lawson in command, with orders to disembark and prepare to march." Lt. Roach added that the orders included directions for camping the Brigade and caring for the animals. The General with his army of some 8,000 men, was waiting for Streight twelve miles up the Bear River, twenty miles or so west of Tuscumbia. The meeting was vital for the two leaders to finalize plans for the feint of Dodge's 8,000 man army toward Rebel forces near the small village of Town Creek, Alabama. It was simply a ruse, a hope, that Streight's departure into enemy territory would not be noticed in the tumult of attack. The idea was not to risk troops in a full scale assault, but to push the smaller Rebel forces back using a front line of rifle, sniper, and small cannon fire. General Dodge agreed to push about five miles past Town Creek to the town of Courtland, Alabama.

In fact, fifteen miles or so east of Tuscumbia, the waters of Town Creek for which the village is named, were swollen and deep from heavy rains of the previous few days. So, General Dodge's "attack" stalled at the waters of the creek, muddling on for the balance of the night and most of the next day, as little more than individual, but considerable, sniper fire from both Union and Confederate troops across the swollen waters...plus a few - largely ineffective - cannon balls lobbed across by each side.

During the hours of their strategy session, and his horse ride to and from General Dodge's command post, Streight was unaware that he was in for yet another decidedly unpleasant surprise. "I returned to Eastport about midnight," he continued, "and was informed that a stampede had occurred among the animals, and that some of them had got away."

Again, Lt. A.C. Roach explains the fractious incident in a bit more detail. "In justice to all parties concerned, it would be well to mention a circumstance which contributed much, no doubt, to the failure of the expedition. While disembarking and picketing the animals, a stampede was created among them, when nearly 300 of the best we had escaped."

Actually, news items published about a week later in the Southern city of Rome, Georgia gave a much more pervasive, and likely, slant on the stampede. General Dodge had marched to bear Creek with 5,500 men and was joined by 2,500 more making his force, aligned on the west bank of Bear Creek, 8,000.

On the east bank of the creek Dodge was faced by a Brigade commanded by Confederate Brigadier General Philip Dale Roddey. In fact, Roddey had himself raised the 4th Alabama Calvary Regiment as a Lt. Col. there in Tuscumbia in October 1862. After a number of successes in middle Tennessee through that winter he had quickly been promoted to Brigadier General and continued on to become one of the best known, most successful, most respected Rebel cavalry commanders in Alabama. It was reported a few days later in the newspaper of Rome, Georgia, that it was some of his men who secretly crossed bear Creek into the area held by Dodge's Union forces, slipped into Streight's camp and caused the stampede by knocking down a crude fence and firing guns in the air.

"Daylight the next morning," the obviously dismayed Streight said, "revealed to me the fact that nearly 400 of our best animals were gone. All that day and part of the next was spent in scouring the country to recover them, but only about 200 of the lost number were recovered. The remainder fell into the hands of the enemy." Streight readily acknowledged that the loss of the horses was a "heavy blow" to his command. Besides detaining the unit for nearly two days at Eastport, and wearying men and horses in scouring the countryside looking for the lost ones, it caused still further delay at Tuscumbia to replace them.

Streight again made note of the continuing consequence of the poor and ill animals he had originally been issued. "Quite a number of the mules drawn at Nashville," he grumbled, "had to be left at Eastport, on account of the distemper before mentioned; several died before we left."

But finally, with commendable effort by all hands, Streight's Brigade was able to move on. "We left Eastport on the afternoon of April 21," he reported, "and reached General Dodge's headquarters the following morning about 8 o'clock." From this it is clear that during the afternoon and night hours of Tuesday, April 21, 1863 and through the dark hours, dawn, and early morning of Wednesday April 22, 1863 we are on an all night march with the Boys From Lake County. "

"We then proceeded in the rear of General Dodge's forces," Streight continued, "which were continually skirmishing with the enemy as they advanced as far as Tuscumbia." Clearly the men of Streight's Brigade were advancing without sleep ... unless some, or even many, of them might have napped in the saddle during the night. The ones on foot certainly could not have done so. Dodges 8,000 men had advanced across Bear Creek. General Roddey's much smaller force, about 1,100 men with 4 cannon, had little choice but to fire and slowly retreat back toward Tuscumbia. At the same time, Streight was still looking for good mounts, "scouring the country to the river on the left and to the mountains on our right," he explained, "and collected all the horses and mules that could be found." To be sure, the ones scouring the countryside for more horses could not have been napping in the saddle.

"We arrived at Tuscumbia about 5 p.m. on April 24," Streight stated. It was the last Saturday of that spring month in 1863. Now... there would be two days to catch up on missed sleep. "Here General Dodge furnished me some 200 mules and 6 wagons to haul ammunition and rations."

Dodge also furnished Streight with vital information concerning a Rebel officer who would quickly become a most ardent foe. That fact was not fully true at the moment ..at least not quite yet, but would certainly soon be so... the next day. "General Dodge informed me that there was no doubt but Forrest had crossed the Tennessee River, and was in the vicinity of Town Creek; hence he agreed to advance as far as Courtland, on the Decatur Road, and, if possible, drive the enemy in that direction, but if they (the enemy) turned toward Moulton (the route of Streight's Raid) our cavalry, under General Dodge was to be sent in pursuit."

In fact, that help never followed Colonel Streight, although it was sorely needed. It surely boded yet another significant reason for failure of his mission. And that reason could perfectly be placed on the wily daring for which Confederate Cavalry General Nathan Bedford Forrest became famous. It is amazing how quickly information could be shared in those Civil War years...but it must be remembered that in populated areas telegraph was available. The next day, being informed of Dodge's incursion, Forrest crossed the Tennessee River into Town creek with 1,000 men and 6 cannon, being joined by 600 more men of the 11th Tennesee Cavalry. In doing so, Forrest took command of a force of 2,700 men and 10 cannon.

But just as quickly, the next day, Tuesday, April 28, 1863 in a typically risky, bold, move, he split the small force..., sending 700 men and several cannon around to the rear of General Dodge's army of 8,000. There, they certainly did not have enough strength to win a pitched battle, but created enough noise, rifle and cannon fire, and guerilla attacks to cause Dodge to turn around, push them back through Tuscumbia and retire to his main camp at Corinth, Mississippi. Worse, Dodge failed to pursue the small 1,200 man cavalry force, with just 2 cannon, which Forrest took with him... as he himself, charged off after Streight's Brigade.

It was at this juncture that the vibrant little city of Tuscumbia endured the worst time of it's already long life. Dodge reported that he "burned all provisions, produce, forage, all mills... destroyed everything of aid to the enemy. I took stock of all kinds." It is with these events so recently behind them that Col. Streight, The Boys From Lake County, and their fellow soldiers, now cavalrymen, find themselves heading...on into the dark and rain.

Major William Krimball Circa 1862

Chapter Five

The Boys From Lake County

This saga of America's Civil War, by it's very name, shares much of the history of largely un-remembered, rifle bearing, Union soldiers from just one locality, Lake County, Indiana.

In the National Archives of the United States of America in Washington, DC, where my wife Sandee and I held the original, hand written, Regimental records of the 73rd Indiana in our hands... and read with awe the penned entries...we fully hoped for a wealth of personal observations of those in Company A..., the Boys From Lake County.

As mentioned earlier, though, what we found is that in most instances, Company A records were simply commingled into integrated Regimental ones... their military engagements mainly described within the context of the operations of the 73rd Indiana Volunteer Infantry. Generally, though, we could discern information concerning the location of individual Companies. In other words, we can be certain that the men of Company A were indeed part of a certain day's battle action, march, or camp report. And so, we can share where they were and what they were doing on most days of their Civil War service to America. In this sense we are able to paint a graphic portrait of both their in-camp, seemingly endless, waiting...as well as the battle ferocity and casualties of their Civil War engagements.

More important, we've been fortunate to be able to piece together and share much of their individual story from other sources. To be sure, after nearly one hundred and forty passing years, the records of a great many individual deeds and daily chores have been lost, forgotten, or simply faded out of sight in the pages of documents or books no longer published.

But... in the hand written records of the 73rd Indiana Volunteers, we found another reason why mention of the combat actions of individual soldiers are rare in formal report records of the Civil War. In battle recounts, the commanding officer would usually comment: "...there are several men I would like to commend for especially heroic conduct today. But, since I cannot be everywhere at once and likely was not able to see the same heroic conduct from many others...I feel it unfair to single out any one individual. So, I'm just going to say that my entire unit performed dutifully and heroically in this day's action." In such a model of fairness, integrity, and consideration for their men, officers often lost for all time a record of the names of many individual soldiers who should have been remembered for their deeds of heroism.

Notwithstanding, it becomes clear that the Boys From Lake County were greatly typical of most volunteers, from both the North and South. Since we know a substantial amount about them, their time in our history...who they were, where they came from, their movements, how they conducted themselves in battle, what happened to them... they become a phenomenal model by which all Civil War soldiers may still be remembered, described, honored.

The more we partake in the assembling of historical data, the more it becomes evident that both Union and Rebel rifle bearers came from the same kinds of towns, villages, counties, or farms. Weather seasons may have been quite different in parts of the North and South, and perhaps in some cases, family heritage. But all spoke the same language, albeit sometimes with sharply varying degrees of accent. It is undeniable, though, that all had the same basic belief in freedom and democracy that was already America's heritage by the opening salvos of the Civil War in 1861.

When debate roared to it's ending, and the call to war came, the ranks of both armies were eagerly and rapidly filled. Citizens of both the North and South shared a deep, abiding belief in the rightness of their cause, in America herself. In the

The Boys From Lake County

final analysis...sadly enough considering the horrendous human and animal loss during the Civil War...that faith is what has made our United States of America one of the greatest experiments in human freedom and democratic governing ever seen in the history of our planet. Both Confederate and Union soldiers believed deeply that they were fighting for home, family, and the future of our Nation. And both were willing to die for Her. The Boys From Lake County were no different.

In fact, when the announcement of the formation of Indiana's 73rd Volunteer Infantry Regiment was published, the Boys From Lake County responded so quickly they became Company A, the first company of the new unit. It was initially recruited by Capt. William Krimball of the town of Crown Point, the county seat of Lake County, Indiana. Krimball's officer commission was dated Tuesday, August 5, 1862. His 100 men were all assembled from Lake County, the larger towns of Crown Point and Lowell, several smaller villages, as well as a nearby area of Lowell known as the Three Creeks Township.

An early "History Of Lake County" was written in 1872 when memories of the Civil War were still fresh and painful, letting us be there, share again the feeling of those days. It was penned by the Reverend Timothy H. Ball, a Lake County Baptist minister. His words echo the sentiment of Lake County citizens of that era far more fully:

"Amid the political changes and excitements which marked in this land the sixth decade of the nineteenth century," he said, "Lake County, formerly Democratic, became strongly Republican...and entered heartily, in 1860 into the campaign which resulted in the election of Abraham Lincoln.

"When, therefore," he continued, "that shot was fired, at twenty minutes past four o'clock on the morning of April 12, 1861, against the granite wall of Fort Sumpter, which inaugurated the great Civil War in America; and when the tidings were flashed along the wires that Fort Sumpter had actually surrendered to the Rebels, and that, on the historic 19th of April blood was shed in the streets of Baltimore; and when the President's call for volunteers was heard; it was expected that the loyal citizens of Lake County would thrill in that intense wave of excitement that poured over the North, and press forward at once for marching orders, that they might hasten to the scene of conflict." (The reader will notice here that local writers of that era seemed prone to write in sentences that were a full paragraph in length, ideas separated by semi-colons instead of periods.)

"The entire population of Lake County in 1860," continues the Reverend Ball, "was 9,145. The number of families was about 1800. So many of our young men went into Illinois regiments that the whole number of our citizens enlisting cannot be determined. So far as can be ascertained, as many as one thousand men from those eighteen hundred families entered the Union army."

In organizing Lake County's Civil War unit, Richard W. Price, of Lowell, was named First Lieutenant of Company A, and Philip Reed, also of Lowell, became Second Lieutenant. Alfred Fry, of Crown Point, was Company A's initial First Sergeant, also referred to then as an Orderly Sergeant.

In fact, Alfred Fry represented the symbol of American men who spend a great deal of their lives as industrious civilians, while in times of National need demonstrating an adventurous, full grown, inborn talent for military engagement and leadership.

Before joining Company A of the 73rd Indiana Volunteers as one of the Boys From Lake County, Fry was already a veteran of the Mexican War, having served as a private, then as Corporal, in Captain Joseph P. Smith's company along with thirty-two other enlisted men from Crown Point.

"Sergeant Fry apparently thrived on army service" says the Lake County History of 1934, "and not only survived the Mexican War, that took the lives of over half of the company, not through any thrilling experiences, but by disease, accidents, sun-stroke, and starvation...but he likewise survived the Civil War, being promoted through the ranks, and returning home as Captain..." of Company A, 73rd Indiana Volunteer Infantry Regiment in 1865.

Just eleven days after Captain Krimball's commissioning, Company A, the Boys From Lake County, rendezvoused with others of the 73rd Regiment, and were mustered in at Camp Rose near South Bend, Indiana on Saturday, August 16, 1862. Their contracted term was for three years of service. On that same day Captain Krimball was promoted from Captain of Company A, to Major, and given command of the first Battalion of the Regiment.

Consequently, at the same time, First Lieutenant Price was promoted to Captain of Company A, his position being assumed by Second Lieutenant Reed who was promoted to First Lieutenant. Thereby, on Friday, August 22, 1862, Alfred Fry received his first officer commission as Second Lieutenant of Company A.

Of four other initial Sergeants in Company A, Henry Pratt of Crown Point served as such until honorably discharged on Saturday, February 28, 1863, Andrew Sprague of Crown Point until honorably discharged Wednesday, November 25, 1863, and Thomas W. Loving of Crown Point until his death of illness at Nashville, Tennessee on Wednesday, September 30, 1863. George S. Clark of Lowell was promoted to Second Lieutenant, with the date un-noted.

The 1934 "History of Lake County" defines an indirect, but astounding, reference to the lack of time for training afforded Company A, the Boys From Lake County, and their 73rd Indiana Regiment before being ordered into troop march and the threat of combat.

"Under this early leadership." the volume relates, "Company A went with the 73rd Regiment to Louisville, Kentucky, and was ordered from there to Lexington, Kentucky where they had hardly arrived when defeat of Union forces at Richmond, Kentucky on August 30, 1862 necessitated a forced march back to Louisville."

So...mustered into the 73rd Regiment on Saturday, August 16, 1862..., within the fourteen days to Saturday, August 30, 1862, the Boys From Lake County had undergone two major moves and were in the process of a forced march back to Louisville. There seems to have been virtually no meaningful time for specific military training.

Of course, much of our Nation was still frontier in that era. Moreover it follows that America was largely a rural, farming environment in Civil War years. Most men knew weapons well, using them for protection of their homes and families and for hunting to add food to the family table. In fact, before mustering into the Army, many could kill a squirrel or turkey with a, meat saving, head shot from 50 paces away.

Even so, one man sent a letter home to his family, during one of the stops on those earliest of marches, saying, "...we shot off our guns yesterday morning. Mine kicked me over, and they kicked me for falling." Obviously, they were still greatly in need of training nearly two weeks after being mustered in, even though they were already "on the move" and at daily risk of employing their weapons or being shot at.

Having one of the long, huge bore, weapons of the Civil War "kick over" an unsuspecting and untrained soldier is far from surprising. The basic weapon of an infantry soldier in that era was the single shot, muzzle loading percussion rifle musket.

Foremost among these was the Springfield, manufactured at the U.S. Armory in Springfield, Massachusetts, but also at other locations. All were simply called "Springfields" by the rifle bearers. By the end of the war, it's total production neared 1.5 million weapons. The Springfield had a 39 inch long, rifled, barrel and could fire a .58 caliber bullet effectively at targets 500 yards distant. (That's 1500 feet, more than a quarter mile). After the Confederate capture of the Federal Armory at Harper's Ferry, Virginia (later West Virginia), more than 64,000 Confederate copies were produced.

A comparable contender to the Springfield, the best of that era's foreign made rifles, was the British Enfield. More than 800,000 of these rifles were imported, with portions of that total bought by both the North and South. The Enfield fired .577 caliber bullets approximately the same distance as a Springfield.

42

The difference between a rifle and a musket is explained by the fact that the inside of the musket barrel is smooth. When fired, the round lead ball (bullet) explodes forward, un-streamlined, tending to wobble as it rushes through the air, thereby greatly diminishing accuracy.

The rifle barrel has a spiral groove inside. The lead bullet is cylindrical rather than round, with a pointed nose which cuts more cleanly through the air. The barrel's spiral groove gives the bullet a spin which hugely improves both distance and accuracy of the shot.

While rifles were preferred for their long range and accuracy, a large number of older, smooth bore, muskets of both domestic and foreign manufacture saw a great deal of service during the Civil War as well.

Most notable among these was the 1842 Springfield musket. This weapon had a 42 inch long, .69 caliber barrel, firing one solid .69 caliber round lead ball, along with three smaller buckshot. It was manufactured until 1855 at Springfield, Massachusetts and also at Harper's Ferry. Records indicate that 172,000 were made. Some 10,000 of these were later rifled in the pre war period...meaning that the spiral groove was cut in to the existing barrel and a new pointed bullet replaced the round ball and pellets. In fact, though, the bulk of those 1842 Springfield muskets remained un-modernized, and were issued, as far less accurate smooth bores.

Without the extra range of fire, soldiers armed with the big .69 caliber musket found themselves seriously handicapped against an enemy armed with rifles that could shoot accurately from 500 yards away. In his personal writings about the Civil War, General, and later President of the United States, Ulysses S. Grant observed that using the 1842 Springfield musket, "you might fire at a man all day from a distance of 125 yards without him ever finding it out."

It was this huge bore musket with which many Volunteer units were armed ...and records indicate it was this same old, outdated, .69 caliber, 1842 Springfield musket which the Boys

From Lake County carried into battle. Needless to say, with it's huge .69 caliber, it had a "kick" like a mule when it was fired. Hence the wry complaint from a neophyte soldier of being "kicked over" when he fired it for the first time.

The great many Volunteer army units who used it learned quickly that to be most effective they must wait until the enemy was within 100 yards or so. In other words "wait until you can see the whites of their eyes." At that close range, with such a huge lead ball and three smaller ones, the weapon was simply devastating when a volley was fired from many muskets into closely spaced ranks of advancing enemy.

In fact, during the opening years, many of America's Civil War battles were fought "European Style" with tightly knit lines of men standing shoulder to shoulder, advancing toward each other in an open field, each side firing en-masse, point blank, into the oncoming ranks. The side who could re-load and fire the fastest, killing or wounding the greatest number in the other ranks, would be victorious... while the opposite ranks seeing masses of their comrades falling to the ground might scurry into retreat from the slaughter...sometimes in the helter-skelter of panic.

By the war's mid years it became obvious to both sides that combat in such a style, while enormously courageous, resulted in devastating, foolish, human loss. During latter war years much more of a guerilla style was often employed with soldiers using any type of cover available, hastily dug trenches, dirt embankments piled by shovel, thick wooden fences, or trees as protective cover while firing into enemy positions. Mass advancements and charges were still made in major engagements, but even then men moved toward the enemy firing in more wide-spread, crouched stance, making it harder for opposing riflemen, who then had to "pick off" the oncoming enemy one at a time. Cannon, of course, were different. A heavy, flying, cannonball could plow through, and take out, many of the enemy with one carefully aimed shot. Cannon loaded with many smaller lead pieces called "grape shot" might be devastating to even a wider spread unit of oncoming soldiers.

The forced march back to Louisville was a long, weary ninety miles - never to be forgotten - for the new troops of the 73rd Indiana Volunteer Infantry and it's Company A, the Boys From Lake County. A "forced march" in army lingo meant hurrying afoot for long hours of a day, and even on into the night, often at double-step time. According to the "History of Lake County" numerous solders died of sunstroke, and many became violently ill from heat, dust, and lack of proper sanitation involved in connection with inexperienced troops. This record, too, fully supports their almost total lack of training at that point, even though they were under fighting orders and movements. The Boys From Lake County seem to have all survived that experience, although "official records" says the 1934 History,"indicated that one man, Newman G. Eadus, was missing in action, at Lexington, Kentucky, Saturday, August 30, 1862."

After the defeat at Richmond, Kentucky, the 55,000 man Union Army of the Ohio was reorganized under General Don Carlos Buell. The 73rd Indiana Volunteer Infantry Regiment, along with Company A, the Boys From Lake County, was assigned to Maj. Gen. Thomas L. Crittenden's II Corp of the Army of the Ohio. Buell's army was facing the Confederate forces of General Braxton Bragg.

It is a fact of history that these un-known, un-famed, Boys From Lake County, along with their fellow soldiers of the 73rd Indiana Volunteer Infantry served under the command of, or fought against, several of the most famous and interesting of Civil War Generals.

General Buell was a West Point graduate, a career officer of the Class of 1841. Prior to the Civil War, he'd already served in the Seminole and Mexican wars, wounded at the battle of Churubusco. Later, he was appointed adjutant-general of the Union Army's Department of the Pacific. As the Civil War began on April 12, 1861, Buell was assigned to Washington, arriving in September 1861 to assist the storied General George B.

McClellan (also a West Pointer) in organizing the immense and highly successful Army of the Potomac. In command of the army for operations in East Tennessee, Buell led the capture of Nashville. He also fought along side General Ulysses S. Grant on the second day of the horrific Battle of Shiloh, and was a commander of Union forces in the nearby Battle of Corinth.

Maj. Gen. Thomas Leonidas Crittendan was a classic example that our Civil War was often a conflict of brother against brother. Born in Russellville, Kentucky, he was the son of Senator John J. Crittenden, brother of Confederate General George B. Crittenden, and cousin of Union General Thomas T. Crittenden. A lawyer, he was a member of the Kentucky bar. In years after the Civil War he was State Treasurer of Kentucky. Earlier, Crittenden had led the 3rd Kentucky Volunteer Infantry as a Colonel and aide to General Zachary Taylor in the Mexican-American War. After that conflict he was appointed as U.S. Consul in Liverpool, England. In an attempt to prevent the Civil War Crittendan introduced Congressional legislation meant to ease the concerns of Southern States headed toward secession.

Braxton Bragg, born in North Carolina, was one of only eight men to reach the status of full General in Southern forces. He was certainly one of the Civil War's most controversial Generals, and the brother of Confederate Attorney General Thomas Bragg. Before the War he'd shown great leadership qualities in the Seminole and Mexican wars...afterward a Louisiana planter. He entered the Confederate Army soon after War was declared in 1861, serving in the Louisiana Militia as a Colonel. Still in that same year he was promoted to Major General commanding the Department of Louisiana. Soon he was elevated to Brigadier General commanding operations against Fort Pickens in the harbor at Pensacola, Florida. He led a Confederate Army Corp at the Battle of Shiloh. His success in that bloody engagement brought him promotion to full General and command of all Confederate Armies in the West.

In General Thomas L. Crittenden's II Corps...Company A, The Boys From Lake County with their fellow members of the

73rd Indiana Regiment, marched quickly again from Louisville, advancing south on the Bardstown Road following, searching for Bragg's Rebel forces known to be in the area. They reached Springfield, Kentucky on Monday, October 6, 1862.

On Tuesday and Wednesday, October 7th and 8th they were deployed on a hillside in reserve, and watched the battle of Perryville, Kentucky. In fact, having one Regiment held in reserve was a common tactic of Civil War battle strategy. Standing close by, they could quickly be advanced as required into an area of the battle in greatest need of reinforcement.

The Battle of Perryville developed when in mid-July 1862 General Braxton Bragg, commanding the Confederate Army of Mississippi, along with Confederate General Kirby Smith, set in motion a raid into Kentucky from two different routes. People of Kentucky were divided between Union and Confederate loyalty. Bragg and Smith hoped to lure thousands to the Southern side, volunteers to the Rebel Army, as well as drawing Union troops out of the State of Tennessee. Unhappy with the lack of enthusiasm by many Kentuckians in the Confederate cause, Bragg had brought about the appointment of a Confederate governor in Frankfort, the state capital.

By late September 1862, the Confederate armies of both Bragg and Smith, had made their way into northern Kentucky. Distracted by another enemy force, though, Bragg did not react to the approach of Buell's 60,000 man Union Army towards Perryville...and paid no attention to the possible aid of 16,000 nearby Confederate troops commanded by General Leonidas Polk. The night of Tuesday, October 7, 1862, elements of Union and Rebel regiments fought over water rights at a place called Doctor's Creek.

The hotly-contested Battle of Perryville, began the next morning Wednesday, October 8, 1862 with Buell's Union Army of the Ohio facing portions of Bragg's Confederate Army of Mississippi. Bragg got there early in the morning and assaulted the left side of Union army units. Buell intended to meet the attack with his entire force, but orders didn't reach his commanders in time and they were late meeting the attack. The ferocity of battle reeled back and forth, fiercest fighting taking place in a northern sector of the battlefield where Benjamin Cheatham's Confederates struggled against Union forces of Alexander McCook's lst Corps. At center, the aggressive Union division of famed commander Philip Sheridan drove back Confederates toward the town of Perryville. One Union brigade under Colonel William Carlin, hurrying to support Sheridan, even charged into the streets of the town. The battle ended at dark, Union forces suffering the most with 4,211 casualties. There were 3,396 in losses for Confederates under General Braxton Bragg.

Although Bragg's army suffered less than Buell's, the Confederate commander awoke to the fact that he faced the entire Army of the Ohio, and ordered an immediate retreat. Sadly, in spite of more than 7,600 combined battle losses, neither side gained meaningfully at the Battle of Perryville. It seemed mainly a lack of coordination between Confederate Generals Braxton Bragg and Kirby Smith that doomed a complete Southern success of their invasion of Kentucky. Equally bumbling, Union commander General Don Carlos Buell, and his troops...including the Boys From Lake County... did follow the Confederate retreat, but Buell commanded the effort in such indifferent, unsuccessful fashion that he was eventually removed from command of the Army of the Ohio. For a commander, not pushing a retreating army intensely, can be a major missed opportunity.

Afterwards, Company A, The Boys From Lake County, amidst the 73rd Indiana Volunteer Regiment, were marched directly over the battlefield among General Crittenden's II Corps and others of the Army of the Ohio. They pursued General Bragg's Confederate army only as far as a village named Wild Cat, not far from Glasgow, Kentucky. They were then marched back to the west and southwest through Kentucky with Buell's army, reaching the Tennessee line near Gallatin on Friday, November 7, 1862.

In fact, trooping immediately over the battlefield after the battle of Perryville, Kentucky, though held in reserve and never shooting nor being shot at, gave the Boys From Lake County their first real "look" at the suffering and death of war. No battlefield has ever been a "pretty" place just after the shooting ceases. Approximately 620,000 men, 360,000 Northerners and 260,000 Southerners, died in the Civil War's four-year conflict, a figure that tops the total fatalities of all other wars in which America has ever fought. Of these, approximately 110,000 Union and 94,000 Confederate men died of wounds received on the battlefield. The rest died of disease.

On the now quiet battlefield which the Boys From Lake County must have seen.., quiet, that is, except for moans of the wounded... when rifles and cannon were stilled..., the dead lay face down, face up,.. mouth often sagged open, eyes glazed, rifle perhaps still clutched in a hand, often simply lying beside, or dropped in leaning position against an earthen bank or fence. Just as much in evidence were still living wounded. With more than 7,600 casualties that day at Perryville, the Boys From Lake County likely had a close look at both.

Needless to say, the slow, stagger of wounded headed back from the battle front was as painful as the sight of the bodies of those killed in action. There were shattered limbs bound in dirty rags used as slings. Body and head wounds were covered with bloody, soiled bandages. Others limped and heaved their way along, a foot rolled in dirty, bloody rags...using crutches made from hastily cut tree branches. In all engagements the wounded suffered in heat of sun or shivered in cold depending on the time of year, uniforms holed, ripped, soiled, bloody.

America's Civil War exploded at a time when the practice of medicine was just beginning to develop into more modern treatment methods and medications. Truly terrible casualties and the Civil War's high amputation rate were the result of the type of rifle ammunition used...the big Minie Ball. About the size of a quarter, it was a bullet of soft lead, tending to mushroom when it hit bone, tearing a gaping wound. It caused enormous injury, often damaging bone and tissue past hope of repair. With it's weight, an abdominal or head wound was far too often fatal.

A shot to an arm or leg usually shattered bone. Bullets carried dirt and germs into the wound, causing a high rate of secondary infection. Of about 180,000 wounds to arm or leg among Union troops, 30,000 or so brought about amputation of limb. About the same rate of amputation was found among Confederate soldiers.

Every effort was made to treat wounded men within 48 hours...(author's note: two entire days...?) Most primary care was administered at field hospitals located far behind the front lines. Those who survived were transported by bouncing, two wheeled cart, or four wheeled wagon, ambulances...unreliable, overcrowded...to army hospitals located in some nearby city or town.

After directly crossing that battlefield, The Boys From Lake County spent several weeks in the vicinity of Gallatin, Tennessee marching back and forth trying to catch Rebel Morgan who was operating in the region.

Morgan was another of the famous, enterprising, Confederate Generals of which the Boys From Lake County were well aware. A calvary raider, and determined individualist, John Hunt Morgan found it far from easy to comply with constraints placed by his superiors. Born in Alabama, he'd served in the Mexican War as a First Lieutenant with the lst Kentucky Regiment. Unlike many volunteer officers, he did indeed see action in that conflict. Moving to Kentucky as a Lexington merchant between wars, Morgan organized the Lexington Rifles Company of the Kentucky State Guard in 1857. When Civil War came, even though his state never did secede, he chose to join the Confederacy.

Rising rapidly in rank from Captain after forming his own Morgan's Kentucky Cavalry Squadron in 1861, he led them in central Kentucky and at the great battle of Shiloh. Morgan was then promoted to Colonel, leading a regiment during the Corinth siege and two regiments on a raid through Kentucky from July 4, to August 1, 1862. This raid, together with that of Nathan Bedford Forrest, greatly hampered the advance of Union General Don

Carlos Buell on Chattanooga. In October 1862 shortly after the collapse of the Southern campaign in Kentucky, he led a brigade on another raid through his adopted state of Kentucky. During the Murfreesboro Campaign, from December 21, 1862, through January 1, 1863, Morgan led a mounted division into Kentucky, against Union supply lines. Promoted then to brigadier general, he received the thanks of the Confederate Congress for his exploits.

Following an engagement known as the Tullahoma Campaign he again received permission to enter Kentucky. On this raid from July 2 to 26, 1863, he violated Bragg's instructions not to cross the Ohio River. Crossing over into Indiana, he moved into Ohio, skirting Cincinnati, though the city went into a panic. Pursued by cavalry and militia, he was finally captured near New Lisbon, Ohio, on July 26th, after most of his command was taken prisoner. Confined in the Ohio State Penitentiary, he escaped on November 26, 1863. Again Morgan was placed in command in East Tennessee and later in Southwestern Virginia. He was surprised and killed at Greeneville, Tennessee, on Sunday, September 4, 1864.

In their back and forth searching after Morgan and his forces, several times the Boys From Lake County and their fellow 73rd Indiana Volunteers reached his camp a few hours after he and his troops left, but found none of them. At one time, though, on that first morning near Gallatin, November 7, 1862, nineteen Confederates were captured while still asleep, fatigued from their raiding. Finally, on November 26, 1862 the Boys From Lake County marched into Nashville, Tennessee.

In little more than a month they were headed into the first big battle of their Volunteer Army service. That engagement, the battle of Murphreesborough, Tennessee, also known as the Battle of Stones River, was one of the Civil War's ten bloodiest clashes. The Boys From Lake County with their fellow soldiers of the 73rd Indiana had a vital part in it.

By then the Boys From Lake County and their 73rd Indiana Regiment were assigned to the 3rd Brigade, 1st Division, Left

Wing, 14th Army Corps, in Major General William S. Rosecrans' massive Army of the Cumberland. Along side them were the 51st Indiana - commanded by Col. Abel D. Streight, 13th Michigan - commanded by Col. M. Shoemaker, 64th Ohio - commanded by Lt. Col. A. McIlvain, 65th Ohio - commanded by Lt. Col. Cassil, and the 6th Ohio Independent Battery - commanded by Capt. Cullen Bradley. Col. Charles G. Harker of the 65th Ohio commanded the 3rd Brigade. Of course, it was he who passed down the orders from Major General Rosecrans for the Brigade, to march southeast of Nashville toward a large force of Confederate troops threatening the city of Murphreesborough, Tennessee along the banks of Stones River.

In the exact words of Col. Harker, the Brigade "...left Stewarts Creek about 10 a.m. on Monday the 29th ultimo (December) marching most of the time in line of battle." Harker does not explain it, but there was a plantation called Stewarts Creek in the vicinity of Nashville. It seems likely those plantation fields had been the camp ground for the men of his Brigade, including, of course, the Boys From Lake County.

Actually, though, the Boys From Lake County headed toward Murphreesborough even earlier. Col. Gilbert Hathaway in his report to Col. Harker remarked..."In compliance with your request...the Seventy Third Regiment Indiana Volunteers... left Nashville on the morning of the 26th (Friday) taking the Murphreesborough road, encamping that night near La Vergne." Obviously, the 73rd Indiana, with Company A - the Boys From Lake County, was one of the 3rd Brigade units chosen to move out ahead, to lead in the operation.

The next day (Saturday) Company A and their fellow members of the 73rd Indiana Regiment marched in line of battle through fields and Cedar thickets amidst a drenching rain, encamping at night on Confederate camp grounds, which bore abundant evidence of having been hastily evacuated. "In the course of the day," Col. Hathaway said, "we passed several of his (Rebel) camp grounds, strewed with many signs of very recent occupation. Some sharp skirmishing was had today by one of my flanking companies."

Col. Hathaway reported that the enemy had been in the area in "considerable force," and that information sent back to his commanders was no doubt invaluable in guiding them to be sure enough Union troops were sent to counter Confederate's massed, for what turned out to be, the Battle of Stones River. "... A company from my command," Col Hathaway continued, " and one from Colonel Streight's (51st Indiana) crossed the river to a camp still in possession of the enemy's pickets, where we found more than 100 cavalry sabers, several rifles, and other arms which were taken possession of without much resistance, and brought into our camp." Streight added another item which must have been greatly welcome to his men. "The next day being Sunday." he said, "we remained quiet in camp."

On Monday morning the line of march was resumed, the Boys From Lake County and others of the 73rd passing through the same kind of country as on Friday and Saturday (very rough and broken.) "We came to Stone's River," Hathaway said, "not far from where the railroad crosses the stream, and about 2 miles from Murphreesborough, the enemy being strongly posted on a rise of ground on the opposite bank."

After nightfall the Boys From Lake County, among all others of the 73rd Regiment, waded across Stone's River... formed up in line of battle, and quickly marched up the hill, their skirmishers keeping up a vigorous fire with Rebels who backed away from the Union advance. Halting just under the brow of the hill, riflemen of the 73rd waited an attack..."which we had every reason to expect, and no doubt would have experienced," said Hathaway, "...had it not been that the very boldness of our advance intimated them. We were near enough to distinctly hear (Confederate) officers urge their men forward, appealing in the name of their 'country and their rights' to make the attack; but they came not." (To us now, it bears the sound of human voices in Civil War combat that still echo over this span of 140 years.)

The next day, Tuesday December 30, 1862, skirmishing was "indulged in" with "successful issues." Heavy firing was kept up to the right and left of the 73rd Indiana's position most of the day.

On the morning of Wednesday, December 31st, Confederates made a more vigorous attack on the right wing of the Union forces than at any time before. The 73rd Indiana along with the Boys From Lake County, were ordered into that direction and soon were engaged in the combat. The 65th Ohio Regiment was stationed in a piece of woodland, and in obedience to orders, Hathaway led the 73rd Indiana to their support. Coming up behind them, they found the 65th Ohio engaged with a heavy column (of Rebels) which was pressing them with great force.

"Well did they sustain themselves," Hathaway related, "till by great superiority of numbers, they were compelled to give way. Passing over my command, which at the time was lying down, we in turn were instantly engaged. Twelve rounds were fired with great spirit and effect." (Remember that the 73rd Indiana was using the old, huge, .69 caliber musket with a big, quarter-dollar sized, Minie Ball and 3 buckshot...simply devastating at such close range. A "round" meant that of a 300 rifleman regiment, 150 would fire while the other 150 quickly reloaded, readying in seconds to fire again. Therefore, in that instance, something near 1800 musket shots were likely fired into a closely packed advancing enemy unit within a very few minutes.)

"...it was seen that the enemy was retreating in disorder, taking an oblique direction to the left," Hathaway said. "I ordered an advance, and well indeed was it obeyed-pressing forward on the double quick." Ground lost by the 65th Ohio was regained, with the Confederates still fleeing before the 73rd's attack. Hathaway found, though, that the Boys From Lake County and others of his 73rd Indiana had gone too far. Realizing they were ahead of any support to his left... and that the battery of cannons which had been covering his right had been withdrawn, Hathaway then saw that the Rebels had brought up reserves, advanced over an open field to their left..."and subjected us to an enfilading (cross) fire for several moments of a most destructive character."

"Being thus left entirely alone." Hathaway lamented, "and finding it impossible to withstand such fearful odds, I withdrew in a somewhat disordered state, but soon rallied and again took position in front. My horse having been shot in the early part of the engagement, I was compelled to remain on foot the remainder of the day. That night we bivouacked on the same ground as the night before." From that time to the evening of January 3rd, The Boys From Lake County along with all of the 73rd Indiana were in the front, more or less exposed to cannon shells of the Confederates, sustaining some loss thereby.

Colonel Hathaway did not report it, but the History of Lake County published in 1934, tells us that all color guards (flag bearers) of the 73rd were killed during the Battle of Stones River...and, also, that the rapid advance toward retreating Confederate soldiers after the 12 volleys were fired, was in fact a bayonet charge.

On the morning of Wednesday, December 31, 1862, the day of their most severe combat, Colonel Hathaway reported that his regiment had just 309 enlisted men, 19 line officers, and 3 field and staff officers. The casualties of the entire 73rd Indiana Volunteer Infantry Regiment on that day were 22 enlisted men killed and 49 wounded...with 36 missing. Captains Miles H. Tibbets, Company F and Peter Doyle, Company I died in battle. 2nd Lts. Emanuel Williamson, Company I, and John Butterfield, Company K were wounded. Major William Krimball, originator of Company A but by then commander of the 73rd's First Battalion was slightly wounded in a knee. "My judgement." said Colonel Hathaway, "is that fully one-half of those missing are killed or wounded, and part of the others taken prisoner." In total Col. Hathaway counted 111 men killed, wounded or missing during the Battle of Stone's River at Murphreesborough...more than one-third of the 73rd Regiment's men at that time.

Company A, the Boys From Lake County lost two men killed...John H. Early of Crown Point, and Edward Welch of Winfield.

The "History of Lake County," published in 1934...likely with the advantage of tales told by soldiers who returned home after the war...expanded on Col. Hathaway's account. "On January 1st, the 73rd, supported by artillery brought up during the night, awaited the enemy who advanced at a run with one of their famous Rebel yells. But this charge was broken up by cannister (cannon fire containing many small pieces of lead as more modern armies might call shrapnel.) The 73rd held it's front line position without further loss until three o'clock in the afternoon." From that time they were "annoyed" by enemy sharp shooters who had worked around into woods on their right. 20 riflemen from the 73rd's Company B joined 100 men from other regiments, chased 300 sharp shooters out of the woods and discovered a position of hidden enemy cannon emplacements.

The huge Battle of Stone's River at Murphreesborough, Tennessee ended with Confederate withdrawal and the victorious Union army occupying Murphreesborough early on Sunday, January 4, 1863. As far as we have determined, official records do not mention this additional, sad, fact. According to mementos kept by rank and file fighting men of the 73rd Indiana Volunteers, though, the bodies of soldiers killed at the Battle of Stones River lay in the field where they fell for an entire week before removal and burial.

The Boys From Lake County along with others of their 73rd Indiana Infantry Regiment were assigned as part of the occupying force at Murphreesborough until April when they were called back to Nashville and re-assigned to duty with Streights Raid.

Chapter Six

Who Were They?

And so, now we know, as the Boys From Lake County... and their fellow soldiers of the 73rd Indiana Volunteer Infantry Regiment... move out on the night of April 26, 1863 as part of Streights Raid, they had become tough, battle hardened, combat veterans.

Colonel Charles G. Harker commanding their 3rd Brigade...in his report to Major General William S. Rosecrans commanding the giant Army of the Cumberland, said of their valor at Stone's River, "Too much praise cannot be bestowed upon Colonel Hathaway, commanding the Seventy Third Indiana Volunteers." In Civil War reports the actions of units were usually reported in the name of their commander. There is no doubt, though, that Col. Harker was speaking of the valor, not only of the Boys From Lake County, but all the men of the 73rd. To be sure, Col. Harker made these commending remarks along with those mentioning several other regiments who performed with great initiative, success, and valor in the Battle of Stones River at Murphreesborough.

In fact, Major General Rosecrans, commander of the entire Union Army of the Cumberland, on Friday, January 3rd, 1863, complimented the 73rd Indiana Regiment for their heroism in the Stone's River campaign. The Regimental commander requested, and Union Army leaders approved, that the 73rd Indiana Volunteer Infantry Regiment add the words "Stone's River" on it's Regimental flag. Such was only allowed when a unit played a significant part in a given battle. Lieutenant Alfred Fry of Crown Point conducted himself so well during the five day Battle of Stone's River that he was promoted to Captain of Company A, replacing Captain Richard W. Price of Lowell who resigned from the army on January 19, 1863, because of his injuries. At the same time, J. Ralph Upthigrove of Crown Point was promoted to Second Lieutenant... and then on February 16, 1863 advanced again to First Lieutenant. Near that time Oliver G. Wheeler of Crown Point was promoted to First Sergeant of Company A. As we shall confirm in a later chapter, Wheeler survived the Civil War and lived long years after as a well known citizen of Lake County.

Because of impeccable record keeping in the 1934 "History of Lake County" we are able to name, to remember, and therefore to honor in this volume, virtually all of the men who originally enlisted in Company A, 73rd Indiana Volunteer Infantry Regiment.

In the following original roll, those 38 listed as "Mustered Out" served until the very end of the Civil War and returned home to Lake County. Six others listed transferred to regular units at the end of the War and continued army careers, at least for some period of time. Earlier discharges were usually because of injuries or illness. Those who gave their lives in the cause of the Civil War are listed as Killed in Action. Those listed simply as "Died," with the place of their death named, died mostly of disease, though some may have died of wounds even long after a battle. In fact, soldier deaths from disease during the Civil War were far greater than those in combat, at a scale of approximately 3 to 1. A little remembered fact of the diseases which were incurable in those years - as we are able to graphically portray in a later chapter - was their life-long, debilitating effect on veterans, who otherwise did not suffer greatly from combat wounds.

In his 1872 "History of Lake County" the Reverend Timothy H. Ball published this poem commending these men and so many others like them. Reverend Ball does not indicate whether it was he who composed the verse, or whether he reprinted it from some other source. To be sure, though, the words say much about the deep held faith in our Republic of average Americans, even after the horror of our Civil War.

"Higher, higher, let us climb,
Up the mount of glory,
That our names may live through time,
In our country's story:
Happy, when her welfare calls, he who conquers, he who falls."

　'Truth is, though, as we know 140 years later...stories of major battles and the names of commanders have "lived on through time." Certainly not, the names of individual rifle bearers who bore the brunt of suffering and death in America's Civil War. That is why we are consoled to record here the names of those who enrolled in Company A, 73rd Indiana Volunteer Infantry Regiment ...to share one last time the physical descriptions of most, as well as their age and occupation at the time of their enlistment. In a sense, we may breath life for them again, at least for whatever period this book may "live on through time."

Originator of Company A, 73rd Indiana Volunteer Infantry Regiment
Captain William Krimball, Crown Point, His Officers Commission dated Tuesday, August 5, 1862. On Saturday, August 16, 1862, the day Company A was mustered in to the 73rd Indiana, Krimball was promoted to Major, commanding the Regiment's First Battalion. He resigned from the Regiment due to injuries shortly after the Battle of Stone's River, in January, 1863.

Commander of the 73rd Indiana Volunteers
Colonel Gilbert Hathaway, LaPorte, near Lake County, a lawyer, member of the Indiana State bar, noted in the 1872 "History Of lake County" as one who "...practiced before our bar." Killed in Action at Blount's Farm, Alabama, Saturday, May 2, 1863 during Streight's Raid.

Officers of Company A

Richard W. Price, Lowell, Captain. Injuries caused his resignation from service, Monday, January 19, 1863, following the Battle of Stone's River.

Philip Reed, Lowell, 2nd Lt. Promoted to 1st Lt. On Saturday, August 16, 1862

Alfred Fry, Crown Point, Promoted from First Sergeant to 2nd Lt., Friday, August 22, 1862

Original First (Orderly) Sergeant Of Company A

Alfred Fry, Crown Point, Immediately promoted to Lieutenant, finally to Captain of Company A.

Sergeants

Henry Pratt, Crown Point. 1st (Orderly) Sergeant. Age 38. 5'6 ½" tall. Dark Complexion. Hazel eyes. Black hair. Born: Rutland, Vermont. Butcher. Discharged February 29, 1863.

George S. Clark, Lowell, 2nd Sergeant. Age 27. 6' tall. Light complexion. Blue eyes. Brown hair. Born; Ontario, NY. Farmer. Promoted to 2nd Lieutenant.

Andrew M. Sprague, West Creek. 3rd Sergeant. Age 27. 5'11" tall. Dark complexion. Blue eyes. Black hair. Born: Ontario, Canada. Farmer. Discharged Nov 25, 1862.

Thomas W. Loving, Crown point, 4th Sergeant. Age 28. 5'11 3/4" tall. Light complexion. Blue eyes. Light hair. Born: LaPorte, IN. Mechanic. Died at Nashville, TN, Sept 30, 1863.

Joseph Bray, Cedar Creek. 5TH Sergeant. Age 40. 5'9 ½" tall. Dark complexion. Blue eyes. Brown hair. Born: Ontario, NY. Farmer. Discharged Feb 25, 1862.

Corporals

Elliott N. Graves, West Creek. Age 39. 5'9" tall. Light complexion. Blue eyes. Light hair. Born: Courtland, NY. Farmer. Discharged Oct 14, 1862.

Leander Morris, Calumet. Age 29. 5'6 ½" tall. Light complexion, Dark eyes. Light hair. Born: Lake Co, IN. Farmer. Died at Nashville, TN, April 30, 1863.

Oliver G. Wheeler, Crown Point. Age 20. 5'8 ½" tall. Light complexion. Hazel eyes. Brown hair. Born: Florence, OH. Clerk. Promoted to 1st Sergeant Nov. 13, 1863. Mustered out July 1, 1865.

Robert W. Fuller, Lowell. Age 32. 5'9 3/4" tall. Light complexion. Blue eyes. Brown hair. Born: Venton, OH. Farmer. Died at Indianapolis August 2, 1863.

Rollin D. Fowler, Crown Point. Age 23. 5'7 3/4" tall. Dark complexion. Hazel eyes. Brown hair. Born: Lake Co., IN. Farmer. Promoted to Sergeant Oct 1st 1863. Mustered out Aug 1, 1865

William F. Davis, Cedar Lake. Age 29. 5'5" tall. Dark complexion. Black eyes. Black hair. Born: Lake, OH. Farmer. Out of service Nov 20, 1862.

Daniel H.C. Barney, Cedar Creek. Age 23. 5'9 ½' tall. Light Complexion. Blue eyes. Light hair. Born: Schenectady, NY. Farmer. Discharged Feb 25, 1863.

Tunis J. Farmer, Crown Point. Age 23. 5'7" tall. Light complexion. Blue eyes. Dark hair. Born: Lake Co, IN. Farmer. Mustered out July 1, 1865 as Sergeant.

Orren A. Chapman, Crown Point. Age 28. 5"10' tall. Light complexion. Blue eyes. Light hair. Born: Lorraine, OH. Farmer. , Transferred to Invalid Corps at Nashville, TN, Sept 1, 1863.

Musicians
Samuel Gordon, Deep River. Age 34. 5"10 ½" tall. Light complexion. Blue eyes. Black hair. Born: Orleans, Vermont. Farmer. Discharged at Nashville, TN, Feb 25, 1863.

Charles A. Stillson, Cedar Creek. Age 47. 5'4 3/4' tall. Light complexion. Blue eyes. Sandy hair. Born: Erie, PA. Farmer. Discharged at Cincinnati, OH, Jan 29, 1863.

Wagoner
William A. Taylor, Cedar Lake. Age 42. 5'9" tall. Light complexion. Blue eyes. Light hair. Born: Erie, PA. Farmer. Mustered out July 1, 1865.

Privates
Lewis E. Atkins, Lowell. Age 22. 5'5" tall. Dark complexion. Gray eyes. Dark hair. Born: Lorraine, OH. Died at Nashville, TN, Nov 22, 1862.

Elijah F. Atkins, Lowell. Age 25. 5'6" tall. Dark complexion. Gray eyes. Dark hair. Born: Muskingame, OH. Farmer. Completion of service unrecorded.

Isaac Ault, Lowell. Age 22. 5'4" tall. Dark complexion. Hazel eyes. Dark hair. Born: Valparaiso, IN. Farmer. Mustered out July 1, 1865.

Wilson Shannon Baughman, Lowell. Age 20. 5'8 ½" tall. Dark complexion. Hazel eyes. Black hair. Born: Tuscarawas Co, OH. Farmer. Mustered out July 1, 1865.

Charles B. Bowen, Merrillville. Age 25. 5'7" tall. Light complexion. Blue eyes. Brown hair. Born: Wyoming, NY. Farmer. Discharged at Indianapolis, IN, July 11, 1863.

George Border, Winfield. Age 30. 5'11 ½" tall. Light complexion. Hazel eyes. Dark hair. Born: Ontario, PA. Farmer. Discharged for disability at Louisville, KY Oct 13, 1863.

George A. Brown, Crown Point. Age 18. 5'5 ½" tall. Dark complexion. Hazel eyes. Black hair. Born: Lake Co, IN. Farmer. Died at Indianapolis, IN, Oct 24,1863.

Arthur Bryant, Lowell. Age 40. 5'7" tall. Light complexion. Blue eyes. Light hair. Born: Lake Co, IN. Farmer. Discharged at Indianapolis, IN, Oct 8, 1863.

John Childers, West Creek. Age 19. 5'9 ½' tall. Light complexion. Blue eyes. Brown hair. Farmer. Died at Nashville, TN Dec 3, 1862.

Alden V. Clark, Lowell. Age 19. 6'1" tall. Light complexion. Blue eyes. Dark hair. Born: Lake Co, IN. Farmer. Discharged at Nashville, TN, Dec. 14, 1863.

Samuel Colvin, Hebron. Age 20. 5'8 ½" tall. Light complexion. Blue eyes. Light hair. Born: Vinton, Ohio. Farmer. Mustered out July 1, 1865.

Thereon Curtiss, Crown Point. Age 21. 5'6" tall. Dark complexion. Blue eyes. Dark hair. Born: Fairfield, CT. Farmer. Discharged at Nashville, TN, Feb 10, 1863.

Orren DeWitt, Lowell. Age 20. 6' tall. Light complexion. Blue eyes. Light hair. Born: Ontario, NY. Mustered out July 1, 1865 as Corporal.

Newman (Laman?) G. Eadus (Etus?), Crown Point. No Statistics. Missing in action Sept 30, 1862.

John H. Early, Crown Point. Age 20. 5'8 1/4" tall. Dark complexion. Hazel eyes. Black hair. Born: Franklin, VA. Farmer. Killed at Stone's River, Dec 31, 1862.

Even S. Evans, Crown Point. Age 19. 5'6 3/4" tall. Light complexion. Blue eyes. Black hair. Born: Richland Co, OH. Farmer. Mustered out July 1, 1865 as Corporal.

Henry. H. Farrington, Lowell. Age 21. 5'9" tall. Light complexion. Blue eyes. Light hair. Born: Lake Co, IN. Farmer. Sergeant Nov 13, 1863. Mustered out July 1, 1865.

Philip Fisher, Winfield. Age 18. 5'9" tall. Light complexion. Hazel eyes. Dark hair. Born: Crawford, OH. Farmer. Discharged at Gallatin, TN, March 13, 1863.

Luman A. Fowler, Jr., Crown Point. Age 18. 5'7 ½" tall. Light complexion. Blue eyes. Light hair. Lake Co, IN. Farmer. Discharged at Gallatin, TN, Feb 20, 1863.

Alber K. Frazier, Merrillville. Age 24. 5'6 ½" tall. Light complexion. Hazel eyes. Dark hair. Born: Montgomery, IN. Farmer. Mustered out July 1, 1865.

William Frazier, Merrillville. Age 18. 5'3 1/4" tall. Light complexion. Black eyes. Black hair. Born: Fountain, IN. Farmer. Died at Nashville, TN, Dec 15, 1862.

Jasper N. Fuller, Lowell. Age 21. 5'7 ½" tall, Light complexion. Blue eyes. Light hair. Born: Vinton, OH. Farmer. Died at Gallatin, TN Jan 29, 1863.

Elisha W. Fuller, Lowell. Age 27. 5'7" tall. Light complexion. Blue eyes. Brown hair. Born: Vinton, OH. , Discharged at Louisvlle, KY, Oct 14, 1862.

Michael Gerlach, Crown Point. Age 20. 5'10 ½" tall. Light complexion. Blue eyes. Light hair. Born: Germany. Farmer. Transferred to Invalid Corps, Nashville, TN, Sept 1, 1863.

(Author's note: The 1934 "History of Lake County" also lists a John Gerlach, Crown Point, "...who affected the dress and haircut of General Custer." John Gerlach was not listed as an original soldier in the 73rd Regiment, but noted along with other... "faithful surviving members of the Grand Army of the Republic...old residents of Lake County, favored with long life, who exemplified all that was the best of the men of that period, and whose names not only speak for themselves, but for many other veterans..."

Relatives or descendants of these Gerlach men migrated into Camp Walton, Florida in the early 1900's. Camp Walton, later renamed Fort Walton, became Fort Walton Beach in 1953. Molly Gerlach married into the pioneer Staff and Bass families, among the earliest settlers of what has become America's New Riviera ...the Fort Walton Beach/ Destin area of Northwest Florida's magnificent Emerald Coast. By an odd concurrence it is also the place where this writer has lived for more than fifty years...and is penning this history of the Civil War's Company A, 73rd Indiana Volunteer Infantry Regiment into which Michael Gerlach mustered on Saturday, August 16, 1862.

Henry W. Gilbert, Valparaiso. Age 18. 5'6" tall. Dark complexion. Hazel eyes. Black hair. Born: Lake Co, IN. Farmer. Mustered out July 1, 1865.

Noah Gordon, Woods Mill. Age 17. 5'8" tall. Light complexion. Blue eyes. Dark hair. Born: Huron, OH. Farmer. Discharged for disability at Louisville, KY, Oct 13, 1862.

Horace Gordonier, West Creek. Age 19. 5'9" tall. Light complexion. Blue eyes. Brown hair. Born: Lake Co, IN. Farmer. Mustered out July 1, 1865.

Marion Graves, West Creek. Age 20. 5'10 ½' tall. Light complexion. Blue eyes. Brown hair. Born: Dekalb, Ill. Farmer. Died at Nashville, TN Dec 16, 1862.

William J. Granger, Hebron. Age 22. 6' tall. Dark complexion. Blue eyes. Dark hair. Born: McCourt, IN. Farmer. Mustered out July 1, 1865.

Lewis N. Green, Crown Point. Age 19. 5'6 ½" tall. Light complexion. Blue eyes. Black hair. Born: Lake Co, IN. Farmer. Mustered out, July 1, 1865.

Allen Gregg, Lowell. Age 20. 5'6" tall. Light Complexion. Blue eyes. Dark hair. Born: Ontario, NY. Farmer. Mustered out July 1, 1865.

James E. Hale, Crown Point. Age 19. 5'8" tall. Light complexion. Blue eyes. Light hair. Born: Lake Co, IN. Farmer. Mustered out July 1, 1865.

Elias Harkless, Crown Point. Age 23. 5'9 ½" tall. Dark complexion. Hazel eyes. Black hair. Born: Westmoreland, PA. Farmer. Mustered out July 1, 1865.

William Hathaway, West Creek. Age 21. 5'5" tall. Light complexion. Blue eyes. Dark hair. Born: Pulaski, IN. Farmer. Out of Service May 12, 1863.

John Holt, Crown Point. Age 31. 5'3 ½" tall. Dark complexion. Hazel eyes. Dark hair. Born: Buffalo, NY. Mechanic. Promoted to Quarter Master Sergeant Nov 1, 1863.

Peter Johann, Hannah Station. Age 28. 5'5" tall. Light complexion. Blue eyes. Dark hair. Born: Prussia. Mustered out July 1, 1865.

Charles Johnson, Lowell. Age 33. 5'8" tall. Light complexion. Blue eyes. Dark hair. Born: Cataraugus, NY. Farmer. Discharged at Gallatin, TN, Feb 19, 1863
.

Samuel Jones, Lowell. Age 21. 5'7 1/4" tall. Dark complexion. Blue eyes. Black hair. Born: Ontario, NY. Farmer. Transferred, Invalid Corps, Indianapolis, IN, Oct 24, 1863.

Nicholas Knoff, Crown Point. Age 25. 5'9" tall. Light complexion. Blue eyes. Dark hair. Born: Germany. Farmer. Discharged, Nashville, TN, Dec 14 1863
.

Austin Lamphiere, Crown Point. Age 18. 5'5 ½" tall. Dark complexion. Blue eyes. Dark hair. Born: Ohio. Farmer. Died at Nashville,TN Jan 7, 1863.

Lloyd Lamphiere, Crown Point. Age 26. 5'9" tall. Dark complexion. Blue eyes. Dark hair. Born: Addison, VT. Farmer. Mustered out July 21, 1865.

Phillip Lattin (Lidder?), Chicago, Ill. Age 22. 5'8" tall. Light complexion. Blue eyes. Dark hair. Born: Germany. Farmer. Mustered out July 21, 1865 as Corporal.

Jacob Lille, Crown Point. Age 27. 5'7 ½" tall. Dark complexion. Black eyes. Black hair. Born: Germany. Mechanic. Mustered out July 21, 1865.

Jacob (Henry?) Masseth (Massoth?), Crown Point, Age 20. 5'6 1/4" tall. Light complexion. Blue eyes. Light hair. Born: Germany. Farmer. Mustered out July 21, 1865.

John Maxwell, Merrillville. Age 18. 5'6" tall. Dark complexion. Blue eyes. Light hair. Born: Lake, OH. Farmer. Died near Scottsburg, KY Nov 9, 1862.

James W. McCann, Eagle Creek. Age 22. 5'5 ½" tall. Dark complexion. Hazel eyes. Dark hair. Born: Wayne, MI. Farmer. Mustered out July 1, 1865.

Alexander McNay, West Creek. Age 22. 5'8 ½" tall. Light complexion. Blue eyes. Dark hair. Born: Elkhart, IN. Farmer. Discharged, Nashville, TN, Dec 9, 1862.

George Metz (Metry?), Cedar Creek. Age16. 5'7 ½" tall. Light complexion. Blue eyes. Light hair. Born: Germany. Farmer. Mustered out July 1, 1865.

Isaac Moore, Crown point. Age 19. 5'5" tall. Light complexion. Blue eyes. Light hair. Born: Will, Ill. Mechanic. Died at Gallatin, TN, Dec 29, 1862.

John F. Meyers, Crown Point. Age 22. 5'3" tall. Light complexion. Hazel eyes. Light hair. Born: Montgomery, NY. Clerk. Out of service August 1862.

Albert Nichols, Lowell. Age 19. 5'8' tall. Dark complexion. Hazel eyes. Dark hair. Born: lake Co, IN. Farmer. Died at Nashville, TN, Dec 1, 1862.

Martin Nichols, Lowell. Age 21. 5'5 1/4" tall. Light complexion. Hazel eyes. Light hair. Born: Marion, OH. Farmer. Mustered out July 1, 1865 as Corporal.

Mortimer Pattee, West Creek. Age 22. 5'6 ½" tall. Light complexion. Blue eyes. Auburn hair. Born: Porter, IN. Farmer. Mustered out July 1, 1865.

John Paul, Chicago, Ill. Age 19. 5'7 3/4" tall. Dark complexion. Hazel eyes. Dark hair. Born: Germany. Farmer. Discharged, Gallatin, TN, March 8, 1863.

Milo S. Pelton, Crown Point. Age 21. 5'2 ½" tall. Light complexion. Blue eyes. Dark hair. Born: Lake Co, IN. Farmer. Discharged, Murphreesborough, TN, Feb 25, 1863.

David Pulver, West Creek. Age 19. 5'4" tall. Dark complexion. Blue eyes. Dark hair. Born: Lake Co, IN. Farmer. Discharged, Gallatin, TN, March 8, 1863.

John Rooney, Merrillville. Age 29. 5'8" tall. Dark complexion. Hazel eyes. Dark hair. Born: Clark, IN. Farmer. Died at Nashville, TN Feb 8, 1863.

John Rosenbower, Crown Point. Age 18. 5'6 ½" tall. Light complexion. Blue eyes. Light hair. Born: Cook, Ill. Farmer. Mustered out July 1, 1865.

Abel Sherman, Crown Point. Age 28. 5'7" tall. Light complexion. Blue eyes. Dark hair. Born: Canada. Mustered out July 1, 1865.

John M. Smith, Crown Point. Age 31. 5'8" tall. Light complexion. Blue eyes. Dark hair. Born: New York, NY. Farmer. Discharged, Gallatin, TN, Feb 20, 1863.

Jasper (Joseph) N. (M.) Sprague, Merrillville. Age 22. 5'10" tall. Light complexion. Blue eyes. Red hair. Born: Lorain, OH. Farmer. Discharged, Gallatin, TN, Feb 21, 1863.

Asher Stilson, Cedar Creek. Age 25. 5'5 ½" tall. Light complexion. Blue eyes. Dark hair. Born: St. Joseph, IN. Farmer. Discharged, Cincinnati, OH, Jan 29, 1863.

John Stowell, Lowell. Age 30. 5'11" tall. Light complexion. Blue eyes. Light hair. Born: Huron, OH. Farmer. Mustered out July 1, 1865.

Oliver Surprise, Lowell. Age 22. 5'8" tall. Dark complexion. Black eyes. Black hair. Born: Lake Co, IN. Farmer. Transferred, Invalid Corps, Indianapolis, IN, Oct 24, 1863.

DeWitt C. Taylor, Cedar Creek. Age 36. 5'7 ½" tall. Light complexion. Hazel eyes. Dark hair. Born: Buffalo, NY. Farmer. Mustered out July 1, 1865.

John Tanner, Lowell. Age 45. 5'6 ½" tall. Light complexion. Blue eyes. Dark hair. Born: Switzerland. Mustered out, Special Orders, War Dept., May 15, 1865.

George Toman, Crown Point. Age 22. 5'2 ½" tall. Dark complexion. Black eyes. Black hair. Born: Germany. Discharged, Cincinnati, OH, Feb 20, 1863.

William Tremper, Crown Point. Age 22. 5'5 ½" tall. Light complexion. Blue eyes. Light hair. Born: Jefferson, NY. Farmer. Discharged, Gallatin, TN, Mar 24, 1863. Died at Boise, Idaho, Silent Camp, about 1920...at about 80 years of age.

J. Ralph Upthigrove, Crown Point. Age 26. 5'8" tall. Dark complexion. Black eyes. Black hair. Born: Canada. Merchant. Promoted 1st Lt. Mustered out July 1, 1865

James H. Upthigrove, Crown Point. Age 18. 5'6" tall. Dark complexion. Black eyes. Dark hair. Born: Steuben, NY. Farmer. Mustered out July 1, 1865.

Cornelius Vanburgh, Crown Point. Age 26. 5'8" tall. Dark complexion. Black eyes. Black hair. Born: Canada. Farmer. Died at Louisville, KY, Dec 21, 1862.

Mial Vincent, Wood's Mill. Age 21. 5'9 ½' tall. Light complexion. Blue eyes. Light hair. Born: Iona, MI. Farmer. Died at Gallatin, TN, Jan 8, 1863.

Philip Weinand, St. John. Age 26. 5'6" tall. Light complexion. Hazel eyes. Black hair. Born: Prussia. Farmer. Mustered out July 1, 1865.

Edward Welch, Winfield. Age 23. 6'1/2" tall. Light complexion. Blue eyes. Light hair. Born: Canada. Farmer. Killed at Stone's River, Dec 31 1862.

Samuel White, Crown Point. Age 25. 5'5 1/4" tall. Dark complexion. Hazel eyes. Black hair. Born: New York. Farmer. Killed at Blount's Farm, AL, May 2, 1863.

Benjamin Wise, Crown Point. Age 21. 5'10 3/4" tall. Light complexion. Blue eyes. Light hair. Born: Crawford, OH. Farmer. Transferred, Invalid Corps, Nashville, TN, Sept 1, 1863.

Benjamin Willis, Lowell. Age 21. 5'11" tall. Light complexion. Blue eyes. Black hair. Born: Clark, OH. Farmer. Transferred, Invalid Corps, Cincinnati, OH, Aug 29, 1863.

Edmund B. Woods, Merrillville. Age 20. 5'8 1/4" tall. Light complexion. Blue eyes. Light hair. Born: Lake Co, IN. Farmer. Died at Nashville, TN, Nov 29, 1862.

Harvey A. Davis, Lake County. Age 31. 5'8 3/4" tall. Dark complexion. Hazel eyes. Black hair. Born: Seneca, OH. Farmer. Out of Service Nov 24, 1862.

Daniel Barney, Lake County. Age 23. 5'9 ½" tall. Light complexion. Blue eyes. Light hair. Born; Schenectady, NY. Discharge information not recorded.

Ransom Kyle, Lake County. Age 24. 5'6 ½" tall. Dark complexion. Hazel eyes. Dark hair. Born: Knox, OH. Farmer. Discharged at Louisville, KY, April 18, 1863.

<u>Recruits</u>

John Binyon, Cedar Lake. Age 41. 5'9" tall. Dark complexion. Black eyes. Black hair. Born: Jefferson Co, TN. Farmer. Transferred to 29th Regiment, July 1, 1865

Azariah Green, Hebron. Age 21. 5'9" tall. Dark complexion. Gray eyes. Dark hair. Born: Vinton, OH. Farmer. Transferred to 29th Regiment, July 1, 1865

Alexander Guin, Lowell. Age 40. 5'7" tall. Dark complexion. Blue eyes. Dark hair. Born: Jefferson Co, TN. Farmer. Transferred to 29th Regiment, July 1, 1865

George Laman, Crown Point. Age 23. 5'6" tall. Dark complexion. Black eyes. Black hair. Born: Switzerland. Butcher. Transferred to 29th Regiment, July 1, 1865

Amos Mahana, Hebron. Age 19. 5'2 ½" tall. Light complexion. Blue eyes. Light hair. Born: Porter Co, IN. Farmer. Transferred to 29th Regiment, July 1, 1865

Jacob Metz, Cedar Lake. Age18. 5'3" tall. Light complexion. Dark eyes. Dark hair. Born: Lake Co, IN. Farmer. Transferred to 29th Regiment, July 1, 1865

Andrew Stilson, Cedar Lake. Age 18. 5'6" tall. Light complexion. Gray eyes. Light hair. Born: lake Co, IN. Transferred to 29th Regiment, July 1, 1865

Private Wilson Shannon Baughman...was enrolled by D. K. Pettibone (as were most of the original 100 men) at Crown Point on July 29, 1862, and mustered in at Camp Rose, near South Bend, Indiana on Saturday, August 16, 1862 with others of Company A and the 73rd Indiana Volunteer Infantry Regiment. He was born on Sunday, January 30, 1842 in Tuscarawas

County, New Philadelphia, Ohio. His father and mother were Samuel and Rebecca Baughman. His parents, along with his Uncle and Aunt, Jacob and Sarah "Sally" Ritter Baughman, were among the earliest settlers of Lowell, Indiana. He served his full three year commitment, mustered out at the end of war on Saturday, July 1, 1865. On that day the Army owed him $15.26 for clothing. He had been paid $25 of an enlistment bounty with $75 still owed him.

In the National Archives of the United States, Washington DC, we came across similar extended information on two others of the 73rd Indiana Volunteers. Not from Company A, they were both from Company K of the 73rd Indiana...but their descriptions help us to better know the young men of that era, and the 73rd Regiment.

George Boothe. Farmer. From Porter County, Indiana. Age 22 at enlistment on Friday, August 1, 1862. He was enrolled by J. D. Phelps at Michigan City, Indiana for a 3 year term. George was 5' 7 ½ " tall with dark complexion, brown hair, and hazel eyes. Enlisting as a Private, he was promoted to Corporal on Friday, January 20, 1865, and mustered out at War's end with the rest of the 73rd on Saturday July 1, 1865, fully completing his three year enlistment.

Hiram S. Root. Farmer. From Marshall County, Indiana. Age 21 at enlistment on Friday, August 1, 1862. He was enrolled by J. H. Walker at South Crossing for a term of 3 years. Hiram was 5' 7" tall with light complexion, brown hair, and blue eyes. He died of illness on Wednesday, November 5, 1862 near Glasgow, Kentucky. According to a friend and fellow soldier he was buried by the side of the road to Glasgow.

(Author's note) Explanations may help make some information more understandable:

1. Seven "Recruits" were all transferred to the 29th Regiment on Saturday, July 1, 1865, the day most of the Boys From Lake County were mustered out of service and returned home. The records do not explain the reason for the transfers. However, two scenarios are likely and either may apply to any one of them. First, some young men may have preferred military life and simply chosen to remain in service. Second, and far more likely, since they joined Company A late in the War for a fixed period of service, they were required to transfer to a still active unit to finish out their enlistment.

2. About 16 non-combat deaths and discharges occurred among the men of Company A in the Fall of 1862... within just four months after the unit was mustered in. Contagious disease spreading among large numbers of young men, suddenly thrown in close quarters, was a major cause of death and long lasting illness among Civil War troops and veterans. As we've noted before, deaths caused by disease outnumbered those killed in combat by the terrible ratio of about three to one. Modern medical science was in it's infancy during the Civil War. Physicians simply had no sources of treatment for many diseases and knew little of how to control the spread of contagious disease. Perhaps even less was known about the importance of maintaining sanitary conditions around camp and in food supplies.

3. About 26 discharges and deaths were reported among men of Company A during the period from January to late Fall 1863. Many of these were likely the result of wounds suffered in the Battle of Stones River at Murphreesborough, Tennessee which took place in late December 1862 and early January 1863. Company A was hotly engaged several times during that battle and the Regiment itself reported more than one-third of it's troops killed or wounded. The Battle of Stone's River at Murphreesborough has been noted by some Civil War historians as one of the 10 bloodiest battles of the Civil War.

4. Several Company A troops are recorded as having been transferred to the "VRC" with no explanation of what the "VRC" was. Clearly,even by the time the 1934 History of Lake County was written, most people must have known. One hundred and forty years later, we had to research the National Archives when we were in Washington to discover the answer.

"VRC" was the Veterans Reserve Corps, originally named the Invalid Corps. The idea dated to Revolutionary War times, but was re-organized for the Civil War on Tuesday, April 28, 1863 under a War Department General Order. It's purpose was to give soldiers who became unfit for active field duty, because of combat wounds or seriousness illness, the opportunity to serve in other light duty capacities. Men transferred to the VRC needed a recommendation from their commanders stating that previous military conduct made them deserving of further service in spite of wounds or disabilities.

The Veterans Reserve Corp was composed of two Battalions. The First Battalion was made up of men whose disabilities left them still able to handle a musket and some marching. The second Battalion included men whose medical conditions were far more serious, perhaps having lost limbs (as was far too common in the Civil War) or suffered some other more severely debilitating injury. These men could still serve as cooks, orderlies, nurses, or guards in public buildings. There were two to three times as many in the less disabled men of the First Battalion than in the Second. VRC First Battalion soldiers were assigned to guard camps containing Confederate prisoners of war, as well as in small units to arrest bounty jumpers or enforce the draft. They escorted substitutes, recruits, and prisoners to and from the battle front, guarded railroads, and did patrol duty. Some even fought again, manning the defenses of Washington during Confederate Lt. General Jubal A. Early's raid on the city, July 11th and 12th, 1864.

As we move out with the Boys From Lake County on the dark, rainy, muddy night of April 26th 1863 we now know far more about them...the kind of soldiers they, and their compadres of the 73rd Indiana Volunteer Infantry, had become.

To be sure...we now also have more than an inkling as to why they were among the relatively small, select, group of units especially chosen to undertake this highly risky, physically strenuous, raid behind enemy lines.

(Author's note:) As we write these words in Summer of the year 2006, our Nation is fearfully and hotly debating what many Americans call the treasonous publishing of Iraq War military secrets by the New York Times newspaper. Considering such, the following similar plea to Edwin M. Stanton, Union Secretary of War in Civil War years is an astonishing bit of history.

Chicago, Ill., August 7, 1862

Hon. E. M. Stanton
Secretary of War

Since the orders for drafting, large numbers of citizens are leaving this city to escape the draft, and it is strongly urged upon me to ask you for authority to declare martial law again. **There is an urgent and almost unanimous demand from the loyal citizens that the Chicago Times should be immediately suppressed for giving aid and comfort to the enemy.** I solicit an immediate answer. Do not delay, for I fear the people will take into their own hands the power which should only be used under the authority of your Department.

RICHARD YATES, GOVERNOR

What the Chicago Times wrote that was considered by Chicagoans to be "giving aid and comfort to the enemy," has so far escaped our research. But it is clear that even in Civil War years "freedom of the press" was sometimes labeled a severe danger to our Nation in time of war.

However, it was not that the citizens of Chicago and Illinois were trying to evade service in the Union Army. By far, most just wanted to volunteer rather than be drafted. Illinois furnished a great many highly effective and courageous Union Regiments in Civil War years. In fact, Allen C. Fuller, Illinois Adjutant General, wrote Secretary of War Stanton on the same day. "I have the honor to inform you that at least 25,000 volunteers are already enrolled in this State. Thousands of our people are now offering themselves under the last call, and are demanding they shall not be drafted. They are ready to enlist. I do not hesitate to say... fifty thousand from this State (Illinois) can be put into camp in this State by the 1st of next month..."

On that same day, Secretary of War Stanton was also sent a message from Indiana Governor, Oliver P. Morton, saying that the State of Indiana had already raised 14 Regiments...including the Boys From Lake County and their 73rd Indiana Volunteer Infantry Regiment...with one more projected, the 79th, all planned to be full that week. "Many of the men recruited are on furlough," Indiana Governor Morton wrote on Thursday, August 7, 1862, "but will be in camp this week. All have, however, been mustered in by the Lieutenants who recruited them." That was not exactly true of the Boys From Lake County and their 73rd Regiment... who were mustered in on Saturday, August 16, 1862.

Chapter Seven

On... Into The Dark and Rain

The Boys From Lake County, along with others of the 73rd Indiana follow along with the 8,000 troops of General Grenville M. Dodge for two hours. It is about 1:00 o'clock, the earliest hours of the morning of April 27th, that Colonel Streight breaks the column away from the much larger force, leads to the right, sneaking - he hoped - the 1500 man Provisional Brigade to the south toward Russellville, Alabama.

But then...how, in enemy country, does one "sneak" 1500 heavily armed troops, in a column more than a mile long? After all...there are creaking wagons, a few necessary swaying lanterns, hundreds of braying animals, at least two cannon on their carriages towed by mule-drawn limbers (ammunition boxes) creaking, rattling... all slipping, sliding in nearly impassable muddy roads. The men often must grunt and heave to push wagons, cannon, and limbers out of deeper mud ruts.

Before departure General Dodge had given the Provisional Brigade some 200 additional mules, plus eight wagons to haul ammunition and food rations. In fact, Col, Streight does not confirm whether those eight wagons were in addition to others already in use by the Brigade.

Also near the time of departure, Colonel Streight related, "General Dodge informed me that there was no doubt but Forrest (famous Confederate Cavalry General Nathan Bedford Forrest) had crossed the Tennessee River, and was in the vicinity of Town Creek; hence he agreed to advance as far as Courtland (well past Town Creek) on the Decatur Road, and, if possible, drive the enemy in that direction, but if they (the enemy) turned toward Moulton (in the Brigade's direction) our cavalry, under General Dodge, was to be sent in pursuit.

Lt. Roach, in his book "The Prisoner of War..." expounds on that theme. He points out one thing not yet mentioned in messages between Streight and his Commanders...explaining that the Brigade was taking a south-east course toward Rome, Georgia. He continued, "General Dodge, at the same time, advanced with his forces on Courtland, to engage the enemy until we should be beyond pursuit. Had he followed this progamme, which was in fact the object of his move from Corinth - as Colonel Streight expected him to do, and as he assured the Colonel he would do - nothing could have interfered to prevent the expedition being entirely successful in every particular." In other words, Lt. Roach blamed General Dodge completely for the subsequent troubles suffered by Streight's Brigade.

The truth is somewhat different, although General Dodge's failure to fulfill his promise was, without doubt, a severe hindrance to the mission. Almost immediately after the 1500 men veered away from the main force to the south, two other events occurred that bore even more significant grievance for Streight's Brigade for Special Secret Service. However, what happened at that point was far more the machinations of a wily Confederate enemy, than simply a fault of Union General Dodge.

First, Confederate General Nathan Bedford Forrest learned quickly that a column of mounted troops had left the main force and headed south deep into his Confederate territory. It was actually near sunset on Tuesday, April 28, 1863 that a leading resident of Tuscumbia, James Moon, found General Forrest in camp near Town Creek. Moon had made a dashing, clandestine ride on horseback weaving his way through fighting units of Union Blue. He was the man who alerted Forrest that a column - he estimated at 2000 - mounted Union troops was at Mount Hope, headed toward Moulton.

Second, Forrest immediately took a calculated gamble that was typical of his daring, aggressive military genius. Though his forces were far smaller than Union General Dodge's, he quickly split them...sending half around behind Dodge's 8,000 men to create a loud, rapid fire, diversion...while himself leading the other half in hot pursuit of Colonel Streight and his 1500 raiders.

Forrest's strategy worked!...far too well for the Boys From Lake County and their fellow members of the 73rd, amid Streight's Brigade. General Dodge immediately feared a sizable Confederate force was attacking the rear of his forces, stopped his advance at Town Creek... far short of Courtland...and never sent his cavalry to protect the back of Streight's Brigade from General Forrest's assaults.

The Battle of Town Creek simply turned into a day of rifle snipers and the roar of cannon, fired mostly randomly and ineffectively at each other over the waters of a rain swollen Town Creek...and then a retreat by General Dodge back to Corinth, during which his forces purposely ravaged the small city of Tuscumbia to deprive the Confederate enemy of whatever he could.

As Streight's Brigade struggled, slipping, sliding through deep mud and darkness of an inky black night, it was raining very hard and progress was frustrating... slow. "One hundred and fifty of my men had neither horses nor mules," Colonel Streight reported., "and fully as many more had such as were unable to carry more than saddles; hence fully 300 of the men were on foot."

Streight expected, when he left Tuscumbia late on the night of Sunday April 26th that the greater part of his command... that is the ones who had horses or mules... would be able to reach the next significant town, Moulton, Alabama about forty miles distant, by the next night. "But, owing to the heavy rains..." Colonel Streight lamented, "...and consequent bad condition of the roads, it was impossible." In stark consideration of that major impediment, Streight sent a rider back to General Dodge with a dispatch informing him that the Brigade would halt for the night at a village named Mount Hope and wait for the men who were on still foot to catch up.

Streight also pointed out the severe, ongoing problem with mounts for the men of his converted cavalry. "We continued to scour the country for horses and mules," he related, "but so many of those drawn at Nashville were continually failing, that although we were successful in collecting a large number, still, many of the men were without anything to ride. Which ones...? The Boys From Lake County...? We simply no longer can be sure. None of the historical reports tells us.

Lieutenant A.C. Roach in his book "The Prisoners and How Treated" adds much to our sense of being there. "The first night...our mounted force, camped in the vicinity of Mount Hope a village in Lawrence County, Alabama having made a march of thirty four miles, over mountainous and almost impassable roads. Colonel Streight took up his quarters at the house of one of the most wealthy and influential citizens of the place; and withal an arrant traitor."

(Author's note: Here Roach, inadvertently indicates clearly a major point of dissension between Northern and Southern states. As a man of the North he believed Southern secessionists were "traitors" to the United States of America. While those of the South believed just as deeply that the Constitution of the United States was not an enforced document but one which had been joined freely by all States and therefore the right to "un-join," or secede, was just as absolutely inherent in the Constitution.)

"His daughter, though,..." Roach continues, "a highly educated and accomplished young lady, professed to sympathize with us and our cause, and did everything in her power for our comfort. In fact, her actions went so far to prove her professions of loyalty, that Colonel Streight ordered the Quartermaster to pay her for a beautiful riding pony taken by one of our tired and sore-footed "boys" - it being General Rosecrans' orders to pay all loyal citizens for whatever property taken for the benefit of the command."

(Author's note: Was this, in 1863, the first hint of the "Women's Movement...? To be sure, those of us who are a bit older know there have always been women, in every age, who spoke their own minds, directed their own destinies, and provided wise leadership within their families and communities..., as we shall soon see again...all without giving up the charm, femininity, and moral values which enriched the lives of their menfolk. Or might it have been that her father was so enraged over the "Yankee" invasion that she feared he would do or say something that might get him killed...and was soothing the enemy for his protection. Either is the epitome of wisdom and courage...and it is a shame that history, so far as we can determine, does not record the names of these leading Alabamians. It is a matter described in this history, as well, that there were many northern Alabama citizens who did not favor their State's secession from the Union.)

And so we rest, as much as we can in such weather, on the night of Monday April 27, 1863. "On the night of the 27th at Mount Hope," Colonel Streight says, "I received word from General Dodge, stating that he had driven the enemy, and that I should press on.

(Author's note: How could General Dodge have been so wrong... putting the Brigade in greater danger? Certainly, considering his previous complete cooperation, under direct orders from higher commanders, it was simply a sincere but damaging, error. It is highly likely that General Dodge was just not able to gather complete facts about the whereabouts, nor size, of the fast moving cavalries of Confederate General Nathan Bedford Forrest and General P. D. Roddey of the 4th Alabama Cavalry.)

"On the night of the 27th at Mount Hope" continues Streight, "my command had not all come up yet, nor did they until about 10:00 a.m. the next day." At that time the entire unit left camp, heading on toward Moulton, Alabama where they arrived about dark. Confederate Cavalry General Forrest and his men were already near...doing their wily work.

"Up to this time," Streight reports. "We had been skirmishing occasionally with small squads of the enemy, but I could hear of no force of consequence in the country." Then Streight related better news. "All of the command but about fifty men were now mounted."

In his book, Lieutenant Roach describes Moulton a bit more fully. "Our advance, consisting of Captain Smith's two companies of cavalry, charged into the town about sunset, putting to flight and capturing part of Colonel Roddey's command. In the county jail...had been confined for longer or shorter periods, and at different times, those citizens of Lawrence County, Alabama who, amid the stirring and exciting scenes of a gigantic Civil War, and surrounded by armed traitors, still defended the old flag, and battled manfully for the glorious principles of constitutional liberty. Many of these patriotic but persecuted men were, previous to the War, friends and neighbors of the soldiers of Captain Smith's command, who were themselves refugees from their homes and families, having nearly a year previous broken the thousand ties that bound them to their homes and firesides, their wives and little ones, to battle even unto death for the holy cause of liberty and human freedom. We remained at this place only long enough for the men to prepare some slight refreshment for themselves and feed their animals."

The Brigade rode (with 50 still marching, of course) from camp in Moulton about midnight on Tuesday, April 28th headed in the direction of Blountsville, Alabama via a cut in the mountains, then called Day's Gap. (As we write these words in the year 2006 the place is called Battleground...and no one there seems now to have ever heard of the name Day's Gap)

"The two previous days," Streight reminds us, "it had been raining most of the time, and the roads were terrible, though on the evening of (Tuesday) April 28th it bid fair for dry weather, which gave us strong hopes of better times."

It is well worth a few paragraphs, at this point, as you will see far more fully in coming days, to reflect a bit on the two Confederate cavalry leaders who almost immediately fell into vigorous pursuit of Streight's Brigade.

General Philip Dale Roddey, along with his 4th Alabama Cavalry, is certainly somewhat remembered in the wider annals of America's Civil War. In the State of Alabama, however, Roddey remains a hero, an icon. In a fateful coincidence, he created the 4th Alabama Calvary Regiment in Tuscumbia, the town from which Streight's Brigade has just begun it's raid. Roddey organized the unit in October of 1862, by combining a group of independent companies which had been assembled in the Alabama counties of Franklin, Lauderdale, Lawrence, Marion, and Walker.

For a brief time assigned in Tennessee, the unit returned to Northern Alabama in the Spring of 1863 to defend against Union raids into that area. Roddey and his 4th Alabama Cavalry, often working under the command of General Forrest, were famed for being able to hit the enemy hard, as well as at the speed of fast horses. The 4th was involved in a long list of actions, often small, sudden, fierce...others major battles such as Chickamauga... in some of those suffering severe casualties. Some were assaults against fleet, invading, Union Cavalry...but usually the 4th served as an advance ahead of main forces, first into enemy contact, giving infantry behind them adequate warning so officers could properly deploy their troops. The Regiment was active throughout the entire Civil War, until a majority of the mounted troopers were captured at Selma, Alabama on Sunday, April 2, 1865, just seven days before Lee's surrender at Appomattox, Virginia. Most who eluded capture on that day surrendered soon after at Pond Springs, Alabama, the home of Confederate General Joseph "Fightin' Joe" Wheeler. A few others just quietly disbanded, slipped away, and went home.

Confederate Cavalry General Nathan Bedford Forrest was born on Friday, July 13, 1821 in Chapel Hill, Bedford County, Tennessee. The first of twelve children in a poor family, he was the son of blacksmith William Forrest . After his father's death, he found himself the head of his family at the age of 17. Through hard work and determination, Forrest was able to raise himself, his mother, brothers and sisters from poverty. He discovered himself to be an astute businessman, eventually owning several plantations, and briefly prior to the Civil War, was a slave trader based on Adams Street in Memphis, Tennessee. In 1858 he was elected as a Memphis city alderman. He took care of his mother, put younger brothers through college, and by the time the Civil War broke out in 1861, had become a millionaire, one of the richest in the South. In fact, his holdings were reputed to be worth $1,500,000, an astounding fortune in 1861.

When War was declared on Friday, April 12, 1861 Forrest enlisted as a Private in the Confederate army. On Sunday, July 14, 1861 he joined Captain J.S. White's Company E, Tennessee Mounted Rifles. Early on, the Confederate States of America forces were poorly equipped. Forrest offered to use his personal fortune to furnish a cavalry regiment of Tennessee volunteers. Rebel Army officers and the Governor of Tennessee, astonished that anyone of Forrest's wealth and prominence had enlisted as a soldier of the lowest rank, commissioned him a Colonel. In October 1861 he was given command of Forrest's Tennessee Cavalry Battalion.

Forrest had no military training or experience. Clearly, though, he was a man blessed with inborn military genius, having an innate sense of successful tactics and vibrant leadership abilities, soon recognized as an outstanding battlefield officer.

Though Tennessee was a state sharply divided in loyalties between Union and Confederate causes, Forrest's aim was to recruit men for the South eager for battle, promising them that they would have "ample opportunity to kill Yankees."

As a man, Forrest was physically imposing, 6'2" tall, 210 pounds, and as such, he could be intimidating in comportment. He was known as a fierce rider and deft swordsman, skills used to great effect during battle.

Forrest's leadership was outstanding at the Battle of Confederate Fort Donelson on the Cumberland River, February 1862, against Union General Ulysses S. Grant, heading a cavalry charge which captured a Union artillery battery. When Grant's Union gunboat and infantry forces prevailed and his Confederate Army superiors were negotiating surrender of the Fort, Forrest angrily walked out of the meeting saying he "had not led his men into battle to surrender." 4,000 of them followed him out of the Fort and across the river. Soon after, as the fall of Nashville loomed, Forrest took command of the city, evacuated several government officials and carried millions of dollars worth of vital Confederate weapon manufacturing machinery to safety.

A month later, Forrest again demonstrated his personal vigor, prowess and military leadership. Late in the battle at Shiloh, he charged the Union line, driving through it. In the midst of enemy without any of his own troops around him, he first emptied his pistols and then pulled his saber. A union infantryman on the ground beside him fired a rifle at Forrest, hitting him in the side, lifting him out of his saddle. Steadying himself and his mount, with one arm he lifted the Union soldier by the shirt collar, and used him as a human shield to avoid more injury. Forrest, apparently, was the last man wounded at the horrific Battle of Shiloh.

Recovered from injury, Forrest was back in the saddle, commanding a new brigade of green cavalry regiments by early summer. In July, with these untested men he achieved another stunning success with a raid into middle Tennessee. On Sunday, July 13, 1862, his men defeated a force twice their number at the First Battle of Murphreesborough, capturing the city. These were just the first of many victories Forrest would win. He remained undefeated in battle until the final days of War, and then lost only when faced with overwhelming numbers. In fact, these early successes earned him a promotion to Brigadier General in command of a Confederate Cavalry Brigade.

In battle Forrest was quick to take the offensive, using speedy deployment of horse cavalry to position his troops, where they would often dismount and fight. Commonly he would seek to circle the enemy flank and cut off their rear guard support. These tactics foreshadowed the mechanized infantry of World War II, bearing little relationship to pre-Civil War cavalry traditions of reconnaissance, screening, and mounted assaults with sabers.

In December 1862, Forrest recruited a new brigade composed of about 2,000 inexperienced recruits, most of whom lacked weapons with which to fight. Ordered into a raid to disrupt Union communications of General Grant at the Vicksburg campaign, Forrest again showed his military genius, leading thousands of Union soldiers in west Tennessee on a "wild goose chase" trying to locate his fast moving forces. Forrest never stayed in one place long enough to be located, raided as far north as the banks of the Ohio River in southwest Kentucky, and came back to his base in Mississippi with more men than he'd started with, all fully armed with captured Union weapons. As a result Union General Grant was forced to delay strategy of the Vicksburg assault.

Forrest continued to lead his men in smaller scale operations, as well as major engagements such as the Battle of Chickamauga, where he served with the main army pursuing retreating Union forces, taking hundreds of prisoners. But his greatest victory, perhaps, was on Friday, June 10, 1864, when his 3,500 man force clashed with an 8,500 man Union force at the Battle of Brice's Crossroads. Again, Forrest's mobility of force and superior tactics won an astounding victory, inflicting 2,500 casualties against a loss of only 492 of his own men, and sweeping the Union forces completely from a large expanse of southwest Tennessee and northern Mississippi.

Forrest led other raids that summer and fall, including a famous one into Union held downtown Memphis in August 1864, and another on a huge Union supply depot at Johnsonville, Tennessee, causing millions of dollars in damage. In December, he fought alongside the Confederate Army of Tennessee in the disastrous Battle of Franklin-Nashville, again showing his military genius by commanding the Confederate rear guard in a series of actions that allowed what was left of the army to escape. For this, he earned promotion to the rank of Lieutenant General.

In 1865 Forrest, against overwhelming Union forces, did not succeed in his defense of the State of Alabama. His opponent, Union Brig. Gen. James H. Wilson, was one of the few to ever to defeat him in battle. Forrest still had an army in the field in April, when news of Lee's surrender reached him. He was urged to flee to Mexico, but chose to share the fate of his men, and surrendered on Tuesday, May 9, 1865. In the four years of war, Forrest is said to have had 30 horses shot out from under him, and he may have personally killed 31 of his Union enemy.

Forrest was a first and instinctive genius at the tenets of "mobile warfare" that became so vital in following wars. Southerners of school age learned that his idea was to "get there fustest with the mostest", even if it meant pushing his horses at a killing pace, which he did more than once. A report on the Battle of Paducah stated that Forrest led a mounted cavalry of 2,500 troopers 100 miles in only 50 hours. He became well known for his early use of "guerrilla" tactics, seeking to constantly harass the enemy in fast moving raids, to disrupt supply trains and enemy communications by destroying railroad track and cutting telegraph lines, as he wheeled around the Union Army's flank. His success in quick hit-and-run tactics is reported to have driven Union General Ulysses S. Grant to fits of anger.

Forrest died in October 1877 in Memphis, just twelve years after the end of the Civil War, reportedly from complications of diabetes. He was buried at Elmwood Cemetery. In 1904 his remains were disinterred and moved to Forrest Park, a Memphis city park.

So now it becomes all too clear by whom the Boys From Lake County, fellow members of their 73rd Indiana Volunteer Infantry Regiment, and others of Streight's Brigade are being stalked as they move out on this ill fated raid. It will also become pridefully obvious in subsequent days..., as they move out from Moulton toward Blountsville, Alabama... what an enormous degree of courage, skill, and determination these Union men are able to wield against Confederate field officers and cavalrymen of such brilliant military accomplishment.

The Boys From Lake County

Chapter Eight

At last...the sun!

Afar the Alabama hills swept round in billowy lines,
The soft green of their bowery slopes was dotted with dark pines,
And from their tops a gentle breeze, born in the cloudless sky,
Stole through the valley where a stream was slowly warbling by,
And as it passed it brought a cloud of odor in its plumes,
Of violets and columbines, and milk-white plum tree blooms,
The coolness and the perfume o'er my weary senses crept.

* * * * *

I hear the bugle, I hear the drum, I have but one hour to stay.
Alas! My dreaming words were true, I woke and knew it all,
I heard the clamor of the drum, I heard the captain's call,
And over all another voice I oft had heard before,
A sound that stirs the dullest heart, the cannon's muffled roar.

These beautiful, rhythmic, words were written by a soldier..., obviously a poet..., Sergeant S. F. Flint of the 7th Illinois Volunteer Infantry Regiment. The poem was penciled at Town Creek, Alabama on Tuesday, April 28, 1863, the eve of battle.

Fellow un-famed writers share all too well the painful, often lost, effort to be published... and even then to be found, read, acclaimed. This writer is delighted with the opportunity to publish Sergeant S. F. Flint's poem here...so that after one hundred and forty years his vibrant, poetic, description of Northern Alabama's Tennessee River Valley in the Spring of 1863 may live again, and help us own the sense of being there in that time.

As we know, the Battle of Town Creek was indeed a mild one. Flint was lucky to be there and not amidst the coming travails of the Boys From Lake County and their fellow troopers of Streight's Brigade.

In fact, Sergeant Flint was from Galesburg, Illinois. It is a poignant sidelight that not only did he survive the Civil War, but was promoted to Lieutenant of his 7th Illinois Volunteer Infantry Regiment. In 1878 the people of Illinois established a Memorial Hall (Hall of Flags) at Peoria to display battle flags and other Civil War mementos of Illinois Regiments. The dedication of that museum was held with great pomp and ceremony. Lieutenant S. F. Flint of Galesburg, Illinois - fifteen years older by then - is recorded as having written another poem especially for that proud and tearful event. The following stanzas of his verse, just a portion of what he wrote, were read aloud during the observance:

So bear them on and guard them well
In yonder proud Memorial Hall.
The flag - the cause for which we fell
Swear brothers it shall never fall.

No traitor's hand its glory mars
While yet a man is still alive
Who bore the banner of the stars
From Sixty-one to Sixty-five.

Even in the face of danger and death, an author sees beauty... and aches to write. Clearly, Flint was a good writer. How nice it is to give him long overdue and, we hope, lasting credit for his work.

After those days of cloudy skies, drizzle, down pours, deep mud, slippery ruts in unpaved roads ...the sun shone brightly again at last. And with the sunshine, Spring abounded there in 1863 in one of the most picturesque places in America's South.

In Northern Alabama's Tennessee River Valley, after the tempest, as the Boys From Lake County moved on into their invasion, the sun shone brightly all day. At night there was a full moon. Spring foliage was in full, fresh, green leaf. The nights were cool, the days comfortable, not yet bearing the South's coming summer heat. Because of the rains, streams were high, running. Blooms of Dogwood and Azalea were already fading, but blossoms of Oak-leafed Hydrangea were opening to Spring sunshine.

Along roadsides the Boys From Lake County found patches of colorful wild flowers in abundant bloom. Lieutenant A.C. Roach of Colonel Streight's 51st Indiana Regiment, in his own writing, recorded that, in quiet evenings, the men could hear "the lonely call of the Whip-poor-will." To those of us who were raised in the countryside of America's South, it is the sound of home.

In between broad expanses of pastures, and farm fields for row planting, lay great virgin forests of tall Pine and Oak trees. Along with some Poplar, Hickory, Gum, Chestnut, and Sycamores, their cluster formed a green roof, shutting out sunlight, denying the growth of underbrush. In fact, the carpet of dead leaves and pine needles at the foot of the forests was so clear a deer could be seen, between the tree trunks, a half mile away.

Along the great River itself in 1863, Alabama's Tennessee Valley was a prosperous, cultured, progressive, well populated cotton producing region. Twenty miles south of the River, a range of hills called the Sand Mountain Plateau, rise sharply, stretching roughly eighty miles east and west.

Midway between Sand Mountain and the Tennessee River lies a second, sixty mile long, ridge called Little Mountain. The low land in between those two long ridges was called Moulton Valley in it's western section...and Morgan Valley in the eastern area.

The route of the invasion required Colonel Streight to head the Boys From Lake County and the rest of his Brigade straight into the sharp hills of the Sand Mountain Plateau...with Sand Mountain itself the initial steep ascent facing them. In the Spring of 1863 this section was far more thinly populated, with very rugged terrain and natural obstacles to be dealt with. Un-paved dirt roads were merely slim expansions of old Indian trails, which followed natural contours of the mountainous land, keeping to higher ground called ridges, and between the streams. There were no bridges. Roadways crossed the streams only at shallow places called fords, which could be waded easily...except in times of rain and ensuing high water.

Scattered over the Plateau were many smaller ridges and hills natives to the region called "sugar Loaf" mountains. The Plateau, part of America's great Appalachian Mountain chain got it's name from rocky terrain which, millions of years ago, was actually sand under the sea. When the Appalachians were thrust up from sea to mountain, that sea-sand solidified, evolving over eons into sandstone with layers of softer limestone underneath. The sandstone and limestone - cracked and eroded by water run-off more easily than other, harder, types of rock - formed drainage basins for numerous streams and creeks...all flowing southward to Alabama's Warrior River and on into the Gulf of Mexico.

As the sandstone, besieged by eons of time, further cracked, eroded... it was worn deeper by those streams of flowing water cutting through it, into the soft limestone below creating steep, rocky ravines. Though these gorges were often ruggedly picturesque, framed by outcroppings of rock and native flowering shrubs, they comprised a great many of those "natural obstacles" faced by the men of Streight's Brigade.

On the dark, rainy night of Sunday April 26th when the Boys from Lake County and others of their Brigade rode and marched to the south out of Tuscumbia they endured a long slow climb up a low ridge of the Little Mountain range...slipping and sliding in the dark and mud, of course...then down the ridge's southern side to Russellville, in Moulton Valley. It was at Russellville that they turned east into the valley toward the town of Moulton, stopping at Mount Hope because of the weather delay, proceeding the next morning on to Moulton itself. When they left Moulton near midnight on Tuesday, April 28th, obviously, it was not many minutes until they were proceeding on Wednesday April 29th.

"We marched the next day (Wednesday April 29, 1863) to Day's Gap and bivouacked for the night," Strieght reported. Actually the march was not quite to Day's Gap, which was up the crest of Sand Mountain.

Lieutenant Roach explains it in a bit more detail. "This day's march brought us to the base of a range of hills known as the Sand Mountains. Here it was determined to bivouac for the night. The prospect of a few hours of rest and sleep, a luxury that had not been enjoyed by any of us for some time previous, gave to our weary men a feeling of happiness."

There were two other successes that brightened, even further, that first day of sunshine. "We also," said Lieutenant Roach, "picked up during the day's march a number of animals, which were indeed very much needed."

"Every man," Colonel Streight expounded on this good news, "was now mounted, and although many of the animals were very poor, nevertheless we had strong hopes that we could easily supply our future demands,"

The other success was just as cheering. "We destroyed during the day a number of wagons belonging to the enemy," Colonel Streight related, "laden with provisions, arms, tents, etc which had been sent to the mountains to avoid us, but luckily fell into our hands. Again it is left to Lieutenant Roach to add other meaningful detail. "…We captured a number of wagons containing bacon, guns, ammunition, etc. Such of these prizes as were necessary for the complete equipment of our command, were issued to the men, and the balance destroyed."

A third issue of the march of Wednesday April 29, 1863 again gives us telling detail of the politics of America's Civil War. Today, a great many, if not most, Americans outside the South, as well texts taught in public schools, claim that the entire populations of all Southern states were fully rebellious against the Union of the United States, and all in favor of secession.

Nothing could be further from the truth. "We were now…," said Colonel Streight, "…in the midst of devoted Union people (deep in the Rebel state of Alabama). Many of Captain Smith's men (the two companies of First Middle Tennessee Cavalry in the Brigade) were recruited near this place, and many were the happy greetings between them and their friends and relations."

At the same time, during these three days of the Brigade's march into enemy territory while suffering near unbearable, rainy, muddy conditions...men of the Confederate army had also been busy. It was at dawn on Tuesday April 28th that the Confederate Cavalry commanded by General Nathan Bedford Forrest moved into the small village of Town Creek, Alabama to aid in it's defense against the 8,000 troops of Union Brigadier General Grenville M. Dodge.

On the previous afternoon he had crossed the Tennessee River on two steam ferries with 1,000 cavalrymen and six cannon...assuming command of a number of Confederate regiments. Added to his force, they numbered less than 3,000 men and ten cannon in all.

Five hours of cannon and sharpshooter dueling across swollen Town Creek blasted until, as sunset deepened into dark on the evening of April 28th, James Moon rushed in to tell Forrest that a Union cavalry force was moving deeper into Southern territory, already twenty-two miles south. As we know, it was the Boys From Lake County and Streight's Brigade.

And as we remember, Forrest, in his venturous manner, quickly split his smaller force to prepare for several possibilities. In so doing, he left a mere 500 men and 2 guns to face General Dodge's 8,000. But he also sent 700 men and 2 guns around to the rear of Dodge's force to give the Union commander a scare that his men might be caught in a pincer between two attackers. A much smaller unit of cavalry, just 50 men and 2 cannon, Forrest sent galloping the 35 miles or so to Decatur, Alabama to protect his own forces from the possibility of an attack in that direction.

Immediately, Forrest also dispatched the 4th Alabama Cavalry under General Philip Dale Roddey, and the 11th Tennessee Cavalry under Colonel Edmondson after Streight's Brigade...ordering the 4th and 9th Tennessee Cavalry, 900 men with 4 cannon, back to Courtland, Alabama with him to prepare for his own personal pursuit of the Union invasion.

At 1:00 a.m. on the morning of April 29th, Forrest and those units headed out in chilly, drizzling, rain and mud after Streight. At 8:00 a.m. they halted one hour to eat and feed their horses. At 11:00 a.m. they rested again for one hour at Moulton. Forrest, leading the column of cavalry himself, was continually giving the order, "move up men."

Pushing fiercely ahead, in the afternoon they caught up with the other two cavalry regiments of Roddey and Edmondson. Night found them all passing through the small Alabama village of Danville. At 2:00 a.m. on Aril 30th, they rested just four miles from the camp of the Boys From Lake County and their fellow soldiers of Streight's Brigade...ready to begin a surprise dawn attack. But, at that vital juncture, Forrest did yet another daring thing, sending about half his 2,000 men to the east in case Streight's Brigade should aim in that direction...sharply reducing the number of men for available for the dawn siege.

The men of Streight's Brigade broke camp and moved out the next morning, Thursday, April 30th, before daylight. "I will here remark, " Colonel Streight reported, "that my men had been worked very hard in scouring so much of the country, (to find horses and mules) and unaccustomed as they were to riding, made it still worse. Consequently, they were illy prepared for the trying ordeal through which they were to pass."

"I could learn nothing of the enemy in the country," Colonel Streight continued, "with the exception of small squads of scouting parties, who were hunting conscripts."(See note below.) Again, Colonel Streight's military intelligence information was notably incomplete...as he would soon learn.

"I had not proceeded more than two miles, at the head of the column, before I was informed that the rear guard had been attacked, and just at that moment I heard the boom of artillery in the rear of the column."

Author's note. The Civil War word "conscript" meant the same as a "military draft" in America's more recent wars. However, conscription was highly unpopular with both the general public and soldiers during the Civil War... and there had never been a general conscription up to the Civil War itself. The South enacted the first of three conscription laws on Wednesday, April 16, 1862. About a year later the Union followed suit.

Americans on both sides, though, feared such compulsory military service, thinking of it as an opposition to individual freedom. Citizens were also uneasy that conscription law would give too much power to the military. Soldiers, likely from personal experience, heartily disliked conscripts, believing that unwilling troops were poor fighting men, that conscription interfered with voluntary enlistment, and had an aura of desperation after military defeats.

Conscription brought on desertion and "substitutes," as "draftees" could "buy" their way out of serving by paying another man to serve for them. Complaints of discrimination were aimed at both Union and Confederate conscription laws as exemptions permitted men with property to evade serving, putting the onus on immigrants and men with little money. Loopholes were also provided by medical, only-son, and career related exemptions. Friendly doctors proclaimed healthy men medically unfit for service, while some physically or mentally unfit "draftees" were sent into battle with fake medical exams. Another notable problem was enforcement, as many conscripts simply never showed up for duty. Several states attempted to block conscription laws with court challenges to their legality, while at the same time arguing over the quota system assigned to each. Civil War conscription likely produced more disagreement than soldiers because of it's seeming unfairness, lack of popularity, and management difficulties. In fact, draft riots occurred in New York in 1863. Of near a quarter million names drawn, only about 6% actually served, the rest buying their way out. However records seem to show that in the last year of the Civil War, conscripts totaled more than a fourth of Confederate armies in the east.

Chapter Nine

The Battle of Days Gap

Unknown to him in that first moment, in the dawning hours of Thursday April 30, 1863, the boom of cannon at the rear of the two mile long column of Streight's Brigade foretold the second major battle for the Boys From Lake County and their fellow soldiers of the 73rd Indiana Volunteer Infantry Regiment.

The first, of course, had been the Battle of Stone's River at Murphreesborough, Tennessee just five months before. Their part in that battle had been a fierce one, as we know, with the 73rd Regiment losing more than one third of their number killed, wounded or missing. Losses in this ensuing day's action would be far less, but the fight would be just as fierce, if not more so.

To be sure, outer scouting assignments of their Regiment... not always the same men, but different units selected at the moment...had been often under fire in "skirmishes" with small units of the enemy. As noted previously, small skirmishes had been going on in this invasion since not long after their departure from Tuscumbia.

These small, quick "skirmish" firefights were a normal, planned part of the conduct of infantry engagements. Smaller units of rifle bearers called "pickets" or "skirmishers" were usually sent out ahead, behind, and to the side of the main force as scouts. As an enemy approached they would encounter them initially, and be engaged in the first rifle fire, the sound of it giving the main force alert and time to prepare for battle. The "skirmishers" themselves, with their job done and the enemy discovered, would not risk heavy loss by standing to fight. Rather, firing to slow the enemy, they would fade back into the main force, then join them in the more major engagement if that followed.

Of course, with the fast moving cavalry of the adroit Confederate General Nathan Bedford Forrest on their trail, a number of the skirmishes since leaving Tuscumbia were simply his standard hit and run, harassing, tactics. His goal in those small engagements was to interfere with his enemy's freedom of movement, beleaguer, slow them down, and pick off a few of them in each skirmish, without losing too many of his own in killed and wounded. This day, Thursday April 30, 1863, though, would be very long... and, as Forrest had chosen, would be far from a "skirmish."

"I had previously learned that the gap (Day's Gap) through which we were passing," related Colonel Streight, "was easily flanked by gaps through the mountains, both above and below." In other words, Colonel Streight - surely from information provided by men of Companies D and E of the First Middle Tennessee Cavalry units who had lived in that area - knew that Forrest could dispatch part of his forces through ravines on either side, circle the Brigade and come out ahead of him, catching his troops in a pincer of rifle fire from both front and rear. In fact, that was the main job of Captain D. D Smith's boys in Streight's Raid...the reason Streight selected them as part of the Brigade...to act as scouts and guides through an area they knew intimately.

"Consequently," Streight continued, "I sent orders to the rear to hold the enemy in check until we could prepare for action." The front of the Brigade's column was, by then, already on top of 1,000 foot Sand Mountain, with the following troops moving up through the gap. With side approaches blocked by steep ravines and rugged hills on either side of the road at that point, Forrest's attackers were easily held in check. But not for long.

What Colonel Streight feared was turned quickly into fact by the aggressive General Forrest and his quick moving cavalry. "I soon learned," Streight reported, "that the enemy had moved through gaps on my right and left, and were endeavoring to form a junction in my advance." Colonel Streight left it unsaid...but it is virtually certain he learned this perilous intelligence by quickly preparing to do so..., that is by sending skirmishers out to the right and left of his force to see what might be going on. It is just as likely that the "seeing eyes" were those men astride Captain D.D. Smith's quick moving horses. "Consequently,' Colonel Streight continued, "I moved ahead rapidly until we passed the intersecting roads on either flank to the one we occupied."

The surroundings at that place were open, very thinly wooded, and with sand ridges. Streight found that it afforded fine defensive positions. "As soon as we passed that (safer) point ..., we dismounted and formed a line of battle on a ridge circling to the rear. "The right side of their battle line stretched to a steep, craggy ravine...the left flank protected by a marshy run...which is a, sometimes dry, creek bed through which water runs during rainy weather.

(Author's note: This battle line described by Colonel Streight was still highly identifiable in the year 1998, in the tiny Alabama village of Battleground, when we were last there. It was a pasture which the run zig-zagged across, instead of woodlands, by then. However, because of intermittent water run off and marshy conditions, the banks of the creek bed were lined with bushes and easy to recognize. When we saw it, there obviously had been no rain for quite some time....so the creek bed was dry and hard. But remember, it had been raining for several days before the Boys From Lake County and others of Streight's Brigade got there. The reader will now find a roadside historical marker at that spot, telling of the battle. But it's message gives far less than justice to the fierceness of the engagement itself.)

Horses and mules were sent into a ravine to the rear of the right side of the battle line to protect them from the enemy's bullets. The Brigage's commander also immediately deployed a line of skirmishers, starting at both sides of the battle line and encircling the rear of his Brigade. That order was given for two reasons. First was to prevent a surprise from any detached force of Confederates which might be sent around to attack the rear of his Brigade...a tactic which might well be expected from General Nathan Bedford Forrest. The second...in Colonel Streight's own words..."to prevent any straggling of either stray animals or cowardly men." Clearly Streight was, by then, understandably sensitive to losing any more mounts. As to "cowardly men" there certainly had never been a mention of any in previous reports... even in the Battle of Stone's River when the Boys From Lake County and their fellow soldiers of the 73rd Indiana had lost 111 men killed, wounded, and missing...a time when Streight's own 51st Indiana suffered less.

Streight also instantly concocted his own cunning tactic. He ordered Captain D.D. Smith and his two companies of cavalry out front of the battle line, instead of rear guard where they had been. "I instructed him to hold his position until the enemy pressed him closely, when he should retreat rapidly, and if possible draw them on to our lines." With the Brigade lying down at the edge of the hill, they were hidden among weeds, loaded muskets pointed and ready. They had also left space near their center so the two companies of the First Middle Tennessee Cavalry could dart back into the battle line at the last second. In addition, Colonel Streight stationed the two 12 pound mountain howitzers (cannon) near the road, at the center of the battle line. The cannon were also concealed from view. The ruse worked perfectly!

"We had hardly completed our arrangements when the enemy charged Captain Smith in large force, following him closely..." In fact, Captain Smith's troopers did their part to perfection, hurriedly dodging back through the battle line with Forrest's attackers in hot, close pursuit.

No sooner had he come," Streight said, "when our whole line rose up and delivered a volley at close range." As we've said before, close range is the point at which the fire from those outdated .69 caliber 1842 Springfield muskets, with which the Boys From Lake County were armed, was simply devastating. "We continued to pour a rapid fire into their ranks," Streight related, "which soon caused them to give way in confusion." As the Confederates faded back, Streight sent skirmishers out front again to keep a check on what might happen next.

True to form, in light of his highly aggressive, tactical genius, General Nathan Bedford Forrest had planned well, too. He had not sent his entire force into the first attack, holding back a reserve.

"Their reinforcements soon came up," Streight continued, "when they dismounted, formed, and made a determined, vigorous attack." The Union Brigade's skirmishers quickly faded back into the line of battle, joining the other troops in firing into Confederate attackers. And during that second advance General Forrest had ordered his cannon to move upward to within 900 feet of the Union line of battle on the crest of the ridge. His cavalry men, on foot now, pressed aggressively forward... firing as they came...an intensified effort to power through Union battle lines....but were "handsomely repulsed," as Colonel Streight put it.

Now, Streight displayed a sense of aggressiveness in battle fully equal, in the moment, to the famous Forrest's tactics. "As soon as they began to waver," he said, "I prepared for a charge."

Again, as in the vicious Battle of Stones River at Murphreesborough, it was the Boys From Lake County and their fellow soldiers of the 73rd Indiana who were chosen, along with Streight's own 51st Indiana, to lead the way, to carry the peril of that bayonet charge. "I ordered Colonel Hathaway, Seventy Third Indiana, and Colonel Sheets, Fifty First Indiana to make a charge, in order to draw the attention of the battery (cannon.) And immediately threw the Third Ohio, Colonel Lawson, and the Eightieth Illinois, Lieutenant Colonel Rogers, forward rapidly, hoping to capture the battery."

Again, Streight's aggressive counter attack worked exactly as he had planned. General Forrest's Confederate Cavalrymen, after a short but stubborn resistance, had to flee in confusion, abandoning both cannon, and two ammunition caissons. The men of Streight's Brigade captured about forty prisoners, representing seven different Confederate regiments. Also left behind by the retreating Forrest cavalry men were a large number of wounded and about thirty dead on the field. Among those wounded was Captain William H. Forrest, a brother of General Forrest.

"Our loss," lamented Colonel Streight, "was about 30 killed and wounded." Among those who died of wounds was Lieutenant Colonel Sheets of Streight's own Fifty First Indiana …"a brave and gallant officer, and one that we were illy prepared to lose," said Streight. Lieutenant Pavey, on the staff of the Brigade, was severely wounded.

It was by then about 11 o'clock in the morning, with the battle having been continuous since about 6 a.m. "I had learned, in the meantime," Streight explains, "that the enemy were in heavy force, fully three times our number (which would have been about 4,500 troopers,) with twelve pieces of artillery, under General Forrest in person. Consequently, I was fearful that they were making an effort to get around us and attack in the rear of our position. Hence, I decided to resume the march."

Clearly, in these words, it is revealed that Colonel Streight already knew of Confederate General Nathan Bedford Forrest's vibrant reputation for fierce determination in battle, elusive combat tactics...that he was far more than a considerable force to be reckoned with.

Further, on the down side, Colonel Streight's intelligence information was faulty. We know his Brigade totaled somewhere between 1500 and 1800 men...and he was told that Forrest's cavalry was three times that number, or about 4,500 men. Forrest may have come into command of nearly that number when he crossed the Tennessee River into Town Creek, Alabama. But in his plans to deal with both Union General Dodge's 8,000 man force, as well as the pursuit of Streight's Brigade, he split them up, sending them in three directions....just about 1,000 of them under his own command lighting out after Streight. During that morning's continuous, fierce, fighting he had lost perhaps 100 or so killed, wounded, or captured of that 1000. As he regrouped his forces at the foot of Sand Mountain, he was rejoined by two units he had sent on other operations...the 4th and 9th Tennessee Regiments with a total of about 900 men. So the truth is that Forrest had about the same sized force, at least at that point. Colonel Streight and his brigade were not overwhelmed by a force three times their size as he was led to believe... but faced a Confederate force roughly equal to his own.

"Everything was soon in readiness," Streight reported, "and we moved out, leaving a strong guard dismounted in the rear, to check any immediate advance the enemy might make previous to the column getting in motion."

Lieutenant A.C. Roach in his postwar book "The Prisoners..." hurled severe criticism at Forrest's men for their "inhuman and brutal" treatment of the wounded Union men left behind with a surgeon in a field hospital. He says the Confederates came up and deprived them of bread, meat, sugar, coffee, and blankets... as well as medicine and surgical instruments which were taken by the Rebel surgeon." Actually, Roach, of course, had moved on with the Brigade, was not there at the time, and does not allege any actual cruelties beyond stealing. After all...war is hell... and such are the confusions and animosities of it, sometimes on either side

In fact, General Forrest certainly had in mind repeating his assault immediately. But by the time he reorganized his battered forces, gathered in the 4th and 9th Tennessee, and charged up Sand Mountain again, Streight's Brigade was gone...but not very far.

"We were not too soon in our movements," Streight related, "for the column had hardly passed a crossroad, some six miles from our first battleground, when the enemy were discovered advancing on our left." Streight doesn't mention it, but it is highly likely the men who discovered Forrest's oncoming cavalry troopers were again the cavalry scouts of Captain D.D. Smith's First Middle Tennessee Cavalry acting as outlying watchmen.

Sharp rifle fire between the two forces began again at a place called Crooked Creek, about ten miles south of Days Gap (which we know now is called Battleground.) Finally Forrest's attack pressed the rear of the Brigade so viciously that Streight had no option but to prepare for battle again.

"I selected a strong position," Streight continues, "about 1 mile south of the crossing of the creek, on a ridge called Hog Mountain." By about one hour before dark, the whole force became engaged in a fierce fire fight. Forrest's troops first endeavored to force their way around the right side of the Brigade's battle line...then vigorously charged the left side. Again... Confederate General Nathan Bedford Forrest's famous hit and run...then hit again tactics. "...with the help of the two pieces of artillery captured in the morning, and our own two mountain howitzers, all of which were handled with good effect by Major Vananda, of the Third Ohio, we were able to repulse them."

Fighting continued on until about 10 p.m. when men of the Brigade were finally able to drive Forrest's forces from their front, leaving...according to Colonel Streight...a large number of killed and wounded on the field.

This battle, confronted at three locations..., two fierce ones at Days Gap and Hog Mountain, with a sharp skirmish at Crooked Creek in between..., had been raging since 6:00 a.m., sixteen long, perilous, hours.

In fact, at 3:00 p.m., as Forrest and his men came up behind Streight's Brigade again at Crooked Creek they surged forward aggressively, firing heavily. "Shoot everything blue, and keep up the scare," Forrest yelled. At 4:00 p.m. as the Union Brigade forded the creek Confederate attackers scattered through the woods. At 5:00 p.m. both forces were wholly engaged. The Union line held on into the dark of night, but the fire fight, although more brief, seemed as intense as the earlier battle at Day's Gap.

Confederate attackers made charge after charge to the right and left, led by the flash of Union guns. General Nathan Bedford Forrest, fighting in person in the midst of his men, as always was

106

his style, had three horses shot out from under him. About 9:00 p.m. he ordered the 9th Tennessee Cavalry Regiment around the Union right flank, threatening soldiers who were holding the Brigade's horses and mules. Colonel Streight and his men, fearing to losing any more mounts, finally succeeded in driving the Confederates back.

With the Rebels, at least temporarily, repulsed Streight decided to use that opportunity to resume the march, and as soon as his troops could get weapons, supplies, equipment and animals ready, the long column of Streight's Brigade formed up and moved out again. Ammunition captured with the two Union cannon had all been used in the battle at Hog Mountain. Without it the guns were of no further use, so Streight ordered them spiked and the carriages destroyed so they would never again be of use to the enemy, and left behind. ("Spiking" a cannon means to hammer an over sized ram deep in the barrel, permanently clogging it.) Also left behind were the Confederate wagons captured earlier, along with some black Alabamians who had joined them in Morgan's Valley.

Once again, the Boys From Lake County and their fellow soldiers of the 73rd Indiana Regiment were the ones called upon to play a vital, valorous, role in battle. "I had ordered the 73rd Indiana (Colonel Hathaway) to act as rear guard...and I remained in the rear in person...for the purpose of being at hand in case the enemy should attempt to press us as we were moving out." In fact, the Brigade had "just fairly" gotten under way when it became evident that Forrest's Confederates were rushing again to the attack. On that late evening of Thursday, April 30th 1863, the moon was full and shone brightly. The country, as we already know, was open woodland with, as Streight says, an occasional spot of thick undergrowth.

"In one of those thickets," Colonel Streight relates, "I placed the 73rd Indiana, lying down, and not more than 20 paces (perhaps 60 feet) from the road, which was in plain view." Forrest's troopers moved up that road, the head of the

Confederate column passing without discovering the hidden position of the Boys From Lake County and their fellow soldiers of the 73rd.

"At this moment," said Colonel Streight, "the whole regiment opened up a most destructive fire, causing a complete stampede of the enemy." It was another maneuver displayed instinctively by Colonel Streight that was fully equal to the famed hit and run battle tactics of his cunning opponent, General Nathan Bedford Forrest.

But General Forrest tells that tale in a different way. The Confederate leader said he sent three scouts ahead on foot to "feel out" any Rebel force. When those advance men sensed the Union soldiers rise up to fire, they quickly dodged, falling flat and saving their lives. Then cannon were pulled by hand up the quiet sand road, hidden from bright moonlight by shade of the dense forest. Loaded with grape shot and fired, the ambuscade was routed. Whose description is more accurate? The only thing we know for sure is that Forrest and his men, indeed, backed off.

In that area, for the forty miles to the Brigade's next destination point at Blountsville, Alabama, woodland mountains were mostly uninhabited. "Consequently," said Streight, "there is nothing for man or beast." He hoped by pushing ahead, even after fighting for more than sixteen hours, they could reach a place where the men of the Brigade could eat, rest, and feed the animals before the Confederates could come up on them again. Streight also hoped that by holding Forrest and his men back where there was no feed he could force him to lay over a day "at least to recuperate." The Union Brigade commander had also learned, somehow, that General Nathan Bedford Forrest and his cavalry had pushed a day and two nights on a tiring forced march from Town Creek before their attack at Day's Gap.

"We were not again disturbed," Colonel Streight continues, "until we had marched for several miles, when they attacked our rear guard vigorously." Lieutenant Roach says this attack, at a place called Ryan's Creek Ford, occurred about 2:00 a.m., which, by then, would have been in the wee hours of the morning, Friday, May 1, 1863. Streight again succeeded in "ambuscading" Forrest's force, but does not describe how it was accomplished or which unit or units were assigned to the task. Regardless, Forrest gave up pursuit for the rest of the night.

"We continued our march and reached Blountsville about 10 o'clock in the morning," says Streight. From the skirmish at Ryan's Creek Ford at 2:00 a.m. the Brigade rode eight miles to Johnson's Crossing, then four miles to Steppville. It was, two and a half miles further to Mulberry Fork Ford, a fork of the Warrior River which the Brigade waded without interference. Another two miles brought them to Putnam Mountain which they ascended with very little bother from Forrest's cavalry. After that, a two mile trek carried the Boys From Lake County and others of Streight's Brigade to Gum Springs. Finally an additional five miles found them in Blountsville. The battles of Day's Gap and Hog Mountain had occurred at a mountain altitude of about 1,000 feet. Blountsville, Alabama, in Brown's Valley, was lower in the mountains at about 650 feet. But higher and more rugged elevations still lay ahead.

The Boys From Lake County and others of the Brigade had been fighting or in the saddle for twenty eight hours without rest. "Many of our horses and mules had given out," Streight related, "leaving their riders on foot, but there was very little straggling behind the rear guard." Hardly surprising, since few would have wanted to face Forrest's aggressive cavalry alone.

(Author's note: As we've learned, this invasion of Union Colonel Abel D. Streight's Brigade deep into the Confederate South is little famed in the general annals of America's Civil War. It was, however, intensely famous among those who were touched by the furor of it's battles and skirmishes...the people of Northern Alabama..., and especially the citizens of Rome, Georgia.

When the author lived in Rome, in the years 1946 and 1947, those of Rome, almost a century later, were still eager, fascinated, prideful in telling the story. General Nathan Bedford Forest was yet passionately regarded as the savior of Rome... his statue overwhelming on the main avenue downtown, and with Rome's leading hotel bearing his name.

Historian Rucker Agee of Alabama, drew this conclusion from his intense physical and literary research of the raid: "The Forrest-Streight campaign across North Alabama in the Spring of 1863 is an intriguing adventure which exacted the extreme of human endurance under opposing military leaders of superior ability, tenacity, and resourcefulness. Although the forces employed were small, the consequences of success or failure were of far-reaching effect on the fortunes of the great armies in the west." (Meaning the western part of America's eastern States. For those who might not recall, it was In States east of the Mississippi River where, by far, most of America's Civil War was fought.)

General Nathan Bedford Forrest, himself however, was so famed by the end of the Civil War for his immense success, aggressiveness and unschooled military genius that a number of biographies were written of his life and deeds, beginning in 1868 and continuing on through 1944. One written just after the Civil War was carefully reviewed and approved by Forrest himself, and so is considered virtually an autobiography.

Several authors of those histories were Civil War General Thomas Jordan with journalist J.P. Pryor 1868, George M. Battey, Robert Selph Henry 1944, John Allen Wyeth 1900, General Joe Wheeler, and Bennett H. Young. Agee also mentions Mathes in 1902, Sheppard 1930, and Lytle 1931 and 1939. According to Agee, virtually all contain a chapter on the battles between Forrest and Streight's Brigade in 1863. Each, he reports, presents evaluations not given elsewhere.

However, comments attributed by Agee to several of them shine brilliant light on the intensity of the running fights, as well as the skill and bravery of the men and their commanders on each side. One says the campaign of Streight's Brigade was "one of the most spectacular exploits of the War." Another says it was "one of the most remarkable and desperately contested undertakings of the War." Yet another, "this incident was not surpassed by any similar occurrence during the conflict." A fourth, "one of the most exciting and brilliant campaigns of the War." A fifth, "Forrest had never struck anything so game and so wary as this intrepid Brigade of Streight's." Major M. F. Clift points out that this campaign gave to General Nathan Bedford Forrest the appellation of "the wizard of the saddle."

Although, like most rifle bearers of the Civil War, and so unlike many of their high ranking commanders, they remained un-named, un-famed..., we may see clearly by these words the kind of tough, determined fighting men the Boys From Lake County, and their fellow soldiers of the 73d Indiana Voluntary infantry Regiment, and of Streight's Brigade, really were.

CHAPTER TEN

Whistling Minie Balls of Friday,
May 1, 1863

"At Blountsville," Colonel Streight says, "we found sufficient corn to feed our tired and hungry animals." The men also rounded up a number of fresh mounts from local farms. But the Brigade commander allowed his exhausted soldiers, horses, and mules only two hours to rest and get something to eat.

Fortunately for the Boys From Lake County and their fellow Union soldiers, the little city was located in a farming area known, then, as the valley of corn and plenty. May 1st was the time usually set aside for May Day festivities, including the crowning of a lovely "Queen of May." That Friday, May 1, 1863 would be stunningly different ... turning out to be one of the most rousing days in the town's history up to that era. It was the first review by the citizens of Blountsville of a large force of the Northern enemy...soldiers in Union Blue. Instead of the expected celebration, they found themselves providing corn for more than 1,500 Union Army horses and mules. Then the Alabamians had little choice but to watch as every horse and mule that could be found in their region was taken as badly needed fresh mounts by the men of Streight's Brigade. In addition, they would see a sharp skirmish of rifle fire in the streets of their city, followed by a second deluge of hungry cavalry horses...and soldiers dressed in Confederate Gray.

"We now knew," Streight continued, "that it would be impossible to take the wagons over the roads before us." The next twenty five miles would traverse a steady climb over extremely rugged terrain to the highest point they would reach in the mountains.

Ammunition and food rations, all each could carry, were quickly handed out to the men. The balance of the ammunition was put onto pack mules. The wagons were burned. It was about 12:00 noon on Friday, May 1, 1863 when the Brigade resumed march, headed in the direction of Gadsden, Alabama.

The truth, though, is that the Boys from Lake County and others of their 73rd Indiana and of Streight's Brigade THOUGHT the wagons were burned. At least when they left the wagons, pushed tightly together, piled with mounds of dry brush and small dry tree branches, were afire. Within minutes, however, General Forrest's cavalry saw the rising smoke, discovered the burning wagons, put out the fires, and captured supplies which, by now, were very badly needed.

With Forrest's men moving up so quickly, the Union Brigade's column had just barely got underway when the Confederate cavalry attacked them again. "A sharp skirmish ensued," said Streight, "between Forrest's advance and our rear guard, under Captain Smith." So again we find Captain D.D. Smith and his two companies of the First Middle Tennessee Cavalry guarding the rear of the Brigade, taking the heat. But this fire fight occurred in the edge of town, right in the streets of Blountsville.

Afterwards Forrest's attackers followed tightly for several miles, with rifle fire continually exchanged between the two forces. According to Colonel Streight, though, the Confederates "were badly handled by small parties of our men stopping in the thick bushes by the side of the road and firing at short range." Remember, short range is where the big .69 caliber musket, with which the Boys from Lake County were armed, was most damaging.

Another seven miles brought them, in the midst of a continuous running fight, to the East Branch of Alabama's Black Warrior River where greater depth of the ford on that day brought yet another major obstacle to the Brigade's advance.

At that site "the enemy pressed us so closely," Streight said, "that I was compelled to halt and offer him battle before we could cross." The Union commander ordered his cannon across the ford of the river and effectively placed them on high ground on the opposite side, along with a strong line of riflemen. Then he sent out a powerful line of skirmishers whose heavy fire drove the Confederate cavalry back out of sight of his main force. That gave time for his Brigade to cross the ford "as rapidly as possible", one regiment at a time while the skirmishers, as well as the riflemen and cannon across the river, covered them. After all regiments had crossed, the line of skirmishers was rapidly drawn back in and crossed the river under protective fire of the cannon and riflemen already stationed on the opposite banks for that purpose.

"It was about 5:00 p.m." Streight relates, "when the last of the command crossed the East Branch of the Black Warrior River. We proceeded in the direction of Gadsden without further interruption, except for small parties who were continually harassing us." In fact Colonel Streight again marched his men and animals all night, without rest.

As the last of the Union skirmishers faded back toward their Brigade and crossed the river, Forrest's cavalrymen kept up a vigorous attack. In addition, increasing the pressure, he ordered a small unit upstream and across another ford, from where they were able to double back and briefly attack the Brigade's right flank. It was just another example of General Nathan Bedford Forrest's famed, continuous, hit and run tactics.

At that juncture, however, Forrest wisely chose to stop and give the main force of his men and mounts several hours rest. Although he did send out the much smaller unit to follow the Union Brigade all night, continually sniping at their rear... keeping them moving. It gave the Confederate cavalrymen not only time to rest and sleep, but to eat and feed their horses.

It was earlier on that same afternoon of Friday May 1st, when two local girls... girls mind you... delivered to Confederate General Forrest three of Streight's union soldiers whom they, themselves, had captured, along with their mounts. The story is virtually unknown in any official Civil War records we've searched. It was certainly well enough known locally along that portion of the route of Streight's Raid to have a road side sign telling of it.

Armies of all the ages have been manned by fighting men who are quick witted, aggressive, adventurous, courageous, determined. Of course, in the ranks with them are a great many others of more average qualities who perform dutifully, even bravely when called upon to do so. Sadly, scattered among those, are some who are notably less intrepid, far from keen of wit, deserters when the going is tough, and even a few of criminal compunction.

Long years have hidden the names of the three "prowling" Union soldiers who left their ranks and went to a farmhouse where the two young women were alone. We cannot even mark from which of Streight's regiments they came. All of the Boys From Lake County seem to have been accounted for at the end of the mission. It may be, of course, that they were simply exhausted and hungry for good food. But, by then all of their fellow Brigade soldiers were in like condition. History just does not tell us if they were foolishly young, fearful deserters, or simply bad characters. However local lore also records that the three "invaded" the homestead, and killed two colts. The killing of the colts was a senseless act, hinting that they were simply of the worst sort and the girls lucky not to have been harmed. The history by the side of the road does tell us something of the young Southern women.

Celia and Winnie Mae Murphree, of course, likely immediately recognized the uniforms of Union Blue. News of a large force of enemy troops in a neighborhood spread very quickly even in days before modern, instant, communication.

Although local lore also says the Union soldiers "took food and drink," it seems obvious, considering how the situation turned out, that the young women handled themselves cooly and well, agreeably providing a satisfactory meal upon demand. If the "drink" was of the hard sort... from the family liquor cabinet...that plus the extreme tiredness of the soldiers would explain why the young men "fell asleep." In those years, whiskey, even among families who drank little, was kept for medicinal purposes. To the exhausted troopers, that must have seemed like a great idea... at the moment...and they were soon in deep slumber.

Regardless of speculation on minor details of the encounter...although they seem obvious...upon awakening with a new day the Union soldiers found themselves, not only detained, but looking up into the barrels of their own muskets. Celia and Winnie Mae Murphree apparently had no more trouble with them as they marched the three as captives, at rifle point, to find General Nathan Bedford Forrest and his cavalrymen, bivouacked at a nearby community called Royal Crossing.

In full scale battle, as well as attack after attack, Colonel Abel D. Streight has been an astounding, spirited, scheming strategist, near the equal of the famed instinctive, aggressive, military genius of General Nathan Bedford Forrest. His brilliant defense has caused Forrest and his men considerable loss in killed and wounded. Streight is driving himself and his men to the utmost, though, laboring under the unfortunate illusion that his vigorous, relentless, oncoming enemy has a force three times the Union Brigade's strength. By the evening hours of May 1, 1863 that was far from the truth.

As we know, in three days before, the daring Forrest had ordered several splits in his limited command to accomplish different purposes at the same time. Crossing the Tennessee River into the Battle of Town Creek he assumed leadership of less than 3,000 men and 10 cannon...compared to Union General Dodge's 8,000 man force. On Tuesday, April 28th, as he lit out after Streights Brigade, Forrest left just 1200 men and 2 cannon to throw the scare into General Dodge. And that small force was again split, nearly half ahead and half behind Dodge's 8,000. Also, as we know, the ruse worked perfectly...reeling Dodge's big army back to his main camp at Corinth, without ever sending the cavalry cover promised, and which the men of Streight's Brigade would need so greatly.

After splitting his smaller force again, sending a unit eastward in the hope of getting ahead of Streight's Brigade, Forrest had about 1200 cavalrymen and four cannon as he approached the Battle of Days Gap. Less than 1,000 of them, with four cannon, made it up Sand Mountain to the Day's Gap fight.

Once again, since then, Forrest has dared to send out units to try to get around and ahead of Streight's Brigade. Therefore, here, very late in this day, Friday May 1, 1863 he is down to near 600 men who are in condition to ride and attack.

So the truth is, instead of being pressed by regiments three times his size, Streight was being harassed, viciously attacked by Confederate units that totaled only one-third the strength of his own Union Brigade.

Though much smaller in size now, Forrest's men still had the advantage of riding horses instead of army mules as many of Colonel Streight's troopers had to do. To be sure, many of the mounts Streight's men took from farms along the way were horses ...although some even of those were likely, also, to have been mules. Of course, the two companies of Captain D.D. Smith's men of the First Middle Tennessee Cavalry were riding horses as did all cavalry troops. Horses were faster, quieter, more sure footed at speed, never balky, noisy, stubborn as were the famous army mules.

It is far from surprising, though, that army leaders would send Streight's men out on such mounts. For generations, even far into the time of internal combustion engines and army mechanization, army brass continued to cling to the mule... the old mainstay of army transportation and burden.

Stories from North Alabama mountain country through which the Union invaders passed told that anyone could hear the braying of Streight's mules for miles. Southerners along the route of the raid called Streight's Brigade the "Jackass Cavalry." Worse...because of that noisy braying, echoing for miles up and down the hills and ravines of the Sand Mountain Plateau, the invasion was a far, far harder event to hide.

Colonel Gilbert Hathaway Circa 1862

Chapter Eleven

The Burning Bridges Of Saturday, May 2, 1863

The expectance of continued major attack, along with constant sniping rifle fire behind them - from what Colonel Streight thought was a large force of Forrest's cavalry - pushed the Union Brigade into yet another all night march. As they climbed into the night shaded mountains, eight miles from the fight at Black Warrior River, Streight and his men crossed the Wynneville Creek Bridge, destroying it in hope of slowing Forrest's oncoming cavalrymen. The Black Warrior River ran at an altitude of 580 feet in the mountains, the Wynneville Bridge at 730. Five miles further at 910 feet, they crossed Red Mountain Pass. At near the same height they rode through Walnut Grove in Murphree Valley, a mile farther wading a ford of the Upper Warrior River. Two miles beyond the river, they passed through Red Bud Gap on Straight Mountain. Just two miles past Red Bud Gap, the Brigade, at 1110 feet, crossed the highest point they would reach in the rugged peaks. At near the same level they passed through Howelton, Alabama and Blount Mountain Pass.

From there it was easier, sharply downhill. In just seven miles the Boys From Lake County and their fellow soldiers of the 73rd Indiana and Streight's Brigade, with rifle fire often coming at them from behind, found the waters of Big Will's Creek running high. In the wading of it they wet, and lost, a good portion of their ammunition.

9:00 a.m. found Streight's Brigade crossing Black Creek Bridge near Gadsden, Alabama..., when, says Colonel Streight, "the rear guard was fiercely attacked." As we know, men of Captain D.D. Smith's two cavalry companies knew that region intimately. Their advice was to hurriedly burn the bridge, surely delaying Forrest's Cavalry for a longer period because of the deep river, giving the exhausted men of the Brigade time to sleep, eat, as well as to feed and rest their tired mounts.

After what Streight described as a "sharp fight," the Confederates were repulsed once more. The Union commander ordered the bridge set on fire. By the time Forrest's main force rushed up, indeed it was too late, the fire far advanced, the bridge structure collapsing, unpassable. They could see men of the Union rear guard on the other side, but Forrest's Confederate cavalry was unable to cross the deep river. Captain D.D. Smith's idea seemed to have worked perfectly.

But, again, there came an event which quickly offset what seemed a great advantage for Colonel Streight and his valorous expedition. And, it brought to the fore the second of two whose names have remained widely remembered among the travails of Streight's Brigade.

Near the road and within two hundred yards or so of Black Creek Bridge lived a family named Sansom. Their small, one story, farmhouse was unimposing, an open hall in the center... two or three rooms on either side, much like most Alabama farm homes in the era of America's Civil War. There was only the mother and her two teenage daughters. Mrs. Sansom's husband had passed away four years before. His grave site was there on the farm, at the edge of woods, near a garden gate. Her son was already in the Confederate army, having joined the 19th Alabama Infantry in 1861, one of the first units formed in Gadsden. Like more than seventy percent of Southerners, the family had chosen never to own slaves. Without the support of son and brother, three women were struggling alone to make the farm productive enough to meet their most basic of needs.

Hearing the gallop of horses, gunshots, yelled orders..., the women came outside their house to find cavalrymen in Union blue, the Boys From Lake County and Streight's Brigade. The long column of men, some driving mules pulling two cannon, were moving in haste to clatter their animals across wooden boards of the bridge. A number of them paused briefly to draw water for themselves and their mounts from the well in Mrs. Sansom's yard.

The women watched as the column dwindled to stragglers urged over the bridge by men of the Brigade's rear guard. Across the river the two cannon were positioned, riflemen scattered among trees and bushes...the rear guard preparing to defend as the main force marched on. Others tore up rails from Mrs. Sansom's fence, piling them on the bridge along with masses of dry brush. Flames surged high as they lit the pile afire.

When the main force of his Confederate cavalry galloped up and found the bridge afire, unusable, it was General Nathan Bedford Forrest himself who rode up to the women standing near the fence bordering their yard. While his men scattered into woods along the river bank on both sides of the burning bridge, Forrest explained that he needed to get his men across the river quickly and asked the women if there was any nearby shallow spot at which they could do so.

It was the youngest daughter, sixteen year old Emma Sansom, who quickly spoke up, telling Forrest of a place about three-quarters of a mile above Black Creek Bridge where she had seen cows wade across the river. "If you'll saddle me a horse," she said, "I'll show you where it is."

"There's no time for saddling horses," was the General's reply, "Get up behind me." Of course, considering the riflemen and cannon facing each other across the river that thought was frightening to Mrs. Sansom. Forrest calmed her fears, assuring her that he would "take good care" of the teenager. With Emma sitting behind him, pointing the way, Forrest galloped his mount across a corn field, disappearing into a wooded ravine.

When they reached the ford, Emma quickly slid from the saddle, creeping forward on hands and knees to a position from which she could show him the shallower water. He followed in like manner until she reminded him that they could be seen by the Union forces. At that point General Forrest rose to his feet and moved in front of her, telling the young woman, "You can be my guide, but you can't be my breastwork," as Union Minie Balls whistled around them. This event is related in several of the Forrest biographies and some say a bullet went through Emma's skirts. Standing up, then, in full view of Union riflemen across the creek, she pointed to where he must enter, and where to emerge, from the river. Finding the little known ford saved Forrest and his command ten miles and three hours' time, worsening the circumstances of Colonel Streight and his Brigade.

Following...let's share this direct quote from the Forrest biography "Confederate Wizards of the Saddle" written by historian Bennett H. Young, and published in 1914.

"As they emerged into an open space, the rain of bullets increased. The girl, not familiar with the sound of shot and shell, stood out in full view, untied her calico sunbonnet, and waved it defiantly at the men in blue across the creek. The firing in an instant ceased.

They (the Union men of Streight's Brigade) recognized the child's heroic defiance. Maybe they recalled the face of a sister or sweetheart away across the Ohio River in Indiana or Ohio.

They were brave, gallant men, the fierceness of no battle could remove the chivalrous emotions of manly warriors. Moved with admiration and chivalrous appreciation of courage, they withdrew their guns from their shoulders and broke into hurrahs for the girlish heroine who was as brave as they, and whose heart, like theirs, rose in the tumult of battle higher than any fear.

Forrest turned back toward his horse, which was ravenously eating the leaves and twigs from the bush where he had been tied. The bullets began whistling about the retreating forms. She heard the thuds and zipping of the balls; and, with childish curiosity, asked the big soldier what these sounds meant. "These are bullets, my little girl," he said, "and you must get in front of me. One might hit you and kill you."

Riding with quickening speed, he galloped back to the house. . . . giving orders to instantly engage the foe. He

sent aides to direct the artillery to the newly found ford, and while they were moving with all haste into position, he drew from his pocket a sheet of un-ruled paper and wrote on it:

"Hed Quaters in Sadle, May 2, 1863. My highest regardes to Miss Ema Sansom for her gallant conduct while my forse was skirmishing with the Federals across "Black Creek" near Gadisden, Allabama.
N.B. Forrest, Brig. Genl. Comding N. Ala"

Lieutenant A.C. Roach of Streight's own 51st Indiana Volunteer Infantry, in his 1865 book "The Prisoners and How Treated" mentions the Emma Sansom epic, but in an entirely different way. "On the morning of May 2nd," he wrote,"we crossed Black Creek, near Gadsden, Alabama, on a fine wooden bridge, which was afterwards burned by our rear guard. This, it was thought, would delay Forrest's forces long enough to enable us to reach Rome, Georgia, before he could overtake us again, as the stream was very deep and seemed to be un-fordable. But among a lot of prisoners captured by us in the morning, and paroled, was a young man by the name of Sansom, who, as soon as set at liberty, made his way direct to the pursuing forces of General Forrest, and piloted that officer and his command to a ford where the whole force soon crossed and started again in pursuit of our Brigade. From this incident the Rebels manufactured the following bit of romance:"

According to an unknown editor, "Roach then quotes several pages of an admiring account of the deed of Emma Sansom, just about as it is now accepted. (And as related briefly above) It seems to be a correct enough account, probably taken from some Southern newspaper. It also states that as a reward she asked to have her brother released from the Yankees who had made him prisoner, and that young Sansom was released when Streight was captured.

"The true version of this story is," Roach wrote, "...whenever we captured any prisoners, they were immediately paroled, and not taken along with the command any distance, especially not forty or fifty miles, as this Rebel romance would indicate. And the young Confederate soldier, Sansom, was with General Forrest when our command surrendered, and not withstanding his solemn oath not to aid or comfort in any manner whatever the enemies of the United States, was fully armed and equipped."

Such are the differing, often hostile, reports in the confusions of war. One thing is sure. The people who live there, who best know the region and it's history, are certain the Forrest account is the correct one.

In the public school system of Gadsden, Alabama, In that State's Etowah County you will, today, find Emma Sansom High School. Not far away is a fine, large monument to this courageous young woman...as well as a granite marker erected in 1928. In her retirement years, the era of our lives in which finances are often more problematical for many of us, the Legislature of the State of Alabama, by overwhelming vote, awarded Emma Sansom Johnson an acre of land...even though she was living in Texas by that time.

Much information, though, was substantiated from a letter Emma Sansom, herself, wrote to biographer John Allen Wyeth, M. D. for his book "Life of Lieutenant-General Nathan Bedford Forrest," first published in 1899. She was born in 1847 in Social Circle, Walton County, Georgia. Her family moved to the farm at Black Creek, Alabama in 1852. Her father died and was buried there in 1859. She married C. B Johnson and later lived in Calloway, Texas with her husband and family.

Preparing to mount and lead his men across the newly found ford after Streight's Brigade, Forrest told Emma he had left the note for her in the house, and asked for a lock of her hair. He also, Emma described in the letter to Wyeth, asked that the Sansom women "see that Robert Turner, a Confederate soldier killed in the skirmishing across Black Creek and 'laid out' in their home, be buried in some nearby graveyard."

"My sister and I sat up all night," said Emma Sansom, "watching over the dead soldier who had lost his life fighting for our rights."

From the burning bridge at Black Creek, the Boys From Lake County, amid Streight's Brigade, rode just three miles to Gadsden. Streight halted there only long enough to attack and destroy a quantity of arms and commissary stores which troops of his Brigade found. By then, because of continuous marching without sleep, many horses and mules, as well as men, were so entirely worn out they were unable to keep up with the column. Those fell behind the rear guard and were captured.

Also, by then, it was evident to the Union commander that their only hope was in crossing the river at Rome, Georgia... destroying the bridge behind them. Streight felt sure that would delay Forrest's forces for a day or two, giving his Brigade soldiers time to rest, sleep, eat...and gather fresh horses and mules. He also was fully aware, by then, that it was impossible for the Brigade to continue on if that goal could not be accomplished.

Another event began there in Gadsden, about which the men of the Brigade knew nothing at the moment, but which produced a third local Southern hero of the invasion, along with General Nathan Bedford Forrest and Emma Sansom.

John H. Wisdom, a resident of Gadsden, was a stage coach driver and rural mail carrier. He had, sometime before, been a resident of Rome. Wisdom undertook an eleven hour ride by horseback to warn the people of Rome that the mounted Union Brigade was headed toward their city...giving them time to prepare. He reached Rome at 2:30 a.m. Sunday, May 3, 1863.

Eight miles beyond Gadsden, the Brigade waded Turkey Creek Ford. A bit over three miles more, at about 4:00 p.m. on May 2nd, they found Blount's Plantation where they could procure feed for the horses and mules. "The enemy followed closely," Colonel Streight said, "and kept up a continuous skirmish with the rear of our column. At Blount's Plantation, I decided to halt, as it was impossible to continue to march through the night without feeding and resting, although to do so was to bring on a general engagement."

The troops of Streight's Brigade dismounted. A detail was chosen and assigned to feed the horses and mules. The rest of the troops moved out and formed in line of battle on a ridge southwest of the Plantation fields. Lieutenant Roach explains the situation in detail that lets us be there, share the time, the peril. "...we halted for the purpose of giving the men an opportunity of preparing a hasty meal for themselves and to feed their animals," he said. "But the anticipated pleasure of a cup of steaming coffee, which the Union soldier considers one of his indispensables, was soon dispelled by the report (sound) of musketry in the direction of our picket line. The command was instantly given to prepare for action, and almost instantly every man in the Provisional Brigade seized his gun, and was marching out bravely and defiantly to engage once more the vastly superior force of the enemy, with whom we had contended successfully for three days, (more accurately, it was six days at that point.) and had completely routed and defeated in two regular pitched battles."

It is made clear by Lt. Roach's words that the officers and men of Streight's Brigade, by Saturday May 2nd, still believed they were battling a force of near 4,000 Confederate cavalrymen. Without doubt, it shows just as clearly again the powerful effect of General Nathan Bedford Forrest's hit and run attacks and the massive vigor of assaults by his, at that point, just 600 troopers.

Almost at the same time the Union men reached their positions, the rear guard of the Brigade, which was endeavoring to hold Forrest's Confederate cavalry in check - likely again the two First Middle Tennessee Cavalry companies of Captain D.D. Smith - was severely attacked and forced back into the line of defense. "The enemy," said Streight, "immediately attacked our main line, and tried hard to carry the center, but were gallantly met and repulsed by the 51st and 73rd Indiana, assisted by Major Vananda with two mountain howitzers (cannon)."

So again we see, as a number of times before, that the Boys From Lake County and their fellow soldiers of the 73rd are in the thick of battle, fighting brilliantly, courageously. Lieutenant Roach pictures for us their part in it...lets us hear the roar of cannon, the crack of rifle fire, see gushing plumes of light blue gun smoke, smell the overwhelming, acrid scent of blasting gunpowder, the sickening sight of men hit, falling.

"Colonel Hathaway," Roach writes, "with his regiment (the Boys From Lake County and their fellow soldiers of the 73rd Indiana) was directed to the front and center, to support our two howitzers (cannon), which were doing such fearful execution in the ranks of the enemy, that they seemed to have to resolved to capture them if possible, regardless of the cost in blood. Their efforts, however, were fruitless, for although nearly every gunner and man connected with the two pieces (cannon) was either killed or wounded, Colonel Hathaway (and his 73rd Indiana Regiment) so determinedly maintained his position that the enemy recoiled in the greatest confusion, our own men pouring a perfect hail of lead into his retreating columns."

"They then," continued Colonel Streight, "made a determined effort to turn our right, but were met by the gallant 80th Illinois, assisted by two companies of the 3rd Ohio." Again it is Lieutenant A.C. Roach who fills in more detail. "This action lasted for nearly three hours," he wrote, "the enemy charging our lines from right to left repeatedly, but was as often repulsed with severe loss...retreating badly hurt, his dead men and horses strewing their line of retreat. Our heroes won the day by hard and desperate fighting."

In those hours, though, the Boys From Lake County and their fellow soldiers of the 73rd Indiana Regiment were to suffer a stunning blow. "It was in this engagement,' said Colonel Streight, "that the gallant Colonel Hathaway (Seventy Third Indiana) fell, mortally wounded, and in a few moments expired. Our country has seldom been called upon to mourn the loss of so brave and valuable an officer. His loss to me was irreparable. His men had almost worshiped him, and when he fell it cast a deep gloom of despondency over his regiment which was hard to overcome." In fact, Colonel Hathaway was shot through the chest by a Rebel bullet.

As we know, although he was from neighboring LaPorte County, in his law career Colonel Gilbert Hathaway also practiced in lake County. To the men of Company A, the Boys From Lake

County, his death must have been like losing one of their own. To add to their pain, Private Samuel White of Company A was also killed before dark on that day, Saturday, May 2, 1863.

General Nathan Bedford Forrest and his Confederate cavalrymen, leaving a few skirmishers to harass, and watch, Streight's Brigade fell back to a ridge about a half mile from the Union battle line, and began massing as if preparing for a more determined attack. "It was becoming dark," said Colonel Streight, "and I decided to withdraw unobserved, if possible, and conceal my command in a thicket some half mile to our rear, there to lie in ambush and await his advance."

At the same time, planning ahead, Colonel Streight ordered Captain Milford Russell, of the 51st Indiana Regiment, to take 200 men and proceed with all haste to Rome, Georgia and hold it's bridge until Streight could get there with his main force. Lieutenant Roach says the intent was also to take possession of railroad engines and cars as well as telegraph lines before Confederate reinforcements could be brought in to set up a defense of the city. The 200 advance troopers were not from any one regiment, but selected from the best men, and best mounts, within the entire Brigade.

In addition to the extremely tired condition of men and animals, troubles continued to mount for men of the Union Brigade. The fight at Blount's Plantation made clear the fact that nearly all remaining ammunition was worthless, having become wet while troops were fording the rivers and creeks, especially at Big Wills Ford. Worse, "much of that carried by the men," said Streight, "had become useless by the paper wearing out and the powder sifting away."

The Brigade remained in ambush only a brief time. Forrest's men found out where they lay in wait and began a movement around the Union flank. Streight discovered that invasive maneuver of Forrest's cavalry in time to confront and deter it.

"I then decided to withdraw as silently as possible," Streight related, "and push on in the direction of Rome." So, the men of his Brigade were in for yet another night of riding without sleep, precious little time even to feed themselves, or their animals.

Colonel Streight does not mention it. This information came with them as the Boys From Lake County returned home at war's end... and was recorded in the 1934 "History of Lake County." When the Brigade moved on from Blount's Plantation in the dark evening hours of Saturday, May 2, 1863 they left the Boys From Lake County, and all others of the 73rd Indiana Infantry, as a rear guard to block Forrest's Confederates from another immediate attack against the main force as they moved out.

It is also not detailed, but easy to surmise, that having seen the Confederate cavalry massing on the ridge a half mile away and expecting an attack, the men of the 73rd remained lying in line of battle with .69 caliber muskets loaded and ready. It is also highly likely, that when things stayed quiet, they took turns watching and napping... getting a bit of much needed rest. It was not until midnight that they moved out to catch up with the main column of Streight's Brigade. So we see again, the Boys From Lake County and others of their 73rd Indiana Volunteer Infantry Regiment trusted, relied upon, to take on the toughest of battle assignments.

General Forrest and his men, though, did not bother them again, wisely stopping, resting for eleven hours that night, also waiting for stragglers to catch up to them from Gadsden. It was the first full night's sleep for Forrest and his men since Thursday April 23rd at a town named Spring Hill as he began the chase after Dodge and Streight.

To the contrary, through constant harassment and attack, Forrest's cavalry had denied any full rest for the men of Streight's Brigade since the night of Wednesday April 29th, at the foot of Day's Gap.

Though the Brigade did indeed move on in the direction of Rome, progress was painfully slow now. A large number of the men were walking again, their horses or mules having completely given out. "The remainder of the stock was jaded, tender-footed and worn down," said Streight, "yet, as everything depended on our reaching Rome before the enemy could throw a sufficient force there to prevent our crossing the bridge, every possible effort was made to urge the command forward."

From the battle at Blount's Plantation the weary Brigade members rode nearly eight miles to Leesburg, Alabama. Five miles beyond Leesburg they waded Yellow Creek Ford. Less than a mile later they reached Round Mountain. There a scouting party found the Noble Iron Works and destroyed it. In some histories the factory is referred to as the Round Mountain Iron Works. According to Lieutenant Roach, the Noble Company was located in Cherokee Valley about thirty miles from Rome. "These works," Roach said, "were, at the time, largely engaged in manufacturing ordnance and material for the Rebel army, and employed nearly 1,000 hands."

From Round Mountain the men of the Brigade rode another four miles to wade Little River Ford.

In fact, the column had ridden, many walking of course, without further sniping from Confederate attackers until they neared Centre, Alabama, "when one of my scouts informed me," Streight said, "that a force of the enemy was posted in ambush but a short distance in front." Despite his own exhausted condition, Colonel Streight still displayed quick response, outstanding instinct for battle strategy. In the dark of night, he immediately sent out a line of skirmishers with orders to move forward until fired upon, then to open a "brisk fire", holding the Confederates in position until the main column of the Brigade could pass. "

The plan worked admirably," Streight related. "While my skirmishers were amusing the enemy, the main column made a detour to the right, and struck the main road some 3 miles to the rear of the enemy." Of course as soon as they had passed, their skirmishers faded back into the column of march."I was then hopeful," said Streight, "that we could reach Rome before the enemy could overtake us."

Actually, the thing Colonel Streight did not know was that Forrest and the main body of his cavalry were deep in sleep a number of miles behind him. The reason the Confederates did not attack was, likely, that they were a very small unit of Forrest's scouts, just keeping an eye on the Brigade's movements.

It was 11:00 p.m. on the night of May 2nd when the Boys From Lake County and Streight's Brigade reached the ferry at Alabama's Chattooga River. An hour before, Captain Russell and his 200 men, moving toward the bridge at Rome, had ferried across the river. But, Captain Russell, understandably, in his own state of exhaustion and hurry, forgot to leave a guard to hold the ferry. It quickly became yet another major obstacle for the Brigade.

Streight's principal guide, un-named, though almost surely Captain D. D. Smith or one of his cavalry officers, had been on the mark in his information up to then. And Streight had, earlier in the evening, inquired very specifically as to the character of the terrain ahead. He was assured there were no difficult streams to cross and that the road was good. "Hence we approached the Chattooga River at the ferry without any information as to the real condition of things." What the stunned officer and his men found was that in the brief hour after Captain Russell and his advance force had ferried across the river, "the enemy had seized and run off the boat before we reached there."

"I then ascertained," lamented Colonel Streight, "that there was a bridge some seven or eight miles up the river, near Gaylesville." The Union commander selected new guides pushed his weary Brigade on as rapidly as possible. By then, it was vital to reach the bridge before any Confederates could beat him to it. On the route, the column had to traverse what they called an "old coal chopping" for several miles. It was an area of the forest where trees had been cut and hauled out to make charcoal. Because of numerous trips, hauling heavy trees, many wagon roads were running through it in various directions. "The command was so worn out and exhausted," Streight recorded, "that many were asleep (likely not the ones who were walking) and in spite of every exertion I could make, with the aid of such of my officers as were able for duty, the commands became separated and scattered into several squads, traveling in different directions..." It was not until near daylight that the last of the weary men and animals had crossed the river. One again, a bridge was burned.

And so...with surge of fire, black smoke rising in late night air, the burning of one last..., that bridge over Alabama's Chattooga River..., the day of Saturday, May 2, 1863 slipped into the records of history for the men of Streight's Brigade. It was, no doubt for the Boys From Lake County, the most venomous, personally consuming, gut-wrenching day of their years in America's Civil War.

Captain Alfred Fry Circa 1863

Chapter Twelve

Surrender, Capture, Prisoners... Sunday, May 3, 1863

And so, for the Boys From Lake County and others of Streight's Brigade, Sunday May 3, 1863 began...with that exhausting, sleepless ride and march, continuing, plodding on, through dark wee hours of morning.

Within those same hours, at 2:30 a.m., John H. Wisdom, reached the end of his eleven hour Paul Revere-like ride from Gadsden along the south side of the Coosa River opposite from Streight's Brigade, and galloped into town. Rome, Georgia came awake, surged into a beehive of alarm, action, preparation.

In great haste the word was spread and a number of older men and boys, plus a few Confederate soldiers home on furlough, as well as a small citizen militia under General Black were organized. Bales of cotton were stacked on the city side of the bridge as a defensive barricade, a shield against Minie Balls. Two cannon were set up commanding the road and the bridge itself. Planks were torn up, and large piles of loose dry hay placed on the bridge structure, a burning torch at the ready to set fire when the first Yankee started to cross. Scouting units were sent out to watch for the Union Brigade's approach.

In one of those scouting parities was seventeen year old W. M. Towers who lived on a farm with his mother eight miles from Rome. His father and brother were already off to war, serving in the Virginia Army. As he arrived in town that Sunday morning to attend Sunday school and church, Gen. Black sent him home to alert his neighbors, get his gun, and bring others back with theirs. No one returned but the young man.

"I was stationed with a number of others on the north side of the Oostanaula River (over the span from town)" he said, "probably two hundred feet above the bridge... with Mr. Sam

135

Stewart, Marshall of the town. The advance guard of the enemy, numbering about two hundred men, was at Shorter's Spring, and we expected every minute to see them charge."

C.A. Smith, Conductor of the Rome Railroad, learning that, "the Yankees are below Rome, and that our men need reinforcements," ran a train from Kingston to Rome carrying about seven hundred men. His note to Mr. C.H. Stillwell, perhaps his supervisor, does not say whether the men were Confederate soldiers or armed citizens.

A newspaper, The Rome Courier, reported that General Forrest sent several messengers during those early hours with dispatches urging the Rome "commander" to "hold the Union Brigade at bay a few hours if possible, and at all hazards."

By 7:00 a.m. the citizens of Rome were as fully prepared as their men and weaponry allowed them to be. What seems clear in the records of that day is that they, the citizens themselves, were fully prepared to fight fiercely to defend their "little mountain city."

At dawn, General Nathan Bedford Forrest and the men of his cavalry awoke, quickly ate breakfast and fed their animals. About 5:00 a.m., greatly refreshed by satisfactory meals and a long night's sleep, they galloped off again in pursuit of Streight's Brigade. Their force was noticeably smaller, however, because of severe battle losses in the previous two hotly contested engagements.

With the far more graceful agility of their cavalry horses, they covered the distance much faster than the Union commander's weary mules and barefoot farm animals...and caught up with their exhausted, plodding, enemy. It took them about four hours, to the Brigade's eleven, to cover the same territory.

With a good night's sleep, it was even more facile for Forrest himself to persist in displaying his usual inventive, vigorous, strategy. For, when he and his cavalry reached Alabama's Chattooga River, and found the bridge burned, unpassable..., it barely slowed them down, fully the opposite of what Streight had hoped. They, astride their mounts, simply swam the river. One history recalls that the troopers held weapons and ammunition over their heads, above the deep river waters. Another says they commandeered a rowboat or two and floated munitions across... dragging the cannon wagons, and empty ammunition caissons, along the river bottom. More likely, both versions are correct, the cavalrymen holding their lighter personal weapons and ammunition above their heads, floating heavier munitions and equipment, such as for the cannon, in small boats.

Captain Russell and his 200 men, the advance unit sent by Colonel Streight to secure the span, had fully expected to be at Rome's bridge four hours earlier. In fact, even though they rode all night at "the utmost speed of their exhausted animals" Lt. Roach's account records that they did not reach the bridge until 8:00 a.m.

When Russell and the men of his unit looked across, they seemed to see "a city full of armed men." Roach further describes what Captain Russell and his men found, portions of it surely gleaned from records researched for his book after the War. "...a large number of troops had been hurried from Atlanta, Kingston, and Dalton. Besides the citizens and home-guards, for miles around, had been collected, and put under arms." (In truth, almost no regular troops had arrived. They came in the next day. The "city of armed men" were, indeed, by far, mostly old men and boys of the home-guard and citizenry.)

"Several pieces of artillery had also been put in position commanding the river bridge," Roach expounded, "and every avenue by which the city could be approached." (In fact, there were just two cannon, at the bridge itself.) "The floor of the bridge was torn up and piled with straw and turpentine, ready to ignite in case an attempt was made to force a crossing." (This seems accurate by all reports.)

Some indicate that the small group of armed Rome citizens, who were ordered across the bridge by General Black to watch for the Brigade, fired a few trial shots at the 200 men of Captain

Russell's advance unit. However, there seems no record that, after assessing the situation, Captain Russell even bothered to return fire at the "old men and boys" before him. He simply sent a courier back to Colonel Streight telling him that Rome was fully defended, the bridge unpassable.

The Rome Courier newspaper noted the Southern view of it all, "At 8:30 a.m., " the reporter wrote, "a small body of the enemy's advance (about 200) reached the environs of the city, and were actually bold enough to dismount and feed their horses in sight of the city. They picked up all the horses and mules in the neighborhood, took some of our soldiers and citizens prisoners, and reconnoitered the defenses of the city."

We find no record of prisoners taken by Captain Russells's 200 advance men... except one. On their way a few miles from Rome, they happened on a rural mail carrier who obviously did not recognize the import of their blue uniforms, apparently mistaking them for soldiers of "his" Confederate army.

At first he declined to accompany them, but Captain Russell warned him the "Yankees" were not far behind, and if he did not join them he might fall into "enemy" hands. Not only did the mailman agree to do so, but became quite talkative, giving Russell much valuable information about the prepared defenses of the city. For Lieutenant Roach's book, Captain Russell related that the Georgia mail carrier "turned white as a corpse," suddenly realizing he was in the grasp of Union soldiers. Trembling, the unfortunate Southerner gasped that he "guessed the Yankees had already got him" according to Roach.

After their burning of the bridge over Alabama's Chattooga River, "We proceeded on," Colonel Streight said, "and passed Cedar Bluff just after daylight."

Far from surprising, it was in those same dawn hours that it became painfully clear to the Union commander that his horses and mules simply could not make it to Rome without halting to rest and feed. Large numbers of the original army mules were still continually giving out. "In fact," commented Colonel Streight, "I do not think that at that time we had a score of the mules drawn at Nashville left, and nearly all of those taken in the country were barefooted, (without iron horseshoes) and many of them had such sore backs and tender feet that it was impossible to ride them...but, in order to get as near as possible to the force I had sent ahead, we struggled on until 9:00 a.m., when we halted and fed our animals."

As he recorded in his 1865 book, Lieutenant Roach was highly aware of the critical nature their circumstance - as Colonel Streight surely must have been - when the Brigade moved out from Blount's Plantation the evening before...leaving the Boys From Lake County and others of their 73rd Indiana behind as rear guard.

"Affairs were now rapidly approaching a crises," Roach admitted of the Blount's Plantation departure, "everyone felt that the next twenty-four hours would decide the fate of our expedition. We were now within sixty miles of Rome, the point at which we designed crossing the Coosa River, and if we could reach that place before a force could be thrown in to check our further advance, complete success would be inevitable. For once on the opposite side of the river, and the bridge destroyed after us, the pursuit of Forrest would be effectively checked, and we would then have ample time to recruit the exhausted energies of our men and animals. Besides, if necessary, we could soon obtain an entire fresh supply of the latter, and could then fight or decline battle at our own option. On the contrary, should there be a force collected at Rome sufficient to prevent us crossing the bridge, there would be no alternative left us but to surrender, the exhausted condition of our men and animals rendering escape by any route, strategy, or valor in battle, an impossibility."

The Union commander found then, as he undoubtedly already could see was happening, that the men of his brigade... unaccustomed to riding.., had become so exhausted from fatigue and lack of sleep that it was almost impossible to keep them awake even long enough to feed the horses and mules.

"We had halted but a short time, when I was informed that a heavy force of the enemy was moving on our left, on a route parallel to the one we were marching on, and was then nearer to Rome than we were. About the same time, I received information that our pickets were driven in." (In other words that the Confederate cavalry was attacking again, with the pickets confronting them first, alerting, then fading back into the main force as they were consigned to do.) The command was immediately ordered into line..."

As in every fire fight with the Confederate cavalry, Colonel Streight quickly, instinctively, selected a fine defensive position, placing his men on a battle line facing the direction of Confederate rifle fire...above the enemy..., partially around the brow of a hill. Once again, it was well done, an excellent defensive posture, but one that would turn fatefully against him this time in the most frustrating of ways. Worse, there was never a large Confederate force nearby. Only the substantially depleted, but greatly refreshed, Confederate cavalry of Forrest. It was the same crippling misconception Streight and his officers had been laboring under since the Battle of Days Gap. General Nathan Bedford Forrest had been doing...and continued even more so in those last hours...to sharply reinforce such sparsity of accurate intelligence.

As Forrest's now relatively small unit of cavalry caught up again with the Boys From Lake County and Streight's Brigade, shortly after 9:00 a.m., they immediately were ordered to begin an aggressive skirmish of rapid rifle fire...making as much noise, sounding as large as possible. Forrest spread them out thinly, in a semi-circle at the base of the hill, giving the officers and men of Streight's Brigade the perception that they were surrounded. At the same time the wily General was careful not to make a full assault which would expose the actual size of his command. Forrest and his officers yelled orders to imaginary units giving the impression of large forces moving in. A small unit of troops and cannon were marched round and round the base of the hill, disappearing on one side, reappearing on the other, again and again...reinforcing the feeling that they constituted a much larger force.

At the top of the hill, the Union commander and his officers struggled vigorously to rouse the men to battle. "Every effort was made to rally the men for action," lamented Colonel Streight, "but nature was exhausted and a large portion of my best troops actually went to sleep while lying in line of battle under a severe skirmish fire."

As it happened, at such an illuminating though coincidental moment, Forrest decided to try for capitulation by the Union force. Under the white flag of truce, he sent Captain Henry Pointer, one of his staff officers, requesting that the Union commander and his Brigade surrender, expressing a sincere desire to avoid further blood shed. Colonel Streight agreed to meet with Forrest..., clearly down the hill, in the dust of the road to Rome.

As the two commanders stood talking one of Forrest's horse-drawn cannon, commanded by Lieutenant R. G. Jones, hove into view. Jones lets us be there, share the morning, the vista, of that historic meeting. "I was riding a little in advance of the gun," Lt. Jones says, "when suddenly looking up, I saw General Forrest, Captain Pointer, one or two other officers, and several Federal officers sitting down on the north side of the road. A little distance up the road I saw a crowd of Yankees. Captain Pointer motioned me to halt. He then approached me and said: 'Colonel Streight objects to your coming up so close... drop back a little.' I moved back with the gun and came to 'action front', with one wheel in the road and the other at the edge of the wood. Soon sergeant Jackson came up with the other piece (cannon) and took position in the other half of the roadway."

In brief conference between the two commanders, Colonel Streight asked the Confederate General what his surrender terms might be. "Immediate surrender," Forrest replied, "your men to be treated as prisoners of war, the officers to retain their side-arms (swords) and personal property." Streight proposed a few minutes in which to consult with his officers. Forrest agreed..., though giving Streight a final hard-sell, pointing out that such conference should be done with dispatch. "I have a column of fresh troops at hand, now nearer Rome than you are. You cannot cross the river in your front. I have men enough right here to run over you." Nothing of it was true. But, it fit perfectly with the Union commander's week long misjudgement of the size of the Confederate force.

Back behind his own line of battle, Colonel Streight called a "council of war" with his own officers. "Most of my Regimental commanders had already expressed the opinion that, unless we could reach Rome and cross the river before the enemy came up with us again, we should be compelled to surrender." In the meantime, Captain Russell's courier had returned with the bad news that Rome's bridge could not be taken. Colonel Abel D. Streight discussed the situation as we know it...since we've traveled alongside them, in rain and mud, warm days and cool nights of a northern Alabama Spring, in the dust of hundreds of mules and horses, amidst the roar of cannon and crack of rifle fire, the acrid scent of light blue gun smoke, the frightening sight of death and terrible wound...from far late in the evening of April 26th.

"Our ammunition was worthless," Streight continues, "horses and mules in desperate condition, men overcome with fatigue and loss of sleep, and we were confronted by fully three times our number, in the heart of the enemy's country." All painfully true, except for the actual strength of the Confederate forces. (By the time Streight wrote his report, a year or so after the surrender, he obviously knew of the true, far smaller, size of the Confederate forces he had been fighting. Clearly what he related was the information he and his officers felt certain was true at the time of the surrender decision.)

"Although personally opposed to surrender, and so expressed myself at the time," Streight said, "yet I yielded to the unanimous voice of my Regimental commanders." And so,

Streight at once entered into negotiations with Forrest to obtain the best possible surrender terms for the officers and men of his Union Brigade. To be sure, considering their almost total lack of ammunition, not to mention food and other vital supplies, it would have been utterly foolhardy, even inhumane, to risk more lives on either side in what had become an unwinnable, and therefore meaningless, conflict.

The situation of Streight's Brigade at that point, was a perfect demonstration of the age old military adage...an army's success, it's very survival, depends fully on the quality and safety of it's line of supplies.

Final terms of the surrender, according to Lieutenant Roach were, "Each Regiment to retain it's colors (flags), and the officers and men their private property, including the side-arms (swords) of the officers."

"At about noon on Sunday, May 3, 1863," Colonel Abel D. Streight recorded, "we surrendered as prisoners of war." The Boys From Lake County, along with their fellow soldiers of the 73rd Indiana and others of Streight's Brigade stacked their guns and were marched away from the weapons to an open field.

Confederate General Nathan Bedford Forrest remained uneasy, however, until he got his small command and their loaded rifles between the Union troops and their stacked weapons. At 3:00 p.m. that day Forrest left the field of surrender for Rome with the officers of the captured Union Brigade. Rome's newspaper, the Courier, reported that the captured Union commanders were ushered into the city about 6:00pm. The Confederate General was joined, about that time, by those of his men who had walked from Will's Creek and Gadsden because their mounts had been shot out from under them. They were assigned to guard duty. The large force of reinforcements, for which Forrest had telegraphed, came in by train the next day. They, too, had little to do but guarding of the prisoners.

When their officers were marched to Rome on Sunday afternoon, May 3rd, the Union troops of Streight's Brigade, were left overnight at the community named Lawrenceville where they were surrendered, not far from the village of Gaylesville. Their camp was on a farm the people of Rome referred to as Mrs. Lawrence's...21 ½ miles from town. It was not until the next day, Monday May 4, 1863 that the Boys From Lake County and fellow soldiers of their 73rd Indiana and Streight's Brigade also rode or marched into the city of Rome.

Again, the words of Rome citizen W.M. Towers lets us see, share those moments. "Those men were guarded in an open space where the Shorter Block now stands. (His reminiscences were written in April 1900) Their arms, ammunition, etc., were stored in the rear of a store on the corner of 2nd Avenue and Broad street. During the night the men were overheard discussing a plan to overpower the guard, recapture their arms, and destroy the city. The guard was immediately strengthened. If they had made the attempt it would have been an easy matter for them to have succeeded."

"After General Forrest brought Streight's command into Rome," W. M. Towers continued, "and Colonel Streight had discovered how poorly fortified the town actually was, and defended by only a few old men and boys, with now and then a furloughed soldier, he became very wrathy, so much so that General Forrest thought it advisable to telegraph to Chattanooga for troops enough to guard his prisoners, as his own troops were so worn and exhausted that they could not do it, and it devolved on the old men and boys to perform this service."

The stationary on which W. M. Towers recorded this poignant note of history in April, 1900 read: "Department of Justice, United States District Court, Northern District of Georgia." Our research did not reveal Towers' occupation. However it seems evident the brave young man had matured into a position of some eminence in Georgia in the 35 years after the Civil War.

Seventy six years later, on June 3,1939, a monument was placed at the site of surrender by the Forney District, Alabama Division, United Daughters of the Confederacy. It recalls that there were 1,466 men of Streight's Brigade captured there on May 3,1863. Local newspaper accounts of the day said the

Union Brigade was captured by a Confederate force of 410 men. However the monument reveals that Forrest had only 322 of his troops remaining out of 600 when he forced the surrender of the 1,466. By this count, Forrest's losses in the final two fierce battles had been nearly half his men... killed, wounded, or un-horsed.

As the Union officers were taken under guard into the city of Rome on Sunday May 3rd, "The citizens of the place gave unmistakable proof of their joy to see us, " Lieutenant A. C. Roach said, "...the ladies...thronged the streets with gay dresses, gaudy ribbons, and smiling faces, to greet us." There was noticeable sarcasm in Roach's words. What he clearly meant was that Rome citizens were elated to see the Union officers as captives, their threat to the city defeated. "At least I'm informed," Roach continued a bit bitterly, "that there was no demonstration of joy, when the Union troops entered the town a year afterwards, as conquerors."

"General Forrest, to his credit" Roach further explained, "furnished us with sufficient rations for our subsistence, also with comfortable quarters." (That was for the officers. The Boys From Lake County, with all the other soldiers of Streight's Brigade, when they were marched into the city the next day, Monday May 4th, were under guard in an open field.)

"Though here," Roach expounded, "as in every other Southern city through which we passed, every insult that a low, malignant, unprincipled and debased spirit could invent was heaped upon us by the citizens, who crowded around the cars (trains) to express their contempt for "Yankees," and boast of the superiority and nobleness of the chaivalric Southerner."

In surrender, however, Roach found that which further defines the painful and often confusing political spirit of America's Civil War.

"But even then," he details, "during the brightest days of Rebellion, unmistakable evidence of loyal sentiment was everywhere visible, but so intimidated by Jeff Davis' bayonets, that it dare not openly manifest itself. At some points on our route, when unnoticed by the guard, the ladies would present some of our officers with choice bouquets, whose pressed and faded leaves they still retain as tributes of Southern devotion to the Union, and sympathy for those who have battled for the "glorious flag."

Lieutenant Roach was not alone in foul remarks toward those who constituted "the enemy." The tri-weekly Rome Courier, on Monday, May 4, 1863, printed rather choice comments about the men of Streight's Brigade...some a bit flattering, though obviously not meant to be.

"Report is having it that all North Georgia and Alabama are swarming with Yankees..."

"A large number of horses were in the streets on Tuesday, many of which were identified as having been stolen by the Yankees in their recent raid through the country."

"The Yankees captured by Gen. Forrest are said to have been the pick of Rosencrantz's army. It is reported that Rosencrantz had offered them a bounty of $300 apiece and a discharge from the service to accomplish their objective..." (We have found no record that was true...the men were never discharged until the end of the war unless disabled.)

"This was a daring, well-planned, well-executed expedition, as far as it went. The troops and commanders were regarded as select..."

"But for the noble and gallant Forrest and for his equally noble and gallant men... our little mountain city would at this hour be in ashes, and many of our best citizens robbed and murdered." This reporting is in sharp contrast to General Garfield's order to Colonel Streight..."You are particularly commanded to restrain your command from pillage and marauding."

"We have but one complaint to make. We thought he (Forrest) was a little too lenient to the impudent, boasting, threatening, cowardly Federal officers."

"And better subjects for such infernal designs could scarcely have been selected, for a more villainous looking set of scoundrels it has never been our misfortune to have seen before..."

It cannot be denied, of course, that the Boys From Lake County and others of Streight's Brigade may well have not looked their best when surrendered on Sunday, May 3, 1863. After all they had been almost constantly in the saddle, or marching, since leaving the river steamers at Eastport, on the afternoon of Tuesday, April 21st. For twelve days they had been out in the open, near constantly on the move, with precious little time to shave or bathe. They had endured several days of rain and mud, then six days of warmth, sweat, chilly nights, 124 miles on unpaved dirt roads in clouds of dust stirred by the hoofs of hundreds of horses and mules, several fierce, stressful, perilous pitched battles, constant wonder about sudden death from near continuous sniping rifle fire of the vigorous enemy. On top of all that came the four days of riding and marching entirely without sleep. Is it any wonder that those fine, brave, young men might appear dusty, dirty, unshaven, boots scuffed, uniforms soiled and wet by the wading of river fords, hair unkempt, a bit gaunt from irregular meals, eyes hollow from lack of sleep.

Despite sneering words by some citizens of Rome, Sergeant H. Briedenthal of Company A, Third Ohio Infantry recorded in his diary on May 5th echoes of Lieutenant Roach's praise for the conduct of General Forrest. "We have been treated well since our surrender, by Forrest's men, who have used us as a true soldier would treat a prisoner." From the city of Gadsden a detachment was sent by Forrest back over the line of march to tend wounded prisoners and pick up abandoned arms and supplies.

It was on the morning of Tuesday, May 5, 1863 that the 1,466 captured officers and men of Streight's Brigade..., among them, of course, the Boys From Lake County..., were put aboard a train in Rome, and headed toward destinations which would be of great surprise to some of them.

Chapter Thirteen

Many sent home...,
Some Imprisoned

It should be remembered, as days of preparation for the expedition began, Brigadier General J. A. Garfield in his written orders to Colonel Abel D. Streight, indicated that "should the brigade be surrounded, and retreat cut off," surrender was anticipated rather than needlessly sacrificing lives of Brigade soldiers. Garfield also "herewith furnished a copy of the General Order from the War Department in regard to paroling prisoners, together with the necessary blanks."

Parole and exchange agreements between Northern and Southern armies seemed never fully established as routine, rather in an on-again, off-again fashion. However, up to near that point in America's Civil War, both North and South released or exchanged many prisoners at, or soon after, capture.

Those simply released at capture were required to sign a "parole" form, including a sworn oath to never again take an active part in the War until, or unless, exchanged. In other words, parolees swore to go home and remain civilian citizens at least until exchanges could be arranged. Soldiers on both sides who were exchanged on a one-for-one basis, however, generally were expected to go back to active duty in their Regiments.

Maintaining full armies..., considering heavy battle losses, three times that number who died or became disabled by illness, and the relative ease with which many could use wealth or political connection to avoid military service... created a shortage of fighting men as Civil War years progressed. By the War's mid years, both Union and Confederate military leaders began to find excuses to deny paroles..., sending parolees quickly back into fighting units...as well as discontinuing the exchange of prisoners. This was particularly fostered by the win-at-any-cost-to-the-enemy vigor of Union Generals Grant and Sherman. In fact, it was Union Lt. General Ulysses S. Grant who ended all exchanges in August of 1864.

Temporary prisoner of war camps, used for holding those captured until exchanges could be arranged, devolved into permanent prisons, after the Union ceased the exchange system. The North's cessation of exchanges eventually brought about the infamous Andersonville prison disaster in the South.

Despite incrimination toward Southerners for Andersonville, the Northern prison camps were certainly not praised by Rebels interned there either, and a great many Southern men died in them. Prisoners from both sides groused about "abusive" treatment and "starvation." In general, though, conditions in both Union and Confederate prisons were reported to be much the same. Historical records seem to make it clear that those who managed prisons on both sides took care of prisoners as well as they were able. In fact, it appears a matter of often mentioned record that prisoners were fed as well, often better, than their prison guards and enemy troops in the field. Sadly, though, because of severe, deteriorating Southern economic conditions in the War's latter years, after Northern cessation of exchanges, there were clearly a massive number of deaths within a few months in the infamous Andersonville, Sumpter County, Georgia prison debacle.

The issue of retaining prisoners, rather than paroling or exchanging, began initially by holding officers. The idea, of course, was to cripple battle forces by withholding experienced military leadership.

Such overview of the Civil War parole process for captured soldiers, prisoner exchanges, and the prisons themselves... notably brief and surely incomplete...allows us a hint of what was in the thoughts of Colonel Abel D. Streight and his Regimental officers as they contemplated the necessity of surrender. It is certain, however, through records we've included from April and May of 1863, that officers of the Union Army of the Cumberland, as well Colonel Abel D. Streight and the officers of his Brigade, fully expected that surrender would result in paroles, or fairly speedy exchange back to their own lines.

It is true that rank and file soldiers, as well as non-commissioned officers, of Streight's Brigade were soon exchanged, sent back across the lines into the Union army again. We remember, of course, that after surrender on Sunday, May 3rd 1863, when officers were taken into Rome, it was not until the next day, Monday, May 4th that the soldiers and non-commissioned officers rode into town, and were placed under guard in an open field.

Very quickly, in fact the next day, Tuesday May 5th men of the Brigade were put aboard trains bound for the city of Atlanta. From the vantage point of 71 years, and surely from stories told by the Boys From Lake County after returning home, here is how the 1934 "History of Lake County" describes their captive experiences.

"The enlisted men…were taken to Atlanta where they were corralled in a pen. Under the terms of the surrender they were to be paroled and sent North within ten days with their clothing. These terms were now violated…and they were taken from one prison to another, starved, mistreated, deprived of their clothing, given old worn out clothing, and taken to Richmond." This account makes it sound as though their time of captivity was very long, agonizing.

But here is the exact record of that time, registered in the "Memorandum From Prisoner Of War Records" for one of the Boys From Lake County, Private Wilson Shannon Baughman.

"Captured at Rome, Ga. May 3rd, 1863." (Sunday) We know that Private Baughman and his fellow Brigade members left Rome by train on Tuesday morning May 5th, evidently first for Atlanta.

"Confined at Richmond, Va. May 9, 1863." (Saturday, just four days later) Clearly, their time spent corralled in a pen in Atlanta, was likely uncomfortable, but could not have been long. In other research, however, we found confirmation that Southern troops did indeed sometimes, perhaps often, because of Confederate supply shortages, remove the better uniforms from captured Union soldiers, and give the Northerners old clothes to wear.

"Paroled at City Point, Va. May 15, 1863." (Friday, six more days) City Point, in 1923, became a suburb of Hopewell, Va. In Civil War years, by 1863 however, because of it's strategic location on the broad, highly navigable, James River it was designated as a point of exchange for prisoners of war from both North and South. In 1864 and 1865, during the siege of Richmond and Petersburg, Virginia, City Point became briefly famous as..., by far..., the largest, most efficient, strategic Union supply depot of the Civil War, in fact of any war up to that time. The town was, at the same time, equally famed as an enormous shipping and railway center for the transport of weapons, ammunition, supplies, and troop rations to the fighting fronts.

"Reported at Camp Parole, Maryland, May 18, 1863." (Just three days after) Camp Parole, near Annapolis, Maryland was a temporary prison used for holding men who were captured until exchanges between the North and South could be arranged. The trip was by steamboat down the James River, up the Chesapeake Bay, not far into the broad waters of the Potomac River.

"Sent on to Camp Chase, Ohio May 19,1863. (The very next day) Camp Chase, four miles from Columbus, Ohio, was established early in the Civil War as a prison camp for captured Confederate soldiers. As war progressed and the need for troops increased, both sides held even their own men who were exchanged under guard until they could be transported back into the control of their own Regimental officers...so they might not "fade away into the civilian population." As a matter of interest, Private Baughman had first enlisted with an Ohio cousin in Company F, 88th Ohio Infantry Regiment which was mustered in for the purpose of guarding Camp Chase.

"Reported at Camp Chase, May 23, 1863." This four day trip was "riding the cars" as trains were referred to by soldiers of the Civil War.

On May 29, 1863… W. Hoffman, Colonel Third Infantry, Commissary-General of Prisoners, Washington, D.C. sent a message to Maj. Gen Ambrose E. Burnside, Commanding Department of the Ohio at Cincinnati. "General: I had yesterday the honor to communicate to you the authority of the General-in-Chief to transfer the 51st and 73rd Indiana Regiments on parole at Camp Chase to Indianapolis until exchanged…"

Colonel Hoffman sent a following message to Maj. Gen. Burnside on June 3, "…the following declaration of exchanges… was made on May 30th…the Regiments of Streight's Brigade - 3rd Ohio - 311 men, 51st Indiana - 371 men, 73rd Indiana - 268 men (down from 450 less officers at the start of Strieght's Brigade), paroled at Mount Sterling, likely the 80th Illinois 463 men, and two companies 1st Middle Tennessee Cavalry - 58 men, have been exchanged with a view to serve as guards till their officers who are now held as prisoners at Richmond join them." That totals 1471, very close to the 1466 who were recorded as captured near Rome. However that is still a bit puzzling as it does not include the officers of Streight's Brigade.

And according to Private Wilson Shannon Baughman's, Memorandum from Prisoner of War Records, they were indeed "Sent to Camp Morton, June 3, 1863." Back home in Indiana, officially exchanged back into their Regiments, exactly one month after surrender. Camp Morton, at Indianapolis, therefore became the initial staging ground for reorganization of the Boys From Lake County and their 73rd Indiana Volunteer Infantry Regiment. The record does not show their arrival date, but it was likely the 175 or so railroad miles from Columbus to Indianapolis were covered in the hours of one day. At that point each was given a 15 day furlough.

For the Boys From Lake County and their fellow soldiers of the 73rd Indiana and Streight's Brigade, being prisoners of war for that thirty days was certainly no picnic. There was, of course - in spite of the sense of defeat - relief from wondering if each moment might be their last, as it had been for the week facing fire-fight after fire-fight under vigorous attacks of the Confederate cavalrymen of General Nathan Bedford Forrest.

In all of America's wars, few are the personal descriptions of arduous experiences and the perils of combat itself. A great many combat soldiers remain so pained by the sudden, violent loss of friends, they are reluctant to talk about it. But among scattered commentary of the Boys From Lake County and others of their Regiment, we may at least, piece together a sense of that thirty day trip back to Indiana, and even a bit of their surrender.

Those who were safely on their way home could, by then, admit that they came through the fighting all right but bullets whistled pretty close. At the surrender, they had no ammunition left but what little was in their personal cartridge boxes. The last three cannon shells they fired did not burst, and at capture there were only two shells left.

After surrender they found Confederate privates treated them fairly, officers more harsh. One said they had only eleven crackers in twelve of the days and only enough meat for one meal in that time. "Crackers" were fairly large pieces of extremely hard bread, often softened with water, added to stew, or dipped in coffee to make it easier to bite. It was also noted that Confederate soldiers were on half rations. They would have suffered, it was written, if they hadn't bought food along the way. So their Union dollars obviously were left to them, and accepted by Confederate and Union merchants alike.

The Boys From Lake County and their fellow Brigade soldiers "took it afoot," as they called marching, the thirty-two miles from Richmond to City Point, Virginia. Then they were taken by steamboat down the James River and up the Chesapeake Bay to Camp Parole near Annapolis, Maryland.

Along the way, from the steamboat, they saw with their own eyes America's huge Fortress Monroe near Hampton, Virginia. Even in those years the Fort was already historic, dating prior to 1611 and the first colony at Jamestown. They also saw the wreck of the Union 24 gun, wooden hulled, steam-sailing sloop Cumberland which had been sunk fourteen months earlier by the new Confederate ironclad warship Merrimac (C.S.S. Virginia). In fact the ship had been sunk the day before the famous battle between that Confederate ironclad and the Union ironclad Monitor which occurred on March 9, 1862.

From Camp Parole and Annapolis the Boys From Lake County and their fellow Union troops were transported aboard another steamboat to Baltimore.

From Baltimore came the long train ride to Columbus, Ohio. The histories of Lake County indicate that the men were a bit tired of "riding the cars" but by then...felt they had seen more of the "world" than farm and small town Indiana boys ever expected.

Although later devastating to Union soldiers captured and imprisoned in the economically stressed South...the idea of holding officers worked well for their Confederate captors in this instance. The Boys From Lake County and their 73rd Indiana Volunteer Infantry Regiment remained disorganized, out of action, for about eight months. Their service during that time was limited to guard duty, routine camp maintenance, the daily chores of camp life, while some units of the 73rd were detailed to other Regiments for special projects.

There was another message sent on June 3, 1863 from Lt. Col William H. Ludlow, Agent for Exchange of Prisoners at Headquarters Department of Virginia, Fort Monroe (Union) to Hon. Robert Ould, Agent for Exchange of Prisoners (Confederate).

"Sir: You informed me at our last interview that you were instructed not to deliver any of the officers of Colonel Streight's command captured at or near Cedar Bluff, Ala., about the 1st of May last. I now make a formal demand for them under the cartel and tender to you their equivalents in your own officers now in our hands. If this demand and tender be refused please state the reasons therefore, frankly that the issues presented may be fully understood and promptly met." In fact, it was a "demand" which was not fully met for many months.

Indeed, it had been far from a happy fruition for Colonel Abel D. Streight and the officers of his surrendered Brigade to find themselves headed toward a much different destination than their men. When they reached Richmond, instead of being paroled and exchanged, they were interned in famous Libby prison, entering there on Saturday, May 16, 1863. Many of them were held throughout most final years of the Civil War, although a few escaped and some, after many months, were exchanged back to Union lines.

As we've noted before, the first "History of Lake County" was written by local Baptist minister Timothy H. Ball in 1872 when tales of the war were still fresh and clear. Information was obviously told directly to him by soldiers of Company A, who returned home to Lake County at War's end. Here, in Reverend Ball's exact words, is a record of their entrance into Richmond's Libby Prison.

"When they surrendered they were to be paroled and sent through our (Union) lines. But, they were sent to Richmond, Virginia...and entered the famous Libby prison. Their paroles had been taken from them, and they had been told they were not recognized as belonging to the army, but were highway robbers, bridge burners, negro stealers, and that they would be turned over to the civil authorities of Alabama, and to be tried and hung. On arrival at Libby they were searched, their greenbacks (dollars) taken away and likewise their blankets. Up three flights of stairs, they were placed in a room one hundred twenty five feet by fifty." (Author's note: In the history of Libby Prison that room on the third floor has always since been called Streight's Room.)

In fact, the taking of their money brought one last contact with General Nathan Bedford Forrest...one which again tells us much about his character and integrity.

Although records show they were fed as well as their guards and Confederate soldiers in the field, economic stress in the South, by mid 1863, was already taking it's toll on prisoners and Rebel soldiers alike. Colonel Streight and his officers obviously felt keenly some level of restriction of food, blankets, and other daily personal needs. They complained bitterly that in their surrender agreement they had been promised they would be permitted to keep all personal possessions, of course including money which would allow them to buy food and personal items.

To their credit, after less than two months, Confederate officers who managed the prison agreed to contact Forrest and ask him if complaints of the imprisoned Union officers of Streight's Brigade were true. Needless to say, at that point, capture was complete. Streight and his Union officers had absolutely no control over their surroundings or treatment. Over eons of human war, many a conqueror has simply ignored such protest, leaving surrendered enemy to the mercy of whatever prison guards might wish to do... even amidst promises which brought about capitulation.

Despite his aggressive military genius and fierce conduct in battle, though, Forrest was clearly a man who considered others, including his enemy, in a more personal, forthright manner. Following are the exact words of his reply as they pertain to the question of money and personal property of the imprisoned Union officers of Streight's Brigade:

Headquarter's Forrest's Cavalry,
Dalton, Ga., October 22, 1863

Brig. Gen. John H. Winder,

GENERAL: Yours of September 15, inclosing a copy of Colonel Streight's letter dated July 4 last, together with a copy of yours of July 6, in relation to the articles of capitulation, and $850, is received.

It was agreed that private property would be protected and that the side-arms of the officers (so far as I was concerned) would also until their arrival at Richmond.

Colonel Streight is correct in his statement in regard to the money in his possession.

My quartermaster purchased the horses of the surgeons and paid for them in Confederate money, and at the time that I made the exchange with Colonel Streight was of the impression that the money was the property of the surgeons. I exchanged also about $800 with Colonel Streight, giving him U. S. Greenback notes, mostly in $1 and 2$ bills.

Colonel Streight's command had done but little damage to property, having destroyed only one furnace and one stable.

Your letter would have been answered, but owing to my absence did not receive it until last evening.

Yours, most respectfully,
N. B. FORREST, Brigadier General

We found no record that Colonel Abel D. Streight and his Union officers were the first to be held permanently as prisoners. In fact, Richmond Virginia's Libby Prison was many months into full operation when the leaders of Streight's Brigade were interned there, so likely they were not the first.

During the Civil War some 40,000 to 50,000 captured Union officers were imprisoned in the facility, designed to hold only about 1200. Obviously, therefore, a great many simply passed through. While in the War's early years, the idea was to hold prisoners until exchanges or paroles could be arranged... it was near the time of the surrender of Streight's Brigade that permanent imprisonment began to take hold. From this, it does seem clear that Colonel Abel D. Streight and his Union officers were among the early recipients of long term imprisonment at Libby Prison instead of parole or exchange.

The name of that Richmond military jailhouse complex, built between 1845 and 1852, was in one sense, a misnomer. Located on part of a block at the corners of Cary, Dock and 20th Streets, the three 110x44 foot, four story, loft style buildings were constructed and owned by John H. Enders. Enders, one of the founders of Richmond's tobacco trade, died in a fall through a hatch from a high ladder during the central building's erection. Also a leader in Richmond real estate development, Enders owned a substantial amount of property in the dock area with the Ege family who were his in-laws.

Captain Luther Libby, a native of Maine, leased the west building of the complex from the Enders family in 1854 for his ship chandlery and grocery (marine supply) business. It was he who set in place the famed sign "L. Libby & Son." However, most of his business was with Northern ships, so he closed the operation at the outbreak of war, while continuing to hold the building's rental agreement. From this bit of information we see that, prior to the Civil War, Richmond, Virginia had a substantial number of ships operated by seafaring New England "Yankee" traders mooring at it's James River docks.

Following the Battle of First Manassas (Bull Run) great numbers of Union prisoners flowed into Richmond. Confederate General John H. Winder was given the job of establishing prisoner of war facilities and the Enders buildings were among several which he commandeered for that purpose.

Luther Libby was given only 48 hours to vacate. Though with a son in Confederate service, some historic accounts say that Libby was suspected of Union sympathy, likely because of his prior business with Northern ships. Regardless, though, of political views Libby may have held, the buildings were converted so quickly that no one removed his business sign. So, only incidentally, did the name Libby become synonymous with the Prison, and achieve fame. While General Winder was responsible for the overall development of Libby Prison, it was Confederate Major Thomas P. Turner it's commandant, together with Richard R. "Dick" Turner, listed as it's "keeper," who were in charge of routine management.

Although Civil War history does not establish it with certainty, Philander A. Streator of Holyoke, Massachusetts was likely the first Union prisoner to enter. The best known captured officer held at Libby Prison was Union Cavalry General H. Judson Kilpatrick who led an unsuccessful raid against Richmond.

In daily operations, captured Union officers were guarded on only the top three floors. Although connected by inner doors, the three buildings were fully separate, designated East, Middle, and West. The ground floor of the West building was used for offices and guard rooms. The ground floor of the Middle building became the prison kitchen. In basements of the buildings cells were constructed to hold spies, and prisoners considered more dangerous.

Miss Elizabeth Van Lew, remembered as "the Union agent" in Richmond visited often bringing reading material and food to Union officers there. Historical accounts suggest that she obtained valuable information from those incarcerated at Libby and passed it through her own "efficient" network to Union officials. It is also said that she aided the escape of a number of Union officers...even with a hint after the War that a tunnel had been maintained between Libby and her home in a section of Richmond called Church Hill. That was never true. However, in the Van Lew Collection at the New York Public Library (as of 1961-1965) there were several items on display given to her by Libby prisoners. One was a small, nicely carved, wooden book inscribed "E. V. L. - A Friend In Need."

As in prisons of both the North and South, letters written home complained about lack of food, cold, and lice...yet at Libby many prisoners could buy extra food and receive packages from home. Black servants (captured Northerners) served white Union officers, and there was running water and even primitive flush toilets. Outside observers, invited in by the Confederate commandant, reported that there were plenty of books, games of whist, and classes in Greek. They also found Libby Prison "scrupulously clean and well ventilated, no bad smell, and that "rafters were thickly hung with hams of bacon and venison, beef tongues, bologna sausage, dried fish, and other substantials."

Nevertheless, as far as grousing about prison life, the Boys From Lake County were no different from their Union or Southern counterparts. Here's the prisoner of war account that Captain Alfred Fry (first Orderly Sergeant, then Lieutenant, finally Captain of Company A) told when he returned home to Lake County.

In Libby Prison, Captain Fry (remember Fry was promoted to Captain of Company A on Monday, January 19, 1863 after the horrific Battle of Stones River at Murphreesborough) found a rusty tin plate and a "rheumatic" knife and fork as instruments for housekeeping, and prepared little sacks for holding salt, sugar, pepper, and rice. These were not very well filled. The rations were three-fourths of a pound of coarse corn bread, one gill of rice (1/2 cup), half a pound of meat, and a very little salt. The vermin were the most revolting feature of the prison. No amount of personal cleanliness could guard against the insatiate lice, and only by examining their clothing and destroying them once or twice a day could these hideous creatures be kept from swarming on the persons of the prisoners. For other occupation during the long evenings the prisoners would sing the Star Spangled Banner, Old Hundred, and Old John Brown.

In this dreary abode Fry remained a year, leaving Libby Prison in company with others, Saturday, May 7, 1864 for Danville, Virginia. Thursday, May 12th they left Danville, arrived Tuesday, May 17th at Macon, Georgia, and were marched into the prison-pen, an area of some two acres surrounded by a stockade fence fifteen feet high. Wednesday, July 27th the officers were transferred to Charleston, South Carolina, and placed in the jail-yard under the fire of Union guns on Morris Island. Here the ground was literally covered with vermin. The prisoners were without shelter. They were brought there to save the city from the shells of the Union batteries.

Wednesday, October 5th they were sent to Columbia, South Carolina and arrived in the midst of a terrific rain storm. The prisoners were compelled to leave the cars (trains) and to pass the night in an open field, without food, blankets, tents, at the mercy of the elements, with four pieces of artillery trained upon the ground they occupied. When the storm ceased they were moved two miles to another open field, and here, without even the shelter of a tree or bush, endured the scorching sunshine that followed the storm. Their food rations, to last five days, were five quarts of very coarse corn meal, one quart of sorghum, two tablespoonfuls of coarse salt, and two tablespoonfuls of rice.

While still at Columbia, a wild hog chanced to pass the guard line. As soon as he was fairly entered, a general advance was made, and he was captured. One man seized a leg, another an ear, others twisted their bony fingers into the bristles and closed hands, eyes, and teeth as if for a death struggle. Every man clung to the part he first seized until it was cut off and securely lodged in the kettle for supper. Between four and five hundred half-starved men were soon devouring him. This stray hog furnished the only meat tasted at Columbia, and for this no thanks were returned to the Rebels.

Tuesday, February 14th, 1865, they were transferred to Charlotte, paroled, and sent on to Wilmington, North Carolina. From there, Wednesday, March 1st, the officers entered once more their Union lines. Fry was furloughed home to Crown Point in Lake County, and enjoyed time with his family from Monday, March 13th until Friday, April 14th ,1865 when he reported for duty at Columbus, Ohio. Captain Fry, remained at Columbus a month, was officially exchanged, so then was able to return to Company A, his Boys From Lake County. They were stationed by then at Larkinsville, Alabama near the Tennessee River.

In the meantime, Brigade Commander Colonel Able D. Streight is recorded again within history of the War. Streight, with several other of his officers, escaped from Libby Prison on Tuesday, February 9, 1864. That event was the largest prisoner flight of the Civil War...one in which 109 Union officers tunneled their way out. Slightly over half of them, 59, actually reached safety, while 48 were recaptured, and two drowned.

Again demonstrating Colonel Streight's toughness and determination... he was one of the 59 who reached Union lines. Streight became relatively renowned nationally for his Brigade exploits and that monumental escape...lauded in the North, reviled in the South. For a time, at least, Streight seems to have been as well known as General H. Judson Kilpatrick, Libby Prison's "most famous" prisoner. There was talk, even in some of his biographies, that Streight himself was the instigator and planner for the huge break-out. However in the history of the escape, records indicate that was not true.

In fact, to the contrary, those records show that the escape of February 9, 1864 was actually led by Colonel Thomas E. Rose of the 77th Pennsylvania Volunteers, assisted by Major A. G. Hamilton of the 12th Kentucky Regiment. Rose was one of the unfortunates, captured and returned to Libby. However, he was soon exchanged and returned to Union lines on April 30, 1864. After several days plodding through in icy swamps, Hamilton safely reached Union lines near Williamsburg, Virginia following his escape.

Total planning and digging for the escape took fifty-one days. Conspirators succeeded in sneaking into a cellar under the hospital area of Libby Prison, digging through a wall and then into the earth. There were two failed attempts during that time, tunnels that led to Richmond's sewer system. The diggers, however, found sewer pipes too small to enter.

Digging of the third, fifty-three foot long, tunnel which finally led to escape took seventeen days. Tools used were simply an old pocket knife, some chisels, a piece of rope, a rubber cloth, and a wooden spittoon. Rope attached to the spittoon allowed it to be pulled back and forth..., full, then empty..., to remove dirt from the tunnel. Excavated earth was piled in the cellar, stomped down as flat as possible to conceal it, then hidden under a pile of straw from old emptied mattresses. (Author's note: This tells us what cushioned the sleep of prisoners at Libby.) Diggers first struck outer surface in the middle of an unpaved street....and quickly stopped that up with an old pair of pantaloons (leather military uniform leggings) filled with dirt and stuffed up into the hole. Digging on, they found themselves under a tobacco shed, opening the tunnel to freedom.

Work was secretly commenced by a party of eighty, fellow prisoners knowing nothing about it. Finally a few other friends were notified, and work parties increased. The planners were "fearful to trust the matter to the general knowledge of fellow prisoners, though when work was done and the outlet open, all who were willing to make the attempt were notified of the fact. It was regarded as a most hazardous adventure for freedom, with a possibility of being shot, a certainty of great hardship, and if captured the ball and chain and low diet."

(Author's note: Now here is a historical record which speaks much truth about the amount of daily food eaten by Union officers held at Richmond's Libby Prison.) "A number of officers who desired to escape were compelled to abandon the effort on account of their corpulency, (fat, over weight)) the tunnel being too small to admit their passage through it. Some of them undertook a depleting process to reduce their dimensions, but failed to come down to the required thinness. (Surely does not sound like "starvation" to this inquisitive writer.)

The actual escape began at 7:00 p.m. on Tuesday February 9, 1864, but some officers did not move through the tunnel until 8:00 a.m. the next morning. It took each man about five minutes to get through the tunnel. It was dangerous for more than one in the tunnel at a time because of difficulty breathing. "Each man, as he emerged in the open air, sauntered slowly off taking whatever direction he fancied. They (Southerners of Richmond) all had on our blue army coats, which facilitated escape, nearly all the (Confederate) military in and about Richmond wearing the same coats, having been supplied from the clothing sent through by the (Federal) Government for our prisoners. They allege they were bought from our prisoners, but some doubt is entertained on this subject."

"Colonel Rose, after bidding farewell to his comrades," said Major A.G. Hamilton co-planner with Rose of the escape, "dropped into the basement and made his way through the tunnel. He was the first man out. I was at his heels, and we were followed by Capt. J. F. Gallagher, Major Fitzsimmons, Capt. Johnston, and Lieut. Fislar. Major Hamilton also provides next to the last mention during the Civil War for the commander of Streight's Brigade:

"Major B. B. McDonald waited in the basement for Colonel A. D. Streight, whom he had chosen as his picked friend. (Of the original eighty escape conspirators, it was decided that each would pick an additional close associate and offer the chance to participate in the escape.) And without malice or prejudice, I would like to say right here that this is the only connection with the Libby prison tunnel that Streight had, so far as my knowledge extends. I never knew of an idea that he contributed and never heard his name connected with it as far as the digging party was concerned." (In his account written at some time after the War, it is clear that Hamilton simply wanted to set the record straight on this particular matter.)

"After getting outside the lines around Richmond, they were greatly facilitated by the sympathizing negro. In no case did they apply to them for direction as to their route, without receiving correct information gladly given. They were told how to avoid the Rebel scouts and pickets, and where they would be most likely to strike the Federal lines."

Lieutenant Colonel Alfred B. Wade Circa 1864

Chapter Fourteen

Their Last Months of War

As we've found, Confederate imprisonment of Union officers did, in fact, work well for Southern forces, the lack of experienced officers crippling re-organization of at least some, and perhaps many, Union Regiments. As we've noted before, and as a clear example, the Boys From Lake County and fellow soldiers of their 73rd Indiana Volunteer Infantry Regiment were essentially inactive as a fighting unit for eight months.

Six months after their May 3rd capture, we find them on Monday, November 9, 1863 still doing little but guard duty at Camp Morton, Indianapolis. They are clearly identified in a personal inspection report of that day sent to Colonel William Hoffman, Commissary-General of Prisoners headquartered at Washington, by Colonel A. A. Stevens, Commanding, 5th Regiment Invalid Corps.

"I found quartered in Camp Morton," Colonel Stevens said, "two regiments of exchanged soldiers, the 51st and 73rd Indiana Volunteers, belonging to Colonel Streight's Brigade, captured at Rome, Georgia last spring, their officers still being held as prisoners of war at Richmond, Va. These regiments were doing the guard duty of the camp, and, although composed of good material, were to quite an extent demoralized as the result of having been captured and paroled. The want of a sufficient number of commissioned officers was also a cause calculated to render them insufficient to perform a duty so important as that required of a guard at this post, there being but 7 commissioned officers to a command of 1,300 men, and these had all been commissioned since their capture. Under the above circumstances, I found the guard in no very high state of discipline. The policing (neatness) of the camp, owing to a scarcity of officers, had not been as thorough as it should have been.

In that same report of November 1863 we discover, in fact, further evidence that conditions in Northern prisoner of war camps were often just as discrepant as any in the South, excepting the rare tragedy of Andersonville. "I found the barracks in a bad condition," Colonel Stevens related, "wanting extensive repairs in order to render them fit for occupancy during the winter. The buildings used for hospitals, not having been built for that purpose, were insufficient in extent and appointments for the purpose. I found the prisoners generally supplied with necessaries, though in a poor state of health. The cause I am unable to determine, as our own troops quartered near them and equally crowded enjoyed excellent health." Stevens did add that repairs and new buildings under construction would remedy those flaws.

It was not until Saturday, January 2, 1864 that the 73rd Indiana was reassigned to the Twelfth Army Corps. Their division was a reorganized unit, newly called the "District of Nashville," commanded by Major General Lovell H. Rousseau. The new division included the posts within Nashville where most of the men of the 73rd had already been stationed again for a brief portion of the eight months after November 1863. With them in the First Brigade of two in that division were the 10th Tennessee, 13th Wisconsin, 102nd Ohio, and 18th Michigan Regiments. A further note from commanders who scheduled the reorganization said, "newly organized troops are to remain in their present positions."

On that same day, January 2, 1864, there was a report from a Union Regiment at Huntsville, Alabama which was to have major future import for the Boys From Lake County. It was addressed to Major-General Logan: **"Four bridges burned between this place and the intersection of the Alabama and Tennessee Railroad. The Indian Creek Bridge, 80' long, 8 miles out. Beaver Dam Bridge, 7 miles, 200' long, trestles 40' high, not entirely burned. Limestone Bridge, 4 miles** further, 150' long, and Caving Bridge (?), 21 miles farther, 75' long. The enemy have one Regiment picketing the south bank of the river from Decatur to a point near Paint Rock. J. I. Alexander, Colonel Commanding."

On Thursday, January 14, 1864, a report was forwarded from an inspecting officer to Brig. Gen. J. M. Brannan, Chief of Artillery, Department of the Cumberland, which records the work and condition of the Boys From Lake County and others of their 73rd Indiana in previous months. **"The Seventy-Third Indiana Infantry has charge of all the other guns (cannon) that are in position at Nashville. At the capitol there are four 30 pounder and two 20 pounder Parrotts. At Fort Houston one 24 pounder siege gun and four 6 pounder field guns (this work is unfinished.) At Fort Morton one 30 pounder Parrott, one 32 pounder sea-coast, and one 24 pounder siege gun (the last two are mounted on carriages like casemate carriages without the chassis). There is a 24 pounder siege gun at the termination of Broad Street, one 100 pounder Parrott between termination of Broad Street and officer's hospital (in the camp of the 129th Illinois Regiment), one 100 pounder Parrott near officer's hospital, one 24 pounder siege gun near Lebanon Pike, one 100 pounder Parrott at water-works, and one 24 pounder siege gun on river bank. These isolated guns are mounted like the two before mentioned at Fort Morton, carriage of casemate gun without chassis.**

At the Capitol the magazine is a portion of the basement. The ammunition keeps well, though complaint has been made that it is too damp. Such is perhaps the case in summer rather than in winter. The magazines (ammunition storage) at Forts Morton and Houston are in good order. At each isolated gun there is a small magazine capable of holding about 100 rounds of ammunition. They are very indifferent, but so far the powder has kept pretty well by being taken out and aired as often as the weather would permit. There were from 80 to 100 rounds with each

gun, and in one or two, ammunition belonging to other guns. I directed Captain White, chief of artillery, to leave 50 rounds per gun and send the balance to one of the large magazines. The men are generally very comfortable, some in tents and some in huts. A squad of about 10 men are with each isolated gun. The military appearance, police (neatness), and discipline very fair, drill good, guard duty seemingly well performed."

On Friday, February 12, 1864, there was an isolated mention in a report that the 73rd Indiana Regiment was "small," and we saw in the previous exchange report that the 73rd constituted by then just 268 men. In fact, after their return to Indiana from the battles of Streight's Brigade, capture, and exchange..., one company (not Company A) of the 73rd was down from 100 to 32 men. Obviously, though, despite being "small" in number ...in view of the above Nashville inspection report..., the Boys From Lake County and other men of the 73rd Indiana Volunteer Infantry Regiment had again become exemplary soldiers.

Less than two months later, by April 8, 1864, the Boys From Lake County and others of their 73rd Indiana have experienced two events that sent them back to the fighting fronts.

First, Major Alfred. B. Wade, one of the high ranking officers of the 73rd under the previous leadership of Colonel Gilbert Hathaway had been exchanged from Libby Prison and sent home. Leadership of the Regiment was still clearly in limbo at the time of his arrival. Wade quickly asked army headquarters for permission to be promoted to commanding officer of the Regiment. He was granted that command and promoted to Lieutenant Colonel.

Second the burned bridges of Northern Alabama close by the Tennessee River, and near where they had begun Streight's Raid, had indeed beckoned the Boys From Lake County and the 73rd Indiana back to northwestern Alabama. In the following report from Larkinsville we can pinpoint the location of the Boys From Lake County and others of the 73rd Regiment on that day and confirm Wade's command of the Regiment along with, what seemed to be, his new rank.

Headquarters Seventy-Third Indiana Infantry
Larkinsville, Alabama, April 11, 1864

Sir: I have the honor to report that a squad of 15 men from Company D of this regiment, under command of Corporal William H. H. Reed, met the enemy (supposed by them to number at least 40) near Paint Rock bridge on the 8th instant. Although surprised and driven back after a short contest, yet the Corporal brought his men into camp in perfect order, with a loss, however, of 1 man killed and 1 severely wounded. The loss of the enemy is unknown, but reported by the men and a citizen to vary from 2 to 4 killed and 3 wounded.

Very respectfully, your obedient servant,
A. B. Wade
Lieutenant-Colonel Seventy-third Indiana

So we see by then that the Boys From Lake County and their fellow soldiers of the 73rd Indiana are back in the front lines...facing again the injuries and death of Civil War combat. It is also telling to note that this small engagement on Friday, April 8, 1864 at Paint Rock, Alabama...with the combat death and severe injury of fellow soldiers of Company D...occurred exactly twelve months and one day before the surrender of the Army of Northern Virginia by Confederate General Robert E. Lee at Appomattox, Virginia after the Civil War's last big battle, a place called Saylor's Creek.

It is of further consequence to remember that during their lengthy period of reorganization, the Boys From Lake County missed being sent into the bloody battles of Chickmauga and Chattanooga in the Fall of 1863. Afterwards, the huge, fierce, engagements of the Civil War, were no longer fought in the "western" war zone where they were stationed, but eastward..., the great Battle of Atlanta, Sherman's widely destructive march to the sea, then moving toward closure at the vast, long running battles of Petersburg and Richmond, Virginia.

Clearly, though, from Wade's report..., the peril of fire fights, deaths, and combat wounds would still be a risk, just on a much smaller scale. In fact as we shall see, during the last year of the Civil War, the Boys From Lake County and their fellow soldiers of the 73rd Indiana remained stationed there in northwestern Alabama, guarding the Nashville & Chattanooga Railroad and it's bridges along, or near, the Tennessee River from attacks by Rebel guerillas and cavalry raiders. For much of the time many of them were stationed in defensive blockhouses near bridges. In his pension application, Private Wilson Shannon Baughman specifically notes that Company A, the Boys From Lake County were, for some time, guarding "Little Limestone Bridge." Especially noted are the towns of Larkinsville, Stevenson, Triana, Limestone Point, Paint Rock, Gurley's Tank, Somerville, Athens, Decatur, and Huntsville, Alabama... as well as Prospect, Tennessee.

And, of course, as we shall see all too well in a following chapter, the results of illness and disease will still dog the Boys From Lake County as well as all Civil War soldiers right up to the end of the War...and for many... for the rest of their lives.

In fact, on Wednesday, July 27, 1864, one of the Boys From Lake County, Private Wilson Shannon Baughman, was sent to the Regional Hospital at Triana for an extended stay.

On Friday, July 29, 1864 commanding officer Alfred B. Wade left "Headquarters, 73rd Indiana Infantry, Triana, Ala" at 3:00 a.m. with a small, partial, force of 47 men and one commissioned officer from the Regiment. Wade's report does not tell us whether the Boys From Lake County were with him, or left in blockhouses guarding a bridge. By 5:30 a.m. the whole force had crossed the river at Atkins Ferry. A canoe capsized sending three cannon into the river, recovered by men left behind for that purpose. Wade marched his men south-southwest and entered the town of Somerville in Morgan County, Alabama. There they expected Rebel troops, but found none. On the way, Wade and his men did encounter Rebel cavalry scouts, but since men of the 73rd were not on horseback the Rebel cavalrymen escaped and alarmed the country in advance. "Hearing of a (Rebel) force on Flint Creek, I held the town but half an hour," said Wade, "and then retired via the Fletcher's Ferry and Decatur Roads." By 4:30 p.m. Wade and his men of the 73rd were back in camp, having marched twenty and a half miles in thirteen and a half hours, and crossing the Tennessee River twice. "Four of my men suffered somewhat from sunstroke," Wade related, "but not severely." In the course of the day this unit of the 73rd Indiana captured 4 horses, a mule, 6 guns, and made "demonstrations at Limestone Point and Gillsport to perplex the enemy, which were entirely successful." A few men crossed at Gillsport, but meeting a squad of Confederate cavalry were compelled to return. "Fifteen crossed at Limestone Point and succeeded in procuring forage (feed for horses and mules) retiring without loss before a superior force. Major Alfred B. Wade, 73rd Indiana Infantry."

We found no explanation as to why Wade lists himself again a Major rather than Lt. Colonel as in the report of two weeks earlier. Likely he received verbal confirmation of the promotion from some higher ranked officer, then found that the "paperwork" had not yet, in fact, trickled down through proper channels of the Union Army command. (That happened to this writer as a 17 year old Private in the Alabama Air National Guard. Sure did hurt to have to take off those Corporal stripes.)

Wade also included an associated report from a Lieutenant leading a scouting party from his command that same day.

"The scouting party from this post crossed the river about 2:00 a.m. (Friday, July 29, 1864) They first went to General Garth's and got about 60 bushels of corn, for which they gave vouchers. They then went farther in the country and scouted until 12 o'clock, when they came back to General Garth's and were attacked by a party of Rebels, about 50 or 60 in number, and were forced back to the landing opposite Limestone Point, where they killed a beef, but the owner got no receipt for it. They then crossed the river, fell in line of battle, and found they had lost two men. In about two hours time I sent a scout over the river and found the rebels had gone. I then sent the same scouting party back to find those two men they lost, if possible. They soon found one of them returning to the river, and returned without the other one. But about 5 p.m. he was seen coming to camp on this side of the river, so there were none hurt from this post. It is supposed that there were 3 or 4 of the Rebels killed or wounded, as they were seen to fall from their horses, one of them the commander of the Rebel force. If they were not shot they were not very good horsemen." J. H. Kierstead, Lieutenant, Commanding at Limestone.

In an action of Monday, August 15, 1864, we find the Boys From Lake County and their fellow soldiers of the 73rd Indiana still headquartered at Triana, Alabama.

"I left camp at 3 a.m." says Wade, "with a detachment of 100 men - the whole available force at this post excepting pickets. (Remember many of the Regiment's men were stationed in blockhouses guarding railroad bridges) By means of one flat and one pontoon boat I crossed the Tennessee River with the whole force by 5 a. m. Marched due south one mile, where a corral of thirty horses was discovered. Part of these had been stolen and run south through our lines; some belonged to persons now within our lines, who came over secretly. The balance belonged to soldiers and Major Ragland, upon whose plantation they were found. A squad of my men surprised four (Rebel) soldiers, capturing 2 of them. Leaving a detachment in charge of these horses, I marched south southeast two miles and a half, to the plantation of James Grantlin, and destroyed a saltpeter-work belonging to the Confederate Government. (Rebel) scouts were seen on several roads, but none captured. I then marched the command as rapidly as possible to Valhermoso Springs, six miles from the river. Here the advance guard was fired into by a squad of eight or ten Rebel cavalry. They were easily driven off, when I effectually destroyed another saltpeter-work located at this point, breaking the kettles and burning the building. Returning by the same route I reached camp at 1:30 p.m., having re-crossed the river with 25 head of horses and mules, 4 beef cattle, 3 prisoners, several guns, and without the loss of a man." A. B. Wade, Major 73rd Indiana, Commanding.

On Sunday, August 21, 1864 Brigadier General Robert S. Granger commanding the District of Northern Alabama, of the giant Union Army of the Cumberland, said, "I have ordered the 73rd Indiana Infantry (except one company) along with the 102nd Ohio and 13th Wisconsin to use every effort to keep Clanton (a large force of Rebels) on the south side of the river. Troop movements on both sides were in preparation for a confounding, long running series of engagements that culminated in what was called the Battle of Lynnville. Confederate forces, including those under Clanton, Forrest, Roddey and others were led by Major-General Joseph "Fightin' Joe" Wheeler. Just 5'4" tall and only in his late twenties, Wheeler was one of the most outstanding cavalry generals of the Southern army. Likely, the "except one company" was Company A, the Boys From Lake County. Remember that Private Wilson Shannon Baughman recorded in his pension records that at the time Company A was guarding the Little Limestone Bridge in that area.

In fact, on Friday, August 26, 1864 Private Baughman, is listed as having reported to the Regimental Hospital for a lengthy stay. As mentioned before, he had reported to the same hospital for a number of days beginning on Wednesday, July 27, 1864. He was again listed as being in the hospital on Thursday through Saturday, September 15th to the 17th, and again beginning on Wednesday September 28th. Records do not indicate what he was hospitalized for. However, during that period he contracted Malaria, Dysentery, and Sore Eye (Conjunctivitis)...illnesses from which he suffered the rest of his life.

On Sunday, August 28, 1864 General Granger said, "I ordered the 102nd Ohio, 13th Wisconsin, and the 73rd Indiana to fall back immediately to the railroad - the 13th I sent to Huntsville, the 73rd to Elk River, and the 102nd Ohio to Decatur

Junction." Rebel cavalrymen were using every means to cut the railroad, especially burning railroad ties, bridges, engines and cars to hamper the rapid movement of Union troops. It was vital to protect it.

On Wednesday, August 31st, General Granger said, " I have...the 102nd Ohio, 13th Wisconsin, and 73rd Indiana from river, except one company, at most exposed points commanded by each Regiment...concentrated and provided with three days cooked rations ready to throw them upon any point of the railroad. In fact, on the same day came a report that General Joseph "Fightin' Joe" Wheeler's cavalry had indeed cut the railroad at a town called Wartrace...and again at a spot north of Elk River where portions of the 73rd Indiana had been stationed. As a result, the next day, September 1st, the 3rd Tennessee, the 73rd Indiana and two pieces of artillery were hurried back to Elk River Bridge.

On the morning of Friday, September 2nd, Brigadier-General John C. Starkweather reported leading a small force of Union troops to Elk River and "finding there a section of 1st Ohio artillery and 73rd Indiana Infantry."

"On the morning of (Thursday) September 8th at Elk River," said Brigadier-General Robert S. Granger, "I met Colonel Streight with 2,500 infantry and two pieces of artillery. Colonel Streight stated to me that he was there by order of General Steedman, with authority to do as he pleased, and asked my advice. I advised him to move on and attack Wheeler at Centre Star, and gave him my best Regiment of cavalry for that purpose. So... here we see that Colonel Abdel D. Streight, after his escape from Confederate Libby Prison is back in the fight, now leading a much larger, Battalion sized force. Clearly it is the course by which he was promoted to Brevet (temporary) Brigadier-General prior to his resigning from the army in the spring of 1865.

For the three week long series of feints and engagements called Wheeler's raid, or the Battle of Lynnville, the Boys from Lake County, as far as we could determine, were guarding Little Limestone Bridge..., the rest of the 73rd Indiana sent back and forth between specific assignments and guarding the Elk River Bridge.

On Saturday, September 24th, in a message from Decatur, Alabama, Brig. Gen Robert S. Granger said, "...the force in and about Athens belongs to Forrest's command. (Confederate Cavalry General Nathan Bedford Forrest is still quite busy) One of the block-houses (railroad defense) was summoned to surrender by Forrest. Forrest's force said to be very large. I shall move at once with all the forces at my command. I have retained the 102nd Ohio and the 73rd Indiana.

Later, on that same day, Saturday September 24th, General Granger sent a second message, "Colonel Campbell, Athens, was said to have surrendered the post at that place, the strongest position in the district. Forrest was there at 2 o'clock this afternoon; firing was heard there then. Forrest's force said to be very large. The detachment (Union) sent from here to re-enforce Athens last night, about 350, is said to have been captured within one mile and a half of Athens, after a very obstinate engagement."

(Author's note) In fact, Athens had been held by Union forces for some time. After the Battle of Shiloh in April 1862 the Union Army captured the Confederate, Memphis and Charleston Railroad, using it to push into the South and occupy a number of towns including Athens. Many of the 900 Athens residents claimed to be pro-Union and were cooperative with Union occupiers. On Thursday, May 1, 1862 the Confederate 1st Louisiana Cavalry commanded by Colonel J. S. Scott made an unexpected attack, driving the Union garrison out of town. A hundred or so Athens townsmen grabbed their rifles and assisted, helping to chase the Union troops for about six miles. The next day Colonel John Basil Turchin commanding a full Union Brigade composed of four Regiments counterattacked, overwhelming the much smaller Rebel cavalry unit, forcing them to again abandon Athens. By then Colonel Turchin and his men were angry, feeling the people of Athens had

*betrayed them. Turchin, in effect, gave his men permission
to ransack the city causing notable, never to be forgotten,
damage to stores, shops, and homes along with widespread
thefts of retail goods and personal possessions. Killing of
citizens was never intended, although one expectant mother
and her unborn child died from a miscarriage caused by the
stress of soldiers firing rifles into her home. The soldiers,
and some Union officers, heaped insults on men and women
of Athens, improper proposals were made to women, and
one "servant girl" was raped. This rare event was quickly
termed...by both North and South...as one of the very few
"atrocities" of the Civil War, a conflict fought by both sides
in a spirit of honor and integrity despite fierce battles and
horrific losses. The misdeeds at Athens resulted in an
immediate Union courts-martial for Colonel Turpin and his
officers. Yet again, at about 4:00 a.m. on Tuesday, January
26, 1864 600 Rebel cavalrymen attacked the 100 man Union
garrison at Athens. The two hour battle ended with the Union
force, although much smaller, repulsing the attackers and
bringing about their retreat.*

On Wednesday, September 28, 1864, General Granger received a message from famed Civil War General William Tecumseh Sherman. "I will send General Thomas up the road," Sherman told Granger. "In the meantime you should drive any squads of Forrest's men across Elk (River) and threaten the fords at Lamb's and Elkton; also open up communication with Rousseau, so you can act in concert." Sherman sent his message from Hdqrs, Military Division of the Mississippi, In the field, Atlanta, Ga. Here we are reminded that even the highest ranking of Civil War generals often operated on the battlefield with their troops.

On the same day, Granger replied back to Sherman, "After leaving minimum guards at garrison's and block-houses, I have only 300 cavalry and 500 infantry to operate against Forrest. General Rousseau has nearly all my available force at upper end of the (rail) road. This estimate will leave Decatur without a single mounted man." Again, this tells us just how vital the guard duty performed by the Boys From Lake County, Company A, 73rd Indiana Volunteer Infantry, was in those block-houses along railroads near the Tennessee River in the last months of War.

And..., still at Decatur, on that same day, Wednesday September 28, 1864, General Granger received yet another message. This one is especially curt and to the point. Furthermore, it contains very specific orders that will affect our Boys From Lake County. The order originates from Headquarters, Department of the Cumberland, Atlanta, Ga., George H. Thomas, Major-General, U.S. Volunteers, Commanding.

"Report your whole strength immediately," General Thomas orders. "You can keep Wheeler or any other Rebel raider from crossing the Tennessee River with the force you have now, assisted by the gun-boats, **but Athens must be recovered**. To assist you in doing that I will send troops to you as soon as possible."

From this we see that Major-General George Henry Thomas, in the last year of War, has taken over command of the giant Army of the Cumberland from General Rosecrans and become top commander for the Boys From Lake County. He will be remembered as much more aggressive and successful than his predecessor.

General Granger's reply to General Thomas, immediately on the same day, Wednesday, September 28, 1864, is one of the most revealing as to Civil War daily problems and field operations we have seen in years of research.

"Major-General Thomas: Scout from Athens reports 300 Rebels within three miles of Athens. I am repairing the rail road to that point, and will reoccupy the place as soon as I have a disposable force. Effective force at my command: 18th Michigan Infantry 333; 102nd Ohio 250; 73rd Indiana 411; 13th Wisconsin 461; 10th Indiana 427; 11th Indiana 700; total infantry 2,582. 102nd Ohio 100 and 11th Indiana 100 at Stevenson, Alabama." By order of General Rousseau, 250 men on gun boats. **Infantry**

force much diminished by sickness since my last report, particularly my best Regiments, recently on the river and garrisons of block-houses on margins of streams. Infantry garrisons, Decatur, Huntsville, and twenty-five block-houses and stations on railroad to Stevenson. The abandonment of any would insure the burning of bridge in twenty-four hours by Johnson or Mead. We have also a post on the river occupied by 200 men. We have one on the south at Larkinsville with 750 men, and a Regiment of 400 back of Guntersville.... I have not the least apprehension but I can hold any position taken, but our difficulty is to know where to hold, when we have only infantry to hold so large a body of (Rebel) cavalry. Our infantry are not only eager, but mad, because they cannot get a fight. Our cavalry force: 2nd Tennessee 300; 12th Indiana 170; total 470. Nothing heard from Forrest since 4 o'clock day before yesterday. I have sent 300 men to reoccupy Athens. I have left 300 cavalry and 500 infantry; this will leave minimum garrisons at stations and blockhouses." **(Author's note: This report shows the 73rd Indiana Volunteer Infantry Regiment at about it's usual strength... indicating that Company A, the Boys From Lake County have been ordered out of the block-houses and into the fight for the reoccupation and defense of Athens with others of the 73rd Indiana. The History of Lake County also confirms the Boys From Lake County's participation in the fight at Athens.)**

And finally, dated for the month of September 1864, in the abstract from returns of the Department of the Cumberland, Maj. Gen. George H. Thomas, Commanding, the Boys From Lake County's Regimental commander has officially achieved his promotion, listed as "73rd Indiana, Lieut. Col. Alfred B. Wade" Commander.

On Sunday, October 2, 1864 Brig. General Robert S. Granger, from headquarters at Huntsville, Alabama sent a message yet again recording the fighting ability of our Boys From Lake County and others of the 73rd.

"Major-General Thomas: Athens was attacked yesterday (Saturday) by a portion of General Forrest's command at 3 p.m. Well equipped with artillery, resumed attack this morning. Cannonading very severe between 6 and 8 a.m. today. Lieutenant-Colonel Wade, with his Regiment, 73rd Indiana, which I sent there by your order to reoccupy the place, repulsed the enemy handsomely. (Rebels) moved off in the direction of Elk River, Major McBath with 2nd Tennessee Cavalry (200 men), pursuing."

Our search of historical records indicates that when the cavalry of General Nathan Bedford Forrest again achieved the surrender of the Union garrison at Athens on Saturday, September 24, 1864, as well as the capture of the 350 man Union force sent to assist them...he did not hold the town for any length of time, simply moving on to another fight. There is no record showing that there was a battle when the Boys From Lake County and their 73rd Indiana Regiment marched in to reoccupy Athens...until this one on Saturday and Sunday, October 1st and 2nd. Undoubted, though, is that Athens, like it's neighboring city of Tuscumbia (although not damaged nearly as severely) saw far more than it's share of Civil War conflict. Another notable perspective from this report of General Granger... is that Major-General George H. Thomas, supreme commander of the huge Union, Army of the Cumberland, was the officer who selected the Boys From Lake County and others of their 73rd Indiana to go back in, to reoccupy, to defend the fort and city of Athens, Alabama...a city General Thomas said "must be recovered." Records indicate that 300 men of the 73rd Indiana, part of their 411 at the moment, handled the assignment, and the fight, along with portions of other Regiments. The entire force was led by the 73rd Indiana's Regimental Commander, Lieut. Col. Alfred B. Wade. This records again the great esteem in which the Boys From Lake County and their fellow soldiers of the 73rd Indiana Regiment were held...up to the highest levels of command.

Oddly, there seems no record in the history of Athens, Alabama about this successful defense of their city. Despite such lack of commemoration, the report from Lt. Col. A. B. Wade of the 73rd Indiana forcefully denotes this Battle of Athens as a most notable, and inventive, one among less massive engagements of the Civil War.

Wade wrote the recount at his Headquarters, U.S. Forces, Athens, Ala., Monday, October 3, 1864, "Sir: ...My force consisted of detachments from my own 73rd Indiana Infantry, 10th Indiana (dismounted) Cavalry, and one section of battery A, 1st Tennessee Artillery. A portion of the 2nd Tennessee Cavalry joined me when the engagement commenced, making a total force of about 500 effective men, opposed to which was (Confederate) Brig. Gen. A. Buford's division of cavalry, with one battery of four guns (cannon), estimated by prisoners who had been with him...at 4,000 men. I do not estimate his force as large as this, but from an order found upon the field from Colonel Bartwell, one of his Brigade commanders, it is evident that his whole division invested the place.

The fort at Athens was an earth-work, 180 by 450 feet, surrounded by an abatis of brush (logs or sticks set in the ground, sharpened, pointed toward a position of enemy attack. Not often used in the Civil War) and a palisade 4 feet high (fort wall often made of logs set in the ground), a ditch 12 feet wide, and was 18 feet from the bottom of the ditch to the top of parapets (earthen embankment). In fact, Lieutenant Henry C. March, 115th Ohio Infantry, Assistant Inspector of Railroad Defenses said. "It was one of the best works of the kind I ever saw."

"The pickets on the Huntsville Road were driven in at 3 p.m. on (Saturday) October 1st, said Colonel Wade. "I deployed one company as skirmishers to engage the enemy, who had taken position behind the railroad, and to delay his movements as long as possible. A very heavy rainstorm commenced at this time, which aided this object materially. Firing was kept up on the skirmish line until dark, when I re-enforced it with another company to prevent the enemy from gaining possession of a cluster of buildings near the fort.

The result of the late attacks upon this fort and the one at Sulphur Trestle convinced me that the fateful defect in both works was the want of protection for the garrison against artillery, and for two days previous I had labored to remedy this by constructing a temporary bomb-proof of rather a novel character, it being entirely outside the fort. This work consisted in simply covering the ditch, which was fifteen feet wide and six feet deep, with logs, which with a slight covering of earth, would undoubtedly throw off any shot that might strike. The entrance to this underground apartment, which would be by a covered passage-way under the gate of the fort, was unfinished at the time the skirmishing commenced, but the delay of the enemy in making the main attack proved our salvation. I continued the work as rapidly as possible, and by midnight it was ready for use. During the night the noise made by the enemy's battery (cannon) enabled me to locate the position of their guns with certainty, and the two pieces (cannon) in the fort were brought to bear on them, ready to return their fire as soon as commenced."

"From early daylight until 6 a.m. (Sunday) October 2nd," Colonel Wade continued, "a straggling fire with small-arms was kept up from both sides, principally from the west, where a thick growth of timber approached to within a short range of the fort. I reserved the artillery to operate against the enemy's battery (cannon.) At 6 a.m. he (Rebels) opened fire from one gun in position on the Brown's Ferry Road, southwest from the fort, which was promptly responded to. Ten minutes after, three rifled guns (cannon) opened upon us in quick succession from a slight elevation half a mile north. With such a cross-fire there is scarcely a spot in the fort but what can be reached by a shell, and I immediately moved the troops into the bomb-proof, leaving a sufficient number posted as sentinels to watch for indications of an assault. The enemy's guns (cannon) after a half hour's practice, obtained the range and threw shells into the fort with great accuracy. About sixty rounds were fired, twenty-two of which struck the fort (almost all inside) the balance either bursting overhead or passing beyond. Two shots passed through the Regimental flag of the 73rd Indiana, a tall chimney was crumbled to the ground, one caisson was disabled, and about 30 horses were killed or wounded. Lieutenant Tobin, commanding the section of Battery A , replied to this severe fire coolly and deliberately, and is entitled to much praise for the manner in which he handled his guns (cannon). Ambulances were seen moving about in the vicinity of the Rebel guns, (cannon) and it is believed they did not escape without loss.

"At 8 a.m. the firing ceased," Colonel Wade further explained, "and General Buford sent in a flag of truce, demanding the surrender of the fort and garrison, and empowering his Adjutant-General to grant certain conditions. What those conditions were I did not inquire, but promptly refused to surrender."

Within the many records we've researched, Wade's next information is notably unusual..., far outside the spirit of integrity with which American Civil War tactics were usually employed. "The enemy (Rebels) basely took advantage of this flag (of truce) to move a portion of his troops within 200 yards of the fort, forming, as I supposed, for a charge in case we refused to surrender. I therefore concentrated the artillery and infantry at that point, but subsequently learned that it was simply a cover to enable them to steal six wagons and four ambulances directly from under my guns."

"Respect for the usages of war," Wade continued, "prevented me from opening fire while the flag was in sight, but as soon as it disappeared I opened briskly and drove them from this new position, killing 4. A number were wounded, but were carried off in the wagons. Finding that his artillery practice, hitherto so successful, was perfectly useless here, and not daring to attempt an assault upon our excellent fortifications, the enemy commenced drawing off his troops at once, leaving a body of sharpshooters to attract our attention. Suspecting something of this kind, at 9:30 a. m. I pushed out skirmishers in every direction, and, with the assistance of the artillery, drove them from the field. Major McBath, with the 2nd Tennessee, immediately commenced the pursuit, and ascertained that the whole (Rebel) force retreated down the Florence Road.

Our loss in this action was only 2 slightly wounded; that of the enemy, with the exception of the above mentioned, unknown. The conduct of the troops was all that could be desired. Both officers and men seemed animated by a determination never to surrender."

And so we see the Boys From Lake County and their fellow soldiers of the 73rd Indiana still fighting with great courage and determination after the exhausting conflict and capture of Streight's Brigade. We also see that Lieutenant-Colonel Alfred B. Wade has followed in the footsteps of his previous commanders, Colonel Gilbert Hathaway and Colonel Abel D. Streight, as an equally determined, courageous, and successful battlefield commander. Wade also displays the self assurance and assertiveness to forward his ideas to upper levels of command. "I consider the bomb-proof by which we were protected," he explained, "the main feature of this defense, and estimate the saving in casualties by it to be at least 10 per cent. The moral effect upon the men was great, and the two hours cannonading to which they were subjected only confirmed their belief that they could hold the place against any force that might attack. The fact that a garrison of 600 men was compelled to surrender this same fort only a short time since leads me to call attention to the necessity of having fortified places provided with a good bomb-proof, large enough to contain the garrison."

Further memorializing the esteem in which the Boys From Lake County, their fellow soldiers of the 73rd Indiana, as well as Colonel Alfred B. Wade were held...Brig. Gen. Robert S. Granger had this to say in his message to Union Army command, "The conduct of Lieutenant-Colonel Wade and the troops under his command during this short siege (of Athens, Alabama) was most admirable. I felt satisfied when I placed this officer in command of this post that we should not be again disgraced by a shameful surrender, and that his fort would not be given up without a most heroic defense."

On Saturday, October 8, 1864, from a new headquarters at Decatur, Alabama, General Granger, again locates our Boys From Lake County, at least within a few miles. "Post Athens," he says, has the... "73rd Indiana Infantry, 200; 10th Indiana 100. The remainder of the 73rd Indiana at block-houses and trains, 50. "

On Sunday, October 9,1864 a more precise count of the 73rd Indiana Infantry at Athens is sent to Maj. Gen. George H. Thomas by Brig. Gen John C. Starkweather. "Report from Athens just arrived. Effective force there consists of 73rd Indiana Infantry, 8 officers, 247 men; 125th Illinois, 12 officers, 237 men; 10th Indiana Cavalry, dismounted, 1 officer, 97 men; Battery A, 1st Tennessee, 1st Section, 2 officers, 31 men."

On Friday, October 21, 1864, Maj. Gen. George H. Thomas in a message to his commander Maj. Gen. William Tecumseh Sherman...again records the assignment of the Boys From Lake County and the 73rd Indiana Infantry, " I have...the 13th Wisconsin, 18th Michigan, 73rd Indiana, 102nd Ohio, 75th Pennsylvania, 83rd Illinois, and 115th Ohio, averaging each 250 men. These Regiments are garrisoning block-houses on Nashville & Chattanooga Railroad, Tennessee and Alabama Railroad, Memphis & Charleston Railroad, and the posts of Decatur, Huntsville, and Athens."

The next day, Saturday, October 22nd, Brig. Gen. Robert S. Granger confirms to Maj. Gen. George H. Thomas, "At Athens and in block-houses at Huntsville, 73rd Indiana Infantry, one Company of same at Triana, total 360." Although, as we know, Regimental records do not often identify the operations of individual companies, we suspect that the Company at Triana, Alabama may have been - at least part of that timeframe - Company A, our Boys From Lake County. Private Wilson Shannon Baughman's pension records indicate that Company A was stationed there for some period during that general time span.

As we've reminded before, though, the peril was not over. On Wednesday, October 12, 1864, Brig. Gen. Robert S. Granger learned that the 23,000 man Confederate Army of General John Bell Hood, along with cavalry forces of General Nathan Bedford Forrest, General Philip Dale Roddey, and General Joseph "Fightin' Joe" Wheeler were massing together, heading north through his Union District of Northern Alabama.

Two days later, on Friday, October 14th he received confirming information and began to order troop movements to counter the Rebel offensive.

On Wednesday, October 19, 1864 General Granger received "reliable information" that the command of Confederate General P.G.T. Beauregard was also with Hood's Army making the combined Rebel force one of the most massive in that region during the Civil War. At 11 o'clock that morning General Granger went up the Tennessee River on a gunboat to reconnoiter in person.

On Sunday, October 23rd he received information that the huge army was moving again on the small city of Tuscumbia only 43 miles from his own headquarters at Decatur. Roddeys' forces were already nearby at Moulton and Somerville, Forrest's men just as close at Florence, Alabama, the main portion of the Confederate troops actually nearing Tuscumbia. He also learned from scouts that there was yet another large Confederate force of 10,000 already lurking at Tuscumbia's Bear Creek. The Rebels, he noted, seemed to be intent on moving north across the Tennessee River, obviously with major goals in mind. Eventually, it turned out to be the last large, bloody battle in the western side of the Civil War, an attempt to re-capture Nashville from Union control, in a huge battle called Nashville-Franklin... but not before Union troops in Northern Alabama would have to deal with them.

"Feeling the great importance of Decatur to the Confederates," said General Granger, "and being satisfied that General Hood would attack it in force, I telegraphed the general commanding (Maj. Gen. George H. Thomas) asking for reenforcements of 2,000 infantry and, if possible, 1,000 cavalry. My garrison at this time (Post Decatur) consisted of 102nd Ohio Infantry, 18th Michigan Infantry, 10th Indiana Cavalry, 2nd Tennessee Cavalry, Battery A-1st Tennessee Light artillery, Battery F-1st Ohio Light artillery, and Battery D-2nd Illinois Light Artillery, in all, 1,500 effective men. I had also upon the line of railroad between Athens and Stevenson the 73rd Indiana Infantry, 13th Wisconsin Veteran Volunteer Infantry, and parts of the 11th, 12th, and 13th Indiana Cavalry...I had also upon the river two companies of the 13th Wisconsin Veteran Volunteer Infantry at Whitesburg, another at Claysville...and one Company of the 73rd Indiana Infantry at Triana. I could withdraw only a small portion of the above named forces for concentration upon any threatened point." In fact, Granger could only send 300 of those to Decatur, increasing his force there to just 1,800.

"With this small force," Granger lamented, "I was obliged to man a line of works with a continuous front of 1,600 yards (almost a mile) exclusive of the river." In fact, Post Decatur, which changed hands eight times during the war, was one of the largest of it's kind in Southern States, the only major fort south of the Tennessee River. Morever, in his District of Northern Alabama, General Granger - by order of Major General George H. Thomas - also had set up a strong picket-post at Brown's Ferry and was intensely patrolling the Tennessee River shoreline from there to Decatur. Above that point the gunboats General Thomas and Stone River were patrolling the river itself as thoroughly as two boats could do.

On Monday, October 24, 1864, the commanding officer at Whitesburg reported 15,000 of General Hood's army at Long Hollow..., intending to cross the Tennessee River at different points between Paint Rock and Decatur, Alabama. "Fully believing, however,"that the enemy...was moving upon this place (Post Decatur) as fast as the roads would permit, I again sent (General Thomas) an urgent request...that strong reenforcements be immediately sent me." Thomas ordered the 29th Michigan Volunteer Infantry Regiment to Decatur.

On Tuesday, October 25th, General Granger requested another 1,000 men from Colonel Sipes command at Columbia... which could not be sent. On that same afternoon Granger took a train to Huntsville to see for himself that defenses of his limited command were set up as well as possible. At 7 p.m. he requested 2,000 more reenforcements.

On the afternoon of Wednesday, October 26th a telegram from Colonel Doolittle, commanding at Decatur, brought news that 500 Rebels had indeed attacked pickets there. "I did not think the attack as yet serious," said Granger, " as it could hardly be more than an advance of Hood's army." Nevertheless, General Granger took every man Huntsville could spare and headed to Decatur, arriving at 5 p.m. That small initial fight was just ending as he came back into the post.

During that night of Wednesday, October 26, 1864 the gunboat Stone River brought 1,200 men of the 102nd Ohio and 18th Michigan. A Detachment numbering 80 men of the 73rd Indiana arrived by train from Athens.

With daylight on the morning of Thursday, October 27th, Union defenders of Post Decatur found thousands of Rebels in position in front of them...stretching in a line from the Tennessee River on their left past the Somerville and Courtland Roads, covering two thirds of their front. During the day the remainder of General Hood's army arrived, covering the other third of the front...comprising an enormous force of about 35,000 Confederate troops.

Little fighting occurred that day, as Rebel commanders waited for the entire force to arrive and get into position... although the right of the Union picket line was forced back by Rebel attackers..."but in the afternoon was most gallantly recovered by detachment of the 73rd Indiana Infantry." Which men? Records do not identify them, but Union reenforcements continued to trickle in during the day...295 of the 14th U.S. Colored Infantry under Colonel J. T. Morgan. (Author's note: Northern citizens said their main fight was to free slaves, and they did allow Black Americans to join the Union army..., not in rank with white troops, however, but in separate Regiments. It is also a matter of history that a number of Black Americans in their Southern homeland joined Confederate Regiments, clearly though, in much fewer numbers) There were also 195 men of the 68th Indiana Infantry under Lt. Col. H. J. Espy, and about 70 men of the 13th Indiana Cavalry equipped as infantry under Captain Wilson. Another detachment of the 73rd Indiana Infantry arrived under Lieutenant Colonel A. B. Wade making about 150 of the 73rd Indiana. We know the Boys From Lake County were there, as confirmed in the "History of Lake County." This made a total Union force defending Decatur of only about 3,000 men.

In those years the area around Post Decatur had been fully cleared for a distance of 2400 feet..."almost a level plain, entirely unobstructed." At that point was a ravine and creek..., "commencing on our left and running across the Somerville, Moulton, and Courtland Roads." Beyond the ravine the ground rose in a sparsely wooded slope for 2100 feet..., "bounded by a dense wood stretching across our entire front, and, bending northward, finds the river at a distance of 1,000 yards upon our right."

About 3 a. m. on the morning of Friday, October 28, 1864 Post Decatur and it's surrounding area was completely enveloped in a dense river fog. Under cover of fog Rebels charged Union picket lines, drove them back toward the fort, capturing the ravine and establishing a line of rifle pits all across the front of Post Decatur. In the rifle pits were three full brigades of Confederate infantry and sharpshooters.

About 9 a. m. the fog cleared, so Union officers could see what had happened. "It became evident immediately," General Granger said, "that it was absolutely necessary to dislodge the enemy from this position, as they perfectly covered every gun (cannon) in our principal fort (there were actually three forts at Fort Decatur) and would soon render it impossible to work them with accuracy." With 35,000 Rebel attackers facing his 3,000 Union defenders inside Post Decatur, Granger's problem was enormous. Rising fully to the occasion, however, the General displayed unwavering fortitude, aggressiveness, and an unfailing grasp of military battle tactics...meshing several commands into one slashing counter-attack

"I directed all cannon in the fort within range," General Granger said, "to be shotted with canister (shrapnel) and train (aim) on the rifle pits and fire with the greatest rapidity as soon as the little charging column should make it's appearance." He then ordered the cannon in Fort #2 to load with explosive shells and fire into the right of the rifle pits at the same time. The banks of Fort Decatur were lined with riflemen, ordered to pour a withering rifle fire into the pits as soon as the Confederates showed their heads. Granger then sent the 18th Michigan Regiment (much reduced) with detachments of the 102nd Ohio and 13th Wisconsin, commanded by Captain Moore of the 18th Michigan to sneak up quietly on rifle pits in the ravine under cover of the edge of the river bank. Granger backed up the sneak attack column with another 500 men headed by Lt. Col Thornburgh. To that he added his picket lines and 50 cavalry. The idea was to head out in support of the first column as soon as the sneak attack was discovered by Rebels. At the appointed moment, Moore and his men jumped up and surged forward... giving a shrill yell which was echoed by every man on the rifle lines at Post Decatur.

"The enemy." said General Granger, "surprised and panic-stricken by this impudent movement, rushed from the pits only to encounter a most terrible and well directed fire of shell, canister, and musketry. Large numbers were killed or wounded, while others threw down their arms, and waving their hats in a token of surrender, ran toward our advancing column." In fact, according to Granger, the little band of Union attackers swept almost the entire length of the first line of Rebel rifle pits, up to the very teeth of his main lines, where Captain Moore (his command reduced by ½ because of having to guard the captured prisoners) commenced slowly retreating, covered by the second supporting Union force on his left. The huge Confederate force made no attempt to charge in counter-attack.

Captain Moore, "returned to the fort," Granger related, "having thoroughly cleared this line of the enemy's works, captured 120 men, including 5 commissioned officers, killed or wounded a very large number, with only a loss of 3 men slightly wounded."

With 35,000 troops, why did the Rebel army not counterattack immediately? No record explains why. There are highly likely reasons. First, the stunning surprise of the Union attack, the sudden loss of their position of great advantage, the large number of Confederate men killed, wounded and captured, the intensity of the Union assault. Second, even though their force was enormous the Confederate commander could not know for sure how many Union riflemen were waiting to fire at them from Post Decatur. He had already seen the power of their cannon and the assured determination of their attack. Third, the 2400 feet of open ground an attacking force must traverse to Post Decatur, leaving them wide open to slaughter by rifle fire and cannon loaded with shrapnel. Fourth, since Post Decatur was an important, but incidental target on the way to Nashville, Rebel commanders would not want to lose large numbers of their force.

Even so, the fight was not quite over. During night hours General Granger found that the Confederates had set up a battery of eight cannon on Post Decatur's left flank close to the Tennessee River. Somewhat protected by trees and hilly ground, the battery was just 1,500 yards (an easy cannon shot) from Post Decatur's main front of defense, it's cannon fire also able to reach the entire length of a Union pontoon bridge over the river, and within a short 600 yard cannon range of any gunboat which might be on the river. Rebels then set up a line of rifle pits linking the battery to their main lines and nearly surrounding Post Decatur.

In clever response, during the same night hours, General Granger sent a detachment of Battery A, 1st Tennessee Artillery under Captain Beach across the Tennessee River and ordered it set up behind quickly dug earthworks to aim a crossfire into the rebel cannon battery and rifle pits. The hurried fortification was superintended by Lieutenant Thornburgh, chief of Granger's Union Cavalry. The next morning, Friday, October 28, 1864, "as soon as the fog lifted," Granger said, "this section began to play upon the enemy most successfully, preventing him from getting any more guns into position or using those already in position against our bridge." Granger immediately ordered the 14th U. S. Colored Infantry Regiment to charge the Rebel cannon battery along with a 500 man force in support. Across the river Captain Beach's cannon opened a rapid fire. Captain Naylor of the gunboat Stone River moved in and fired away also, while yet a third battery of cannon moved forward from Post Decatur Fort #2 blasted into the Rebel cannon battery and rifle pits at the same time.

"It was impossible for the enemy to remain in their works under this galling crossfire," General Granger reported. "Under cover of it, the 14th U. S. Colored Infantry Regiment charged in splendid style, captured the battery, made 14 prisoners, and killed and wounded a large number of men. They spiked two guns (cannon)...the enemy rallying and coming upon them in largely superior numbers, they were forced to retire. This they did in good order, bringing their prisoners with them without having a single man captured." Union losses during that assault were 52 killed and wounded, that of the Rebel army much greater. One shell from Captain Beach's cannon across the river exploded a caisson (ammunition wagon) in the Union battery killing 14 men. Granger also related that cannon fire from the gunboats was both accurate and severe, and the Confederate loss must have been very heavy.

"The action of the 14th U. S. Colored Infantry Regiment under Colonel Morgan," General Granger praised, " was everything that could be expected or desired of soldiers. They were cool, brave, and determined, and under heaviest fire of the enemy exhibited no signs of confusion."

During that day, Friday October 28th, more Union reenforcements poured in, joining the line of riflemen on fort banks. There was heavy firing all day from both sides, but the

Rebel army made no effort to charge Post Decatur. About 12 noon Captain Naylor with his gunboat Stone River sailed into position to fire into the rear of Rebel ranks with long range guns. At 3 p.m. the Stone River was joined by the U. S. Steamer General Thomas. Granger sent orders for both gunboats to fire again into the Rebel cannon batteries close to the river, assisted by Captain Beach's cannon across the river and the cannon from Fort #2. Shells fell directly into the Rebel cannon destroying two cannon, killing or wounding many artillerymen, so distracting that Rebel fire toward the gunboats went wild, doing little damage. One shell from the Stone River again exploded a caisson killing 17 men. "It was impossible for men to withstand this attack, "General Granger said, "they deserted their guns, (cannon) a portion of them retreating to their main lines, while many of them rushed down to the bank and sought the protection of trees at the water's edge." Cannon of the gunboats were double shotted with canister (shrapnel) aimed upon troops in the tree line along the river at a distance of scarcely 300 yards, pouring in a "terrible fire." Confederate losses in that brief engagement, about half an hour, "were very severe," General Granger noted. Casualties on the wooden gunboats, although hit a number of times were very slight, 2 killed and 11 wounded.

During dark hours Union forces became aware that some kind of movement was occurring among Confederate forces before them. However, another dense river fog had set in upon Post Decatur, Alabama and it's surrounding area on that night of Friday, October 28, 1864. "On the morning of (Saturday) the 29th" General Granger said, "I became satisfied that the enemy's forces were withdrawing."

To be sure, the Union General again relied on the 14th U. S. Colored Infantry Regiment under Colonel Morgan, who found nothing but a strong rear guard of Rebels. Not surprisingly, the Regiment attacked, but found the Rebel rear guard so strong they were compelled to slowly retreat back to Post Decatur. "I ordered out a strong Regiment to cover his retreat, and he came in, in good order, with but small loss." General Granger said. "At

4 p.m. I sent out a strong detachment and drove the enemy out of his last line of rifle pits, and at dark our original picket line was re-established."

Union losses during the entire attack on Post Decatur were 113 killed, wounded, and taken prisoner. Granger estimated Confederate losses at more than 1,000 men, though a Mobile, Alabama newspaper reported them at 1,500.

A report by Lieutenant Colonel Alfred B. Wade fully confirms that the 73rd Indiana Volunteer Infantry fought in the Battle of Post Decatur and the History of Lake County confirms that our Boys From Lake county were there. "Our loss in the various skirmishes was slight," Colonel Wade said, "being but 1 man killed and 2 slightly wounded. A number were struck by spent balls, but received no injury," No deaths or severe injuries were recorded for Company A.

And so ended the siege of Post Decatur, and with it..., for the Boys From Lake County at least...the last momentous battle of the Civil War. In these last months, though, we've seen how vital was their duty in guarding railroads and bridges along the Tennessee River of Northern Alabama from Confederate attack. And it is clear that small unit patrols, attacks, and fire fights continued on until the last few weeks before their discharge. Though not the Boys From Lake County...the following report is a classic example.

On Thursday, February 16, 1865, Second Lieutenant Willson Dailey from another company of the 73rd Indiana Volunteer Infantry Regiment stationed at Gurley's Tank, Alabama reported that 20 of his men (12 from his command, 8 from Lieutenant Arnold's detachment of pioneers), led by Sergeant Daniel Hensley, had fought and repulsed 50 Rebels of Russel's 4th Alabama Cavalry. Searching for forage (horse feed) they'd been sent to the plantation of a Mr. Peebe, 3 1/2 miles from Gurley's Tank, on the Brownsborough Road. On their return they were attacked by the detachment of 4th Alabama Cavalry under the command of Captain Britton and Lieutenant Olds. Sergeant Hensley's detachment kept up a running fight until gaining cover of woods. After a stubborn fight they repulsed the Rebels, losing only 2 Enfield rifles and equipments as two of their men were captured...but soon escaped and came in. Casualties of the enemy were 1 man killed (Jack Hickman, 4th Alabama Cavalry) and one man wounded (Allen Grant, 4th Alabama Cavalry). "Peebe was recognized by one of our escaped prisoners as one of the attacking party," Lt. Dailey said. "I should like to have the privilege of destroying his plantation."

Although not our Boys From Lake County, this report of one other 73rd Indiana Company tells us several notable things. In addition to recording an example of the kinds of small fire fights which often occurred in Northern Alabama during the Civil War's closing months...it also memorializes the names of four men of the Confederate 4th Alabama Cavalry...two officers in command, one cavalryman who lost his life in combat, and one who was wounded in the last months of War. Further, it tells us that at least some soldiers of the 73rd Indiana Volunteers were equipped with far better weapons by the end of the War. The imported British Enfield rifle was one of the best weapons of the conflict.

A month or so earlier, in September 1864, the Boys From Lake County and others of their 73rd Indiana Infantry were ordered to take and hold the small town of Prospect, Tennessee, and defend it from Forrest's attack, which was successfully done. We did not find a record of this small engagement in Union Army reports. It was a detail of their years of Civil War service related for the History of Lake County when the boys of the Company A returned home. In the winter of 1864-1865 the Boys From Lake County with their 73rd Indiana Infantry were assigned to Stevenson, Alabama...then to Huntsville...then to guard the Mobile & Charleston Railroad and headquartered at Larkinsville, Alabama. The pension records of Private Wilson Shannon Baughman of Company A confirm each of these stations.

At some point in the seven weeks after Lieutenant General Nathan Bedford Forrest surrendered the last Confederate forces at Pond Springs, Alabama on Tuesday, May 9, 1865, the Boys From Lake County and their fellow soldiers of the 73rd Volunteer Infantry Regiment "rode the cars" to Nashville, Tennessee and were discharged from the Union Army on Saturday, July 1, 1865.

And by the way, Sergeant Daniel Hart Hensley...who led the detachment of 20 men of the 73rd Indiana from Gurley's Tank, Alabama on Thursday, February 16, 1865...was born in Logansport, Indiana on January 10, 1844. His father, Richard Hensley, born in Virginia, brought up in Kentucky, emigrated to Logansport in 1829. His mother, Frances Mull, was born in North Carolina. Daniel received a common school education. At 18 years of age, In July 1862, he enlisted under Colonel Gilbert Hathaway into the 73rd Indiana Volunteer Infantry Regiment as a Private...later promoted to Sergeant. Although we have not yet been able to find which of the 73rd Indiana's Regiments was raised in Logansport, Cass County, Indiana...we do know that Daniel shared all of the experiences of the Boys From Lake County which we have described, serving through the entire three years of the Civil War. At War's end, he was discharged with them in Nashville on Saturday, July 1, 1865. On December 25, 1867 he married Miss Eliza A. Mundorff. By the early 1880's Daniel and Eliza had been residents of Hamilton, Butler County, Ohio for ten years. At that time they had two children, Leroy R. Hensley - age 13, and Mabel M. Hensley - age 1. In Hamilton, Daniel was the Secretary of the Gas Works Company, a member of the Odd Fellows, commander of the Grand Army of the Republic, and a member of the First Baptist Church.

Chapter Fifteen

Forrest's Final Address
To His Troops

Late in the era of the 1960's one major American political party began a campaign to, in effect, re-play the Civil War, splintering the unified spirit of our great Nation into a number of segmented, voracious, savagely self-serving, "special interest" groups...all seemingly with little concern for the heritage of strength and unity which is America.

As a direct consequence, and as our Nation has moved beyond the enormous human advances of the 20th Century, on into the 3rd Millenium, many in those groups have taken to fanatically vilifying the integrity, the flag, the patriotism, and courage with which Southerners fought for their view of the future of America during the years 1861 to 1865.

In the intriguing exploration of the records of America's great Civil War, a researcher sometimes comes across a document which so vibrantly describes the gallantry, heartfelt patriotism, and personal integrity..., as well as the monumental Individual courage..., with which the horrendous confrontation between our North and South was fought by soldiers and commanders of both sides...as to be breathtaking.

The following brief address by famed Confederate Cavalry General Nathan Bedford Forrest to his troops at the time of their surrender on Tuesday May 9, 1865 is one of the most telling of those documents we have found. It beams with belief in the American spirit and in a sense of unity for the American experience that was truly never lost... either before, during, or after the Civil War...until that splintering, special interest group, era beginning in the 1960's, and still devastating to America in this Year of our Lord, 2006.

General Forrest's words to his men are, surely, fully commensurate with the magnanimous spirit and human kindness of Union General Ulysses S. Grant toward the Confederate soldiers of General Robert E. Lee as he accepted Lee's surrender at Appomattox, Virginia one month before, on Sunday, April 9, 1865.

HEADQUARTERS FORREST'S CAVALRY CORPS,
Gainesville, Ala., May 9, 1865.

SOLDIERS: By an agreement made between Lieutenant-General Taylor, commanding the Department of Alabama, Mississippi, and East Louisiana, and Major-General Canby, commanding U.S. forces, the troops of this department have been surrendered.

I do not think it proper or necessary at this time to refer to the causes which have reduced us to this extremity, nor is it now a matter of material consequence to us how such results were brought about.

That we are beaten is a self-evident fact, and any further resistance on our part would be justly regarded as the very height of folly and rashness. The armies of Generals Lee and Johnston having surrendered, you are the last of all the troops of the C. S. Army east of the Mississippi River to lay down your arms.

The cause for which you have so long and so manfully struggled, and for which you have braved dangers, endured privations and sufferings, and made so many sacrifices, is to-day hopeless.

The Government which we sought to establish and perpetuate is at an end. Reason dictates and humanity demands that no more blood be shed. Fully realizing and feeling that such is the case, it is your duty and mine to lay down our arms, submit to the "powers that be," and to aid in restoring peace and establishing law and order throughout the land.

The terms upon which you were surrendered are favorable, and should be satisfactory and acceptable to all. They manifest a spirit of magnanimity and liberality on the part of the Federal authorities which should be met on our part by a faithful compliance with all the stipulations and conditions therein expressed. As your commander, I sincerely hope that every officer and soldier of my command will cheerfully obey the orders given and carry out in good faith all the terms of the cartel.

Those who neglect the terms and refuse to be paroled may assuredly expect when arrested to be sent North and imprisoned. Let those who are absent from their commands, from whatever cause, report at once to this place or to Jackson, Miss.; or, if too remote from either, to the nearest U.S. post or garrison for parole.

Civil War, such as you have just passed through, naturally engenders feelings of animosity, hatred, and revenge. It is our duty to divest ourselves of all such feelings, and so far as in our power to do so to cultivate friendly feelings toward those with whom we have so long contested and heretofore so widely but honestly differed. Neighborhood feuds, personal animosities, and private differences should be blotted out, and when you return home a manly, straightforward course of conduct will secure the respect even of your enemies.

Whatever your responsibilities may be to Government, to society, or to individuals, meet them like men. The attempt made to establish a separate and independent confederation has failed, but the consciousness of having done your duty faithfully and to the end will in some measure repay for the hardships you have undergone.

In bidding you farewell, rest assured that you carry with you my best wishes for your future welfare and happiness. Without in any way referring to the merits of the cause in which we have been engaged, your courage and determination as exhibited on many hard-fought fields has elicited the respect and admiration of friend and foe. And I now cheerfully and gratefully acknowledge my indebtedness to the officers and men of my command, whose zeal, fidelity, and unflinching bravery have been the great source of my past success in arms.

I have never on the field of battle sent you where I was unwilling to go myself, nor would I now advise you to a course which I felt myself unwilling to pursue. You have been good soldiers, you can be good citizens. Obey the laws, preserve your honor, and the Government to which you have surrendered can afford to be and will be magnanimous.

N. B. FORREST,
Lieutenant-General

Private Wilson Shannon Baughman, wife Sarah Jane Corkings (Caulkins) Baughman. Children, top right to left, to right…David D., Ida Jane, James Wilson, Frank E., William E. Circa 1882

Chapter Sixteen

Private Wilson Shannon Baughman

Private Wilson Shannon Baughman, Company A, 73rd Indiana Volunteer Infantry Regiment was this writer's Great-Grandfather. These inclusions of a soldier's family, his war, the effects of it, and his life afterward are not shared to aggrandize him, nor those of us who follow.

Needless to say, after more than one hundred and forty years, life's daily tasks, joys, and tribulation are for most... save the relatively few of high rank, fame, or wealth... lost to the knowledge and understanding of succeeding generations. Indeed, after such a long span of years, it is perplexing even to imagine what life was like "back then."

It is a rare occurrence to find 233 pages recording many daily happenings, 140 years and more past, in the life of a person of average means. Our hope is that sharing such will better distinguish all who lived, or fought, in the time of America's Civil War.

And too, it is easy, as we write these words in the year 2006, to think of the Civil War era as a time when most were newly emigrated to America. For some, perhaps many, that was true. In fact, the reader may note that several of the Boys From Lake County were actually born in Germany, Prussia, and Canada. For a great many others, though, families had already been in America for generations.

In records of the year 1800, in Somerset County (just five years before, a part of Bedford County) Pennsylvania, there appears the name Christian Baughman as well as a son Christian.

Far earlier in our Nation's past, on Wednesday, November 20, 1717 a Pennsylvania Warrant was issued to "Michael Baughman of Strasburg in the County of Chester" authorizing him to take up 400 acres "amongst the late surveys made near Conestoga." In 1718 he was listed among the "Dutch Inhabitants" of Conestoga Township, Chester County, which became Manheim Township of Lancaster County, Pennsylvania.

Baughman was listed in histories of early Pennsylvania counties as a "Swiss Mennonite family name of German origin." The name is originally pronounced "Boff-man" although this writer's father changed the pronunciation to "Bo-man" during the First World War, and some others have done so. Other branches of the family spelled the name Boughman, Bachman, Bachmann, Bochman, Bockman, Backman, Bauchman, Baukman, Bowghman, and Bowman. The Bachman and similar spellings are pronounced "Bok-man," as Baughman sometimes is also. Neighboring English settlers referred to the family as "Pennsylvania Dutch." However, they had distorted the word "Deutsch," meaning German. It is thought the Baughman-Bachman family originated at Bottenstein in the Canton of Aargau, Switzerland. Expanding into border areas of France, perhaps Alsace-Lorraine, many fled as religious refugees into the Palatinate area of Germany. It was from there that they began to emigrate into America in the early 1700's. They were considered then to have been among the world's best farmers.

History does not yet reveal whether Michael Baughman sold land holdings in Germany and came to America with substantial wealth. Considering his wide involvement in land ownership, that certainly seems likely. Or it could be, of course, that he just had a genius for land investment. Whichever the case... in a few years on the new American frontier of Pennsylvania, Michael Baughman, with his wife Katherine, gathered into his possession huge tracts of fine land, which he parceled out to his ten children, Anna, Michael Jr., Christian, John, Elizabeth, Barbara, Lissey, Veronica, Magdalena, and Peter. In 1739

Michael and Katherine are recorded as having purchased 1500 acres for 5,000 British Pounds, quite a fortune in itself in that era. As the original three Pennsylvania counties subdivided into many others, the huge land holdings of Michael and Katherine Baughman, and that of their ten children, fell under the names of new counties. In fact, the names of Michael, Katherine, and their offspring appear numerous times in the early land records of Pennsylvania, especially in Lancaster and Lebanon counties prior to 1750. On Friday, March 28, 1755 Michael Baughman made his will naming his wife Katherine and their ten children as heirs, although the brothers and sisters had already been deeded large tracts of land.

Michael and Katherine's son Christian was born "prior to 1730" in Pennsylvania and lived the longest of any of his nine siblings, passing away in 1811 in Lancaster County. His wife Elizabeth had died a year or so earlier.

It appears..., though considering the lapse of 200 years we've not yet been able to certify it..., that the Christian Baughman in Somerset County was that son of Michael and Catherine, moving back to the family's original home in Manheim from Somerset County in his early to mid 80's, perhaps after his own son Christian waggoned west. Even so, if he was not that son of Michael and Katherine, his branch of the Baughman family was sure to have been related...either there in Pennsylvania, or back in Europe.

What is certain, is that the younger Christian Baughman and his wife Fanny moved from Somerset County, Pennsylvania to New Philadelphia, Muskingham (later Tuscarawas) County Ohio, leaving the father Christian behind. Son Christian is recorded as having bought land in New Philadelphia in 1801 and apparently moved then, or by 1803, about the time Ohio entered the Union as a State.

Christian and Fanny took with them their first child, eldest son, Jacob, born in 1798. In Ohio, Jacob's brothers Samuel M.-born in 1808, James, John, and Christian were born along with several sisters. Jacob married Sarah "Sally" Ritter in Tuscarawas County in 1818. Also in Tuscarawas County, Ohio, Thursday, June 24, 1830 son Samuel M. Baughman married Rebecca Woods, born in Pennsylvania. On Sunday, April 10, 1831 son Christian Baughman married Catherine Noel. On Tuesday, September 1, 1840 son John Baughman married Elizabeth Overholt. Records seem to indicate that young Christian and Catherine remained in New Philadelphia... where estate records show his father passed away in 1830. Brothers Jacob, Samuel, James, and John went north a few miles into Ashland and Richland County, Ohio as land owners...farmers. Jacob and Samuel are recorded as owning land together there. Brothers John and James Baughman remained as Ashland County, Ohio residents.

And so, in the 1850 records of Ashland County, Ohio we find the household of Samuel M. Baughman - age 41, his wife Rebecca - age 45, and their six children, Phoebe Elizabeth - age 9, Wilson Shannon - age 8, Thomas Jefferson - age 7, Oliver P. - age 5, and Francis Marion - age 2. From this we hazard a guess that Samuel's middle name might also have been Marion. Wilson Shannon Baughman was born in Tuscarawas County on Sunday, January 30, 1842. Some of his younger brothers and sisters were likely born in Ashland County.

Brothers Jacob and Samuel, though, soon had their eyes on farmland opening westward in the newer frontier of Indiana. On Saturday, September 23, 1848 Jacob Baughman is recorded as having bought 240 acres of land in Section 32, West Creek Township near Lowell Indiana. At about the same time he apparently bought land in nearby Valparaiso, Porter County, living there for about two years.

Jacob and Sarah, Wilson's Uncle and Aunt, did not move immediately to their farm in West Creek, near Lowell. In 1850 we find them sharing a household in Valparaiso, Porter County, Indiana with their recently widowed son-in-law Daniel Fry, and their grandson Urias. Daniel Fry had married their daughter Mary in Tuscarawas County, Ohio, but Mary Baughman Fry had died in Valparaiso. It may be that Jacob and Sarah went to Valparaiso to help out during her illness.

It was not until 1851 that Jacob 1st and Sarah "Sally" Ritter Baughman moved to the West Creek farm near Lowell with their children, one of whom was that son Jacob 2nd, first cousin to Wilson Shannon Baughman. Son-in-law Daniel Fry and grandson Urias moved from Valparaiso to Lowell then also.

Samuel, his wife Rebecca Woods Baughman and their six children also moved to Lowell about that time, along with Jacob's brother-in-law John Ritter and his family. John's wife was Sarah "Sally" Ritter Baughman's sister. Jacob and John Ritter are recorded as among the most noted early settlers of Lowell... Samuel Baughman less mentioned. The Baughman and Ritter families had evidently been close friends and neighbors as far back as Bedford County, Pennsylvania. It is also clear that some close member of their Baughman family took up expansive farmland at Ligonniere, Indiana east of Lowell in Noble County.

In the 1860 records of Lowell, West Creek Township, Lake County, Indiana, just before the outbreak of America's Civil War... we find the household of Samuel M. Baughman at age 52, his wife Rebecca Woods Baughman - age 56, with now five of their children... Wilson Shannon - age 18, Thomas Jefferson - age 16, Oliver P. - age 15, and Francis Marion - age 12. Phoebe Elizabeth was 19 by then and had married Thomas Johnston on Thursday, December 15, 1859.

(Author's note: In the year 1870 we found Samuel at age 62, his wife Rebecca at age 66 with just one offspring left at home to help with the farm, son Thomas Jefferson at age 27. They were still in West Creek Township near Lowell.

By 1880 Samuel M. Baughman at age 72, and his wife Rebecca Woods Baughman at age 76, were alone, moved to Cedar Creek Township, also near Lowell, where his nephew Jacob 2nd owned a farm. Samuel no longer listed himself as a farmer, but as a brickmason. He also noted that he had the "Shaking Palsy." If that medical condition had been a severe nervous system ailment such as Parkinson's Disease, Samuel surely would not have been able to list himself as a working tradesman. What he may have suffered is an inheritable condition physicians now call Essential Tremor...a very frustrating unsteadiness of the hands (under effort) rather than a life threatening illness. It is one which we now know has touched four of us in later generations of Samuel Baughman's family. We can find no record of the passing of Samuel and Rebecca in Lowell...rather indications that they may have followed a son westward to Kansas or Iowa frontier farmland.)

In the Civil War year of 1862, Wilson Shannon Baughman, at the age of 20...the eldest son of Samuel M. and Rebecca Woods Baughman...joined, not one, but two Union Army Volunteer Regiments. It is an irrefutable example of the patriotic fervor that swept so many young men of America as the ferocity of that War became evident.

First, Wilson traveled back to Ashland County, Ohio to join Company F, 88th Ohio Volunteer Infantry Regiment with his 22 year old cousin James Baughman. He listed his residence as Ashland County, Ohio, his occupation as "shoemaker."

The 88th Ohio was mustered in for only 3 months, as many early Northern Volunteer Regiments were. Northerners felt sure the first time the glorious Union Army attacked, Rebel "riffraff militias" would flee the battlefield in panic, and the War would be over. As we've mentioned before, very early in the Civil War, the 24,000 Union and Confederate soldiers killed, wounded, captured, and missing in the horrific, bloody, battle of Shiloh Church in Tennessee, near the Mississippi border gave Northerners a shocking perspective of the courage, determination, and fighting ability of their Southern brethren. Army enlistments changed to three years.

Furthermore, the 88th Ohio was mustered in for the purpose of guarding the prisoner of war facility at Camp Chase, Columbus, Ohio. Clearly both Baughman cousins quickly decided they did not want to stand around doing guard duty...they wanted to go to war. It is also evident that someone back home in Lowell, Lake

County, Indiana wrote or telegraphed Wilson of the formation of the 73rd Indiana Volunteers.

Long before his three months were up, Wilson had obtained permission from officers of the 88th Ohio and was back home in Lake County, enlisting in (Captain Krimball's) Company A of the 73rd Indiana Volunteer Infantry Regiment. His cousin James transferred to Company B, 87th Ohio Volunteer Infantry Regiment.

We've followed Private Wilson Shannon Baughman through three years of Civil War service as one of the Boys From Lake County, Company A, 73rd Indiana Volunteers...sometimes on an hour by hour basis. We've followed him back to Nashville, Tennessee where he was mustered out of the Regiment on July 1, 1865 after surrender of Confederate forces and the end of America's bloodiest of all wars. Likely Wilson, and the other Boys From Lake County who remained of Company A, "rode the cars" soon after, back home to Lake County, Indiana. It will be almost four years until we learn of him again.

During those three battle scarred years of the Civil War, Wilson's cousin Jacob 2nd -13 years older - did not share Wilson's passion for war. Jacob was busy prospecting (very successfully) for gold. Clearly, the first gold rush of 1849 had struck his fancy. But it was not until 1852, when Jacob was 23 years old, that he headed to the gold fields of California with his brother and two others. Unfortunately the history of Lowell does not name which brother, or the others, who went with Jacob.

However, they went by way of New York (likely by train), took a ship from there to the Isthmus of Panama, crossed that narrow strip of land, and took yet another ship to San Francisco. It was not the travel format of "poor" young men in those wild west years. From San Francisco the four went to Dry Creek..., then to Sierra County, California near Donner Pass and mined the Yuba River west of there with "good success." From the Yuba River they moved to Lost Hill near Bakersfield, then to Bush Creek. Jacob mined in California for seven years before returning to Lowell. According to an 1884 history, "they returned in 1859, much better off."

With his gold, Jacob bought land in Kankakee, Illinois, thirty miles or so west of Lowell and farmed there for three years. However in 1860 at the age of 29 he was listed as living in the household of his sister Catherine and brother-in-law Abiel G. Plummer and their children in West Creek Township near Lowell. That likely was on the farm which had been owned by his father Jacob who died in 1855. In 1862 while cousin Wilson headed off to the Civil War with the other Boys From Lake County, Jacob heard of another gold strike in Idaho. He and his fellow prospectors from Lowell headed out overland this time, driving wagons and ox teams to pay their way. They followed the famous Bridger Trail, still just an old Indian path in those years.

According to Lowell historian Richard C. Schmal, after two months of "adventures and suffering" Wilson Shannon Baughman's cousin Jacob and his little group reached Virginia City, Nevada site of the famous "Comstock Lode" gold find. Virginia City was a clamorous place then, populated by nearly 30,000. With enormous gold wealth unfolding, there were visits by famous people, Shakespeare plays, opium dens, newspapers, several fire departments, fraternal organizations, a booming district of prostitutes, and a six story hotel named the International, housing the West's first elevator, called a "rising room."

Jacob mined just two months there at Alder Gulch, moving again to "his old haunts" at Nevada City, California, north of Sacramento. In 1864 he traveled to Salt Lake City, Utah...then to find "good diggings" at Black Gulch, Idaho. From there he went to mine at Helena and Silver City, Montana. Eventually he headed back home to Lowell, Indiana via the Missouri River and famous Fort Benton, the trading post in North Central Montana which was the main "port of entry" for the 1860's Western gold mining rush.

The towns through which Jacob passed were governed by the old Law of the West with marshals, vigilantes, and hangings. Jacob Baughman, the miner from Lake County, must have seen it all. Lake County historian Weston A. Goodspeed said in 1884, "Mr. Baughman had a mining experience, perhaps not equaled by any man in Lake County. He has toiled, suffered, and has been rewarded."

At age 39, on Thursday, May 28, 1868, Jacob married Emma Dodge, daughter of Henry L. and Mary L. Dodge, also very early settlers of Lowell. They had just one child, son Henry Lancaster Baughman, born in 1869. In 1870 Jacob and Emma left their West Creek farm and moved into town, with a 1909 address of Main Street near Clark Street in Lowell. With at least three major land holdings, Jacob was also recorded in 1900 at about age 70 as being the president of a new bank opening in Lowell. Another old Lake County history said, "Jacob Baughman was one of the self-made and substantial men of Lake County."   The first Baughman Indiana connection in Valparaiso must have been very long lasting. Jacob Baughman called Lowell home most of his life. Yet, he passed away in his sleep in June of 1917 at age 87, while "temporarily living" in Valparaiso. The night before he had walked up town and seemed in his usual health. His wife Emma Dodge Baughman had died in Lowell five years before, in 1912.

The two Baughman cousins shared a lust for adventure, Jacob for the West and gold mining, Wilson Shannon Baughman for the battlefields of America's Civil War. Like so many of the more than 600,000 casualties of the War, though, Wilson paid a severe price for his courage and devotion to our Nation. When he was mustered out of Co A, 73rd Indiana Volunteer Infantry Regiment on Saturday, July 1, 1865, Wilson returned home to the farm at West Creek Township near Lowell, Indiana a sick young man. As noted before, nearly four years passed before we find record of him again...except for reports of that illness.

On Tuesday, March 2, 1869 Wilson Shannon Baughman and Sarah Jane Corkings took out a marriage license signed by William W. Cheshire, Clerk of the Lake County Circuit Court. Sarah Jane was born on Thursday, May 18, 1848 in Oneida Village, Oneida County, New York. Her father, Daniel Corkings, was born on Wednesday, December 25, 1799 and lived 80 years 1 month and 2 days. Her mother, Catherine Jane Wilson was born in Canada on Wednesday, July 27, 1808 and lived 87 years 11 months and 25 days...having moved with her family to Lowell, Indiana after a second marriage to a man named Firth. (So now we know where Wilson Shannon Baughman's first name came from. Wilson's son Earl C. Baughman of Saint Petersburg, Florida told us when he was 95 that a forebear of Catherine Jane Wilson was married to an Irish sailor...leading to a guess that the name Shannon was also passed down in the family.)

On Wednesday, March 10, 1869, Wilson and Sarah Jane were married in the Lake Prairie Presbyterian Church in Lowell by the Reverend Hiram G. Wason. Reverend Wason had retired as pastor of the church. However the new pastor had left after just two years and Wason was filling in as temporary pastor until another one could be assigned. There was another reason for Wilson and Sarah Jane to seek his blessings on their marriage. Hiram Wason was also a long time friend of the Baughman family... owning a neighboring farm in West Creek Township.

From the perspective of the development of our Nation, it is of vital note that exactly three months later...to the day... on Thursday, June 10, 1869 construction teams moving both East and West met at Provo, Utah completing the first trans-continental railroad. On that day, the time it took to travel across America from shore to shore decreased from about three months to eight days.

On Monday, December 27, 1869, Wilson and Sarah's first child, son David D. Baughman was born in West Creek Township, near Lowell.

On Monday, July 10, 1871, James Wilson Baughman was born there. Much of his adventurous life is recorded in the Dedication for this book. Like his father's cousin Jacob Baughman, he intensely loved America's untamed West

On Saturday, January 18, 1873 daughter Ida Jane Baughman joined the family. She eventually married George G. Thigpen and moved to Jacksonvlle, Florida where he apparently worked in the sawmill industry. Later settling a few miles south at East Palatka, Florida, Ida Jane became the most successful of Grandfather's family, a large landowner, astute business woman, relatively wealthy, and Postmistress of East Palatka.

On Monday, August 17, 1874 son Frank E. Baughman came along.

About 1878 Wilson and Sarah Jane left home in Lowell, headed west with their young family to Rothville, Chariton County, Missouri...buying 40 acres of farm land from William and Mary C. Eastman. They were following Sarah Jane's sister Henrietta who had married John F. Miller also in West Creek Township, Lowell, Indiana. Like Wilson, John Miller was a Civil War veteran serving as a Private in Company G, 12th Indiana Cavalry Regiment as a Wagoner M.D. (Mule Driver) He had enrolled at West Creek Township for a three year term, mustered in on Friday, December 25, 1863, and (eventually) paid a bounty of $300. At the end of the Civil War he was discharged on Friday, November 10, 1865. However, on that date he had been absent from his unit, ill, and in the U. S. General Hospital at Memphis, Tennessee since Friday, September 15, 1865.

In Chariton County, Missouri, Wilson and Sarah Jane's 40 acre farm was located about a mile West of the 80 acre farm of John and Henrietta Miller "on the road to Rothville." There Wilson built "a small house, with wide boards up and down, 4 rooms, with a clay stick chimney."

At Rothville, on Thursday, March 4, 1880, son William E. "Will" Baughman was born. (When grown, Will served his own time in the U. S. Army during the Spanish American War of 1898. Later he settled in Montgomery, Alabama and worked as an Engineer on the L&N Railroad until his retirement. His final resting place is in Montgomery."

On Thursday, February 7, 1884 payments to William and Mary C. Eastman were complete and "the North West Quarter of the South East Quarter of Section number thirty five (35) Township number fifty six (56) Range number nineteen (19) containing forty acres more or less except that which has been heretofore deeded to said County for road purposes" was deeded to Wilson S. Baughman. The legal document was notarized by Justice of the Peace T. E. Waugh on Friday, February 8th.

On Sunday, October 12, 1884 son Carey was born.

Just five days later on Friday, October 17, 1884, eldest son David D. Baughman died, just two months short of the age of fifteen. We have found no record of whether his death was caused by illness, or some farm or hunting accident, nor where in Chariton County, Missouri he is interred. There is no doubt, of course, that about Monday, October 20, 1884 Wilson and Sarah Jane, their children, and the Millers were attending David's funeral somewhere near Rothville. We learned only after Grandfather James Wilson Baughman was gone of the life and death of his older brother. We've wondered since why he never spoke of him, or of his other two siblings who did not live to adulthood.

On Monday, August 31, 1885, baby Carey Baughman followed his older brother in death, having lived just 10 ½ months. Again, in the absence of Chariton County records of those years we have not found the cause. We know, of course though, by Tuesday, Wednesday, or Thursday of September, 1885 the Baughman and Miller families were gathered again for a funeral.

On Friday, February 5, 1886 son Earl C. Baughman was born to Wilson and Sarah Jane. Earl was the longest lived of all his family...in reasonably good health at the age of 97. He died at the hands of an 18 year old murderer in St. Petersburg, Florida. The teenager had been hired by Earl's son as a caretaker, but claimed to have a "drug" problem. Earl had retired at about age 65 in the early 1950's after fifty years in Pinellas County real estate. His business letterhead read "E. C. Baughman, Registered Real Estate Broker, Notary Public, Acreage-Homes-Business Property." His motto... "Clean Deals In Dirt." In 1979 he had penciled changes on letter head notations to read 65 years in St. Petersburg, 78 years in Florida. At the age of 97 he was still driving a Cadillac of some vintage. His body was found hidden in the trunk of it.

On the day of Earl's birth Friday, February 5, 1886 his twin sister Pearl was born also...but the baby girl did not live past the day. Another truly puzzling lack of family history from Grandfather, since we also had to learn of this in recent research. James Wilson Baughman, himself, lived well past the age of 84, passing away in St. Petersburg on the last day of 1955.

On Monday, March 12, 1888, the last of Wilson and Sarah Jane's children, daughter Flossie D. Baughman was born in Rothvlle. Flossie also followed her mother and brothers to St. Petersburg, marrying C. D. "Earl" Sands, a long time writer for the famous St. Petersburg Sun-Times newspaper...spending a number of years in Puerto Rico on his reporting assignment there.

It was in the same year, 1888, son James Wilson Baughman left home from Rothville at the age of 17...riding the trans-continental railroad across America to California's Imperial Valley. Again... he never said, but our best guess is that he went to visit his mother's sister Aunt Kate Wilson Parks. The reason? Grandfather said only that he left home because his father was "so mean."

Wednesday, January 16, 1889, discharged Private Wilson Shannon Baughman first applied for a Civil War medical disability pension at age 46. On that day, Wilson and his family still lived on the farm in Rothville, Chariton County, Missouri...but his application was made in the nearby, larger, town of Brookfield, Linn County, Missouri. In that paperwork 25 years after the War, Wilson confirmed that his three life long illnesses began when Company A was guarding Little Limestone Bridge in the area of Decatur and Huntsville, Alabama near the Tennessee River, in the months of July to October 1864. He also confirmed that he had lived in just three towns since 1865...Lowell, Indiana, Burlinghaus, Missouri and Rothville, Missouri. Wilson reasserted something we already know...that he was a farmer when he enlisted in Company A, and had been a farmer in all the years after.

On Friday, February 8, 1889 in Brookfield, Wilson signed a form appointing attorney Charles J. Donnelly of Washington D. C. to handle his pension claim. His signature was notarized by Linn County, Missouri Justice of the Peace, T. C. Waugh and witnessed by Wilson's brother-in-law John F. Miller and neighbor Charles M. Wright. Donnelly was a Washington D. C. law firm apparently specializing in military pension cases. Their fee was $25...paid only if the pension was granted.

On Tuesday, April 16, 1889, in Lake County, Indiana...1st Sgt Oliver G. Wheeler and 2nd Lt George S. Clark , Wilson's officers of 25 years before in Company A provided sworn confirmation of the source of his disability. Wheeler was then 47 years old, living in the Lake County city of Crown Point. Clark was 54, living in Lowell. "In July 1864 at Little Limestone Bridge which Company A were guarding Wilson S. Baughman had infirmation or very sore eyes. He was sent to the Regimental Hospital at Triana on the Tennessee River where he was treated for some time and returned to the Company. But his eyes were still bad and continued so until his discharge. Also about October 1864 at Athens, Alabama, Wilson S. Baughman had chills and diarrhea and was finally sent to Huntsville, Alabama to General Hospital for treatment where he remained for some time." The two fellow Civil War soldiers said they'd known Wilson for 29 years...clearly from two years prior to the date Company A was mustered in. Their document was notarized by George T. Maillet, then Clerk of the Circuit Court in Lake County.

On Tuesday, June 11, 1889 the Bureau of Pensions requested from the War Department, Surgeon General's Office a 25 year old report of hospital treatment. On Friday, June

14, 1889 that document for Wilson, S. Baughman, Private, Company A, 73rd Indiana Regiment, under claim # 688241 was hurried back. It confirmed his hospital stays beginning July 27, 1864, beginning on August 26, 1864...again on September 15-17,1864...,September 28, 1864, and then on June 7-8, 1865, and June 11, 1865.

On Thursday, July 18, 1889, Ralph. W. Bacon, then age 58, a long before neighbor in Lowell, Lake County, Indiana provided notarized confirmation of Wilson's disability after the Civil War. "I was acquainted with said Wilson S. Baughman from the year 1867 until the year 1877 (about when Wilson and Sarah Jane left for Missouri) and lived on the adjoining farm and saw him pretty much every day. During those years we changed work during that time more or less and I knew that he was not well. Knew of his taking medicine more or less during that time. Often heard him complain of not being well and heard him complain of having diarrhea. And I did not consider him able to perform more than one half of an able bodied man's day labor."

On Wednesday, September 25, 1889 Wilson was sent for a physical exam in Laclede, Linn County, Missouri, by Drs. W. P. Spurgeon, J. W. Lane, and H. Shook, apparently comprising an officially appointed committee for pension medical evaluations. His pulse rate was 100, breathing rate 22, temperature 98.5, height 5'8", weight 140, age 47 years. "Eyelids-chronic granulation with marked tendency to ulceration. Inability to bear the light. Enlargement of liver. General condition-pale, anemic. Eyelids granulated so the lid when turned back presented a studded condition. Slight opacity of the cornea as a result of granulation."

On Wednesday, October 16, 1889 Wilson was sent a notice by the Pension Department transferring his attorney of record from Charles J. Donnelly, by virtue of an agreement between Charles J. Donnelly and M. G. Donnelly, to the new firm of Charles J. Donnelly & Company.

As our Nation moved into the era of the Roaring Nineties, on Friday, May 9, 1890 physician J. S. Cater, M. D. of Marceline,

Missouri signed a notarized statement detailing his 18 month treatment of Wilson and confirming other diagnoses.

On Saturday, May 17, 1890 Wilson's neighbors T.W. Morris, age 34, of Chariton County and William Hinkle, age 49, of Linn County gave sworn affidavits as to his disability. Both said they had known him since 1880, that he had always been a farmer until the year 1890 when he became a laborer. They confirmed by "personal observation" the truth of his medical problems.

On Monday, July 7, 1890 Wilson sent a sworn affidavit stating that he could not comply with requirements as to testimony of his Regimental Surgeon as he did not know his name or residence. He also stated that he could not prove his condition from date of discharge to the year 1890 by medical testimony because "medical treatment by physicians was only occasionally had when the disabilities complained of were greatly aggravated. Have doctored myself regularly since my discharge with home remedies and patent medicines. Most notable in this document is that Wilson and Sarah Jane have now sold the farm and moved into town as residents of Brookfield, Missouri. Old family stories tell us that she, with daughter Ida's help, ran a boarding house....while Wilson seems to have worked as he could as a day laborer or carpenter. Son Earl C. Baughman said the two women took in washing and ironing, perhaps as a part of the boarding house business. It must have been a humiliating descent for Private Wilson Shannon Baughman from early years as a strong, healthy farmer and courageous soldier.

On Monday, July 21, 1890 Dr. E. R. Bacon of Lowell, Lake County, Indiana provided a sworn statement for Wilson Shannon Baughman, affirming that he had been acquainted with the soldier for about 21 years... "I have been his family physician from the year of 1869 to 1878 and prescribed for him several times for chronic diarrhea during those years as I was frequently at his home. He also had frequent attacks of inflamation of his eyes but do not remember of prescribing for him but a few times, perhaps twice a year on an average. I did not consider him able to perform more than one-half of an ordinary man's labor, on the account of his chronic diarrhea as treatment seemed to do him but little good."

On Saturday, September 13, 1890 Wilson had to fill out and sign before a notary public yet another sworn application for pension under a new Civil War pension law enacted June 27, 1890. It appears when Congress changed the pension law Wilson had to start all over again.

On Tuesday, September 23, 1890 two neighbors...F. M. Brewer, age 47, of Rothville, and Levi leek, age 46, of Brookfield signed a sworn affidavit as to Wilson's medical condition... "We and each of us became acquainted with claimant in the year 1878 and have lived as neighbors ever since, and have known claimant to be disabled about one-half for the performance of manual labor, during all of said time from 1878 to the present time by reason of chronic diarrhea, sore eyes, and chills and fever. Claimants occupation from 1878 to 1889 was that of a farmer, since that time that of a laborer. Claimants disabilities are increasing with age. Claimants habits are temperate and correct. We know these facts from having lived since 1878 in the same neighborhood with claimant and being intimately acquainted with him."

From this concise personal testimony and from that of others who knew him well, we see that Wilson Shannon Baughman had, in fact, not been able to do his farm work at more than half effort since returning home because of three illnesses he contracted in line of Civil War duty.

On Friday, January 30, 1891..., Wilson's birthday...Charles J. Donnelly & Co sent a request to the Commissioner of Pensions in Washington..."Please issue an order for examination at an early date. Claim is about complete."

In the cold of a Missouri winter, on Tuesday, February 24, 1891 Wilson himself sent a handwritten letter to the Commissioner of Pensions..."I wish to ask in regard to my claim for pension No 688241 Co A 73rd Regt Ind Vol whether you can prosecute old claim and get a pension with all your pay from date of application or do you surrender all of the old when you apply under the new and only draw from date of the new application. My attorney in Washington sent me application blank under new law with circular stating that you could file under the new law and still go ahead with your old claim and draw what back pension due you. I herewith send you circular that I have received from him. My intention at first was to stay by my old claim but he sent a second under new law stating it was best to comply and file under new law. I have tried to comply with instructions that he sent. But whether that is enough I don't know. Now he has sent me a fee bill to sign for the Ten Dollars ($10.00) allowed him under the new law whether he intends to abandon the old claim or not. I know that I will not do so if I am entitled to any under the old law. I want that completed first for I think there is no trouble about getting under the new law. Would you please answer this if it is not asking too much. Yours Truly, Wilson S. Baughman, Brookfield, Missouri, Linn Co."

In early Spring, Tuesday, April 14, 1891 brother-in-law, Thomas Johnston married to Wilson's sister Phoebe Elizabeth, sent sworn testimony from Ligonniere, Noble County, Indiana..."I was personally acquainted with the applicant before he enlisted for about six years and lived neighbor to him and worked with him at farm labor. At the time of his enlistment in the Fall of 1862 he was a stought hearty man to all appearance. I met him next day after he returned from the Army in the Fall of 1865. He was sick when he came home, suffering with Chronic Diarrhea and Sore Eyes. For some time after he came home he was unable to perform any manual labor. I should think for about six years after he came home up to the time I left Lake County, Indiana he was able to do ½ a man's work at manual labor. I know these facts from being with him quite often and also from the fact that we worked together when he was able to work. We exchanged farm work. (+his mark) Thomas Johnston." (They'd known each other since Wilson was 14. Thomas Johnston could not write.)

On the day before, Monday, April 13th...from Lowell, Indiana, Joseph A. Little-age 60, and James Pinkerton-age 43 also sent a sworn affidavit stating they had known Wilson since 1855 and

..."know that he was a healthy man free from disability up to the time he enlisted. That when he came home from the Army he was suffering from chills and fever and Chronic Diarrhea and continued to be so afflicted up to the time he left for Missouri." (These neighbors had known Wilson since he was 13.)

It is not until the Fall, Friday, October 23, 1891, that attorney Charles J. Donnelly & Co in Washington, DC sends a query to the Commissioner of Pensions... "Respectfully referring to the above cited claim we would ask why the delay in issuing an order for claimant's examination in view of the fact that claim has been on file since Feb 4, 1889. Claimant's present address is Bevier, Mo."

A month later on Saturday, November 21, 1891, from Bevier, Missouri, Wilson's brother-in-law James Corkins - age 46 - forwarded a sworn affidavit..."I have known Wilson S. Baughman intimately since 1866 and he was at that time suffering from sore eyes, chills and fever, and chronic diarrhea so much so that he could not work more than one third of the time at his occupation of farming. He is now a carpenter and still suffering with the same ailments probably worse now than then, losing much time on account of it. He is strictly temperate now and has been since I have known him." (Jim Corkings was a brother of Wilson's wife Sarah Jane Corkings Baughman. Clearly Wilson and his family have moved to live near, or perhaps in, Jim Corkings household.)

On Friday, January 8, 1892 the Commissioner of Pensions in Washington sent a request to officials in Brookfield, Missouri to "inform this bureau by indorsement on the back of this letter as to the standing in the community and the general reputation for truth of William E. Hinkle, T. M. Morris, F. M. Brewer, and Levi Leek." An identical request went to Lowell, Indiana officials regarding R. M. Bacon and E. R. Bacon.

Two months passed. It was Wednesday, March 9, 1892 when Wilson finally appeared before the examining board of Doctors S. M. Bennan, L. E. Tracy, and T. W. McArthur in Chilicothe, Missouri. His pulse rate was 80, breathing rate 20, temperature normal, height 5'8", weight 148. "General appearance moderately good. Skin sallow. Lungs healthy. Cardiac dulness normal. Apex beat 1 inch below and 1 inch internal to nipple line, evident by palpation and inspection. Heart action quick and irritable. No murmurs. Pulse standing 100. Two dollars for disease of heart. Liver and spleen normal. Stomach flat on percussion and tender to pressure. Two dollars for disease of stomach. Bowels & rectum normal. He has Naso-Pharyngitis. Membrane thickened. Two dollars for Naso-Pharyngitis. He has chronic Conjunctivitis of both eyes. Two Dollars for disease of eyes. No other disability is found to list."

Finally...On Thursday, May 26, 1892 Wilson's first pension claim was approved beginning as of February 5, 1889 at a rate of $8.00 per month. Apparently the Bureau of Pensions paid him back pay for the months up to September 16, 1890 the day the new law enacted on June 27, 1890 went into effect. So Wilson would have received a lump sum of about $160.

On Friday, May 27, 1892 attorney Charles J. Donnelly & Co "respectfully informs the Honorable Commissioner of Pensions that claimant has changed his address from Bevier, Missouri back to Brookfield, Linn County, Missouri."

And...on Wednesday, June 1, 1892 Wilson is sent a certificate signed by John W. Noble, Secretary of the Interior confirming his pension at $12 per month beginning on September 17, 1890, the date when the second Pension Act of June 27, 1890 went into effect. So...Wilson received a second, lump sum, back payment covering about 8 ½ months at $12 per month..or near $100. And now there was a regular income of $12 per month coming in, beginning June 1, 1892. It sounds very little to us in the year 2006...but in 1892 it was a refreshingly notable amount of money, especially to a war veteran who could no longer work with any degree of regularity. This certificate reveals the first time in 27 years since the Civil War that the medical term Malaria had been used...at least in reference to Wilson's progressive illness. The certificate read..."This pension being for Malarial poisoning, chronic diarrhea, disease of eyes, and heart and catarrh (Naso-

Pharyngitis.) Doctors now know just how devastating untreated Malaria is to other organs in the body. For almost three years, records... and Wilson... were silent then, his life in Brookfield going on.

Yet... how sadly has our United States government bureaucracy far too often failed our war veterans who risked life and health to defend this Nation.

As a terrible example...on Tuesday, March 26, 1895, Civil War veteran Private Wilson Shannon Baughman was notified that his pension would be dropped...but "reinstated" at $8.00 per month. It was a whopping one-third cut in income for a veteran who was unable to work more than half time, and was suffering with three severe diseases caught on active duty during war.., complicated by advancing age. That damaging insult was not the result of an act of Congress...but "In accord with the action of Medical Referee Thomas Featherstoubaugh on January 3, 1895," with final signature by C.E. Paul, Reviewer. Stunned, we guess, Wilson and his records are silent for another two years.

On Wednesday, March 3, 1897, Brookfield, Missouri attorney George W. Stoins sent a terse, handwritten request on a post card..."In regard to the pension of Wilson Baughman No 775097. This soldiers pension was reduced some time ago. Will you please restore his pension to what it formerly was."

As America moved into the Spanish-American War years, on Saturday, January 15, 1898 the Bureau of Pensions in Washington requested Wilson to list the full name and maiden name of his wife..., when, where, and by whom married..., what record of marriage existed, and the names and birth dates of any living children. We also noted that pension payments were paid quarterly after a signed voucher was forwarded to the "pension agent."

Almost a year later, on Thursday, December 22, 1898 long ago neighbors Ralph A. Little - now age 60, and James Pinkerton - now age 43, sent another sworn affidavit testifying to his illnesses, and that they knew him before and after the Civil War.

On Monday, January 9, 1899 - indicating how frustrating Federal law and bureaucracies can be - Wilson sent a handwritten letter to the Pension Bureau..."Some time ago I sent for blanks for increase of pension. You sent me one under the new Law of June 17, 1890. But I was drawing $12.00 under that law after getting $8.00 under old law and you cut me down to $8.00 again. I do not think that they rated me right under old law. I should have been rated $12.00 on old law for three disabilitys... Look up my claim and see if I am right. And send me blanks for re-rating & increase and I will fill them out under the old law or else restore me back again under new law of June 27, 1890. Yours in haste, Wilson S. Baughman. (Apparently there was no answer.)

Nearly eight months went by. On Saturday, August 26, 1899, Wilson wrote again. "Some time ago I requested of you about my claim in regard to re-rating and increase or to be readjusted again. (Again reviews the details) My one disability for Sore Eye has increased terribly since last examination and Malarial Poisoning has increased to a large extent and the result of that Chronic Diarrhea has increased also. Please to take up my claim and if you send an order for examination, please to send for Macon County. The board here (Brookfield) I do not like one of the doctors that is on board. This is my third request to you for blanks and for a revision of my claim. Hoping to hear from you soon. I remain yours truly, Wilson S. Baughman."

Well over a year later, on Friday December 28, 1900, still in Brookfield, Missouri, Wilson at age 58 finally received the "blanks" and signed the sworn affidavit before a notary public. Obviously the notary filled in the forms. Some letters in Wilson's signature were beginning to look shaky.

At long last, on Wednesday, May 15, 1901, Wilson met with Dr. J. W. Lane and two others of the examining board at Laclede, Missouri. On that day he had a new address, listed as Marceline, Linn County, Missouri. His pulse rate was 90 sitting, 110 standing, 136 after exercise. His breathing rate was 24, 30, 36. Temperature 98.75. Height 5'7'. Weight down to 135. Age 59 years. "Abdomen very tender in hepatic region. Liver enlarged. Spleen normal. Muscles very flabby. Skin sallow. Old trachoma both eyes. Malarial poisoning. No evidence of "vicious' habits." Exam included many more medical details.

From the few family stories, it Is certain that long and increasing debilitation caused by illness, and the chagrin of not being able to work effectively, was taking it's toll on Wilson's family relationships, perhaps making him hostile, resentful, angry. Remember, 12 years prior, his son James Wilson Baughman had left home at 17 because his father was "so mean." By the sworn testimonies we've recorded, however, in outside relationships he seemed well regarded and respected...his conduct being "temperate and correct." Another aspect of such dynamics is sometimes, if not often, found in military families. In readying for war, it is vital to train officers and soldiers for instant obedience in the face of severe peril. Without question, teamwork and immediate response even in the face of wounds and death, are the factors which save lives and win battles. Unfortunately, such tenacious training is far too often passed on to wives and children by the soldier, with resulting pain and discord within the family. Whatever the underlying cause, it seems clear that by the date of that physical examination, Wilson was living alone at this new address.

On Friday, October 11, 1901, confirmation of that family discord appeared in the Circuit Court at Brookfield, Linn County, Missouri in the case of Sarah J. Baughman vs Wilson S. Baughman. Wilson did not appear, accepting default. Sarah Jane Baughman after 32 years of marriage was granted divorce. It was "decreed by the Court that the plaintiff be allowed alimony in the sum of $600 the same to be declared a lien on... Lots No Thirteen (13) and Fourteen (14) in Block No Thirteen (13) in Dakes Addition to the town, now city, of Brookfield, Missouri." Sarah Jane Baughman was further awarded title to the "household and kitchen furniture." Sarah Jane accepted payment of Court costs.

On November 6, 1901 the Bureau of Pensions scheduled another physical exam for Wilson in Chillicothe, Missouri to be held on February 17, 1902. Wilson failed to appear.

In fact, on or about Sunday, October 20, 1901 Wilson Shannon Baughman had traveled to Jacksonville, Florida to live near his daughter Ida Jane Baughman Thigpin and her family. Wilson's address was 1427 Market Street, Jacksonville. His son James Wilson Baughman had lived and worked there, too...his Grandson Elba Altdoerffer Baughman born there on Friday, September 22, 1899. But they had left the Florida city in December of 1899 or January of 1900.

On June 17, 1902 Wilson was sent a notice by the Bureau of Pensions reminding him of his failure to appear for examination. The notice included a memo... "Status furnished at the personal request of Hon. J. P. Taliaferro."

On June 26, 1902 Wilson replied in a handwritten letter... "Having rec a notice from you through Senator James P. Taliaferro of Florida stating that I failed to comply with an order for official examination before a board of surgeons at Chillicothe, Missouri dated Nov 6, 1901, I will say that I never rec the order being then in Jacksonville, Fla on that date. Came here about 20th Oct. Notified P. M. (Postmaster) at Brookfield, Mo to forward any letters addressed to me to Jacksonville, Fla. But I never rec that order. Notified Dept through Congressman W. W. Rucker of 2nd Dist, Mo of change of address. He was looking up my claim for me before I changed addresses. And could not very well comply with order when I never got it. I was ex on May 15th at Laclede, Mo. Whether Dept got that report I cannot say. I sent in my ex card that I appeared for and was ex on that date. But am ready for another order. Or be ex by special ex if possible. I have no means to go anywhere of any distance. By rights I should have never been turned down from $12.00 to $8.00 and should be restored back where I was under new law. Hoping to hear from you in reply I remain, Yours truly, Wilson S. Baughman, #775097 Late Co A, 73 Regt Ind Vol Inft, Jacksonville, Fla, General Delivery."

On Tuesday, July 15, 1902 the Board of Pensions in Washington sent Wilson a letter. It was brief and of little import in the saga of his pension, simply telling him their inventory of a pamphlet he'd requested was completely "exhausted". One would be sent to him when available again. In the thirteen years of communication with the Bureau of Pensions there had been many printed forms to fill out. However, this was the first time we found a recorded letter that was typed on a typewriter. All previously had been hand written.

On Thursday, July 10, 1902 Wilson met with Notary Public James H. Acree in Jacksonville to fill out yet another sworn "Declaration for the Increase of an Invalid Pension." H. A. Wilson and C. E, Hoyle were witnesses. In the document Sam W. Fox of Jacksonville was appointed as the new attorney of record. Wilson had moved again. His new address was a few miles south of Jacksonville at Palatka, Florida where his daughter Ida Jane Baughman Thigpin was becoming a well to do, leading, citizen.

On Wednesday, July 23,1902 in Jacksonville, Wilson appeared before yet another board of pension examination doctors, Claude Joyner, Jay H. Durkee, and Thomas Williams. His age was 60, height 5'81/4", weight 125, complexion white, eyes brown, hair gray, occupation none. Sitting, standing and after exercise pulse rate 98 -106-106, breathing rate 22-24-28, temperature 98.2. "Malarial poisoning... skin is pale, spleen is enlarged-somewhat sensitive, tongue very slightly coated & very tremulous, some sensitiveness over the epigastrium. Chronic Diarrhea. He is markedly emaciated & shows marked debility. Disease of eyes. Marked cloudiness of lens of both eyes. Pupils respond slowly to light & shade. Snellensplate 4-D.4 at 3 ft, D.3 at 2 ft, D.2 at 2 inches with right eye. D.3 at 2 ft, D.2 at 6 inches with left eye. Cannot read any other with either eye. Heart action rapid, feeble. Sound indistinct. Second sound very indistinct. Lungs. Full inspiration 361/2", expiration 34". We find moist rales over the anterior centeral portion of the chest. General debility. Is very much emaciated, muscles soft & flabby, he shows marked

& extensive breakdown. His disabilities practically amount to a total disability."

On Friday, August 1, 1902, Wilson sent a handwritten note to the Bureau..."Please to send my Discharge to me. I am making application to enter Soldiers Home."

On Wednesday, August 6, 1902 the Bureau of Pensions in Washington replied that Wilson's Certificate of Discharge was not on file in their office. Certificates in lieu of lost discharge were issued by the Record and Pension Office of the War Department. (Mail service, surely by railroad, was obviously very good).

In an undated reply Wilson said "Rec my discharge from my attorney Charles J. Donnelly & Co. P. S. In addressing any communication to me be sure and put my number of Company here in Military Home. National Military Home, Ohio Co (21). Insures prompt delivery. Wilson S. Baughman." An official report recorded that Wilson was admitted to the Central Branch, National Home For Disabled Volunteer Soldiers on Friday, September 26, 1902.

It must have been on the same day he entered, that Wilson fired off another letter to the Pension Bureau again informing them of his change of address, listing the Soldiers Home as in Dayton, Ohio. However the facility appears to actually have been located in nearby Montgomery, Ohio. "What is doing with my claim," he asked, "I have not heard for a long time. Let me know if you receive this." The Bureau responded with yet another order for an examination.

On Tuesday, November 18, 1902 Wilson appeared before Horace Bonner, M D. 114 W 4th Street, Dayton, Ohio for nothing but an eye exam. In comparison to the several previous exams showing severe eye disease and sight loss...this one seems either poorly done, conducted by a doctor incompetent to examine the eyes, or one who simply favored the Bureau of Pensions instead of the disabled soldier.

On Friday, December 5, 1902 Wilson was transferred and admitted to the Marion, Indiana Branch, National Home for D. V. S. On Sunday December 14, 1902 Wilson himself sent a handwritten postcard notifying the Bureau of his move to Marion, Indiana.

On Wednesday, February 11, 1903, Wilson again sent a handwritten letter to the Commissioner of Pensions in Washington...this time from Ligonnier, Noble County, Indiana..."I am anxious about my claim for increase of pension. Is being a long time since I have heard from you. My attorney and I don't know why I should be held up so long since being examined in November by an expert. Is there anything yet lacking or has my divorced wife been making complaints. She now has been divorced from me one year in Oct last and has the custody of the young children after destroying a good home that I paid for in pension money that I rec of the government. Had deed in her name. Was forced to a soldiers home by sickness. Not able to care for myself. Old army sickness. Chronic Dirrhea, Chronic Bronchitis, Cough and Disease of the Eyes getting no better. Now on furlough from the home at Marion, Indiana being transferred from Dayton home to Marion. Have notified my attorney of the change but have not rec any reply from them. I would like an early adjustment of my claim that I may rec some benefit from it. If anything is lacking notify me and I will furnish it. I am visiting my only sister now. Will be here for two or three months. Am doctoring myself now for my complaints. Please address me at this place. P.O. Box 425, Ligonnier, Indiana. Yours Truly, Wilson S. Baughman."

At long last, on Friday, March 6, 1903 the Bureau of Pensions approved an increase of $9 per month in Wilson's pension, back dating it to Wednesday, July 23, 1902, making his monthly income $17. He also would soon after have a check for back pay of about $72...a tidy sum in those years. Attorney Charles J. Donnelly & Co asked on July 2nd why they had not been paid their fee for the increase. In a typewritten letter dated October 14, 1903 the Bureau of Pensions replied... "it does not appear that you rendered any material service in the prosecution of the case. You are, therefore, not entitled to a fee."

With increased income, on Saturday, April 30, 1904 we find Wilson back home in Brookfield, Linn County, Missouri...sending a letter with an application for yet another pension increase. "I send my application for increase of pension and request if an order for examination to be at Chillicothe, Mo or Macon, Mo. Have been before the board at Laclede two different times. Yours Truly, Wilson S. Baughman."

That Wilson was indeed back in Brookfield for several months was confirmed by this writer's father Elba Altdoerffer Baughman who remembered his father James Wilson Baughman and mother Lavina Belle Warrick Baughman (born in East Liverpool, Ohio) leaving him, at the age of five, in the care of his grandmother in Brookfield while his parents went to see the magnificent, incomparable, St. Louis World's Fair of 1904. Father said his Grandfather Wilson scared him and he ran upstairs and hid under the bed. April 30, 1904 also happened to be the day of the Fair's grand opening.

On Monday July 11, 1904, still in Brookfield, Wilson sent a longer letter to the Bureau of Pensions..."It is now going on three months since I made an application for an increase for pension. Rec your card as a receipt for my application but I have not heard from the Bureau of Pensions since. Why so long for an order for an examination before a board of doctors. Of course I am an inmate of a soldiers home. But I do not like to stay in one. It don't suit my condition being troubled with chronic diarrhea and also piles. The diet is against me that they have in those homes. I have been in three and it served me the same way. I would rather live out of them than to have to suffer with my disablitys and don't want to go in one again. By an increase I think I can live out and take care of myself and I think my condition now will warrant me to an increase..."

On Wednesday, August 17, 1904, Wilson appeared before the three doctor board of pension examiners at 128 Vine Street in the town of Macon, Macon County, Missouri. His age 62, height 5'8", weight up again to 135, complexion dark again instead of pale, eyes brown, hair gray. The food and care at his sister

Phoebe Elizabeth Baughman Johnston's farm in Ligonnier must have been helpful to his health. "Vision both eyes 2/30 (instead of the normal 20/20). Not improved by glasses. Tongue furred and fissured. Abdomen tympanitic and tender. Liver enlarged. Rectum inflamed. External and internal piles irritable but not ulcerated or inclined to bleed. We find no indication of Malaria other than enlarged liver, ascribable to chr. diarrhea. (Author's note: we now know that Malarial symptoms come and go, but remain to strike again another day) Heart's action rapid and due to weakness. Lungs normal except for some subcrepitant rales due to Bronchitis. Claimant is so disabled from Dis. of Eyes and Chr. Diarrhea and resulting piles as to be incapacitated for performing any manual labor and is entitled to $30.00 a month. Condition is permanent and not due to vicious habits."

Doctors E. B. Clements, W. P. Rowland, and Olin Naylor signed the exam form. In another milestone of our Nation's development, this is the first typewritten physician's report we've found. In those years the board at Macon, Missouri met at 10:00 a. m. on the first and third Wednesday in each month.

Two weeks later, by Wednesday August 31, 1904, Wilson had moved yet again. His newest address was 145 Dawson Street, Dallas, Dallas County, Texas where it appears his son Frank E. Baughman was living. It shows how easily people moved around this expansive Nation in the early 1900's. His brief letter informed the Bureau of his change of address. "Hoping an early adjustment to my claim for increase of pension. Yours Truly, Wilson S. Baughman."

On Wednesday, September 28, 1904...in spite of doctor's confirmation that Wilson should be drawing $30 per month... Bureau of Pensions Medical Referee Sam Houston signed a form for "no increase," and on October 3, 1904 the Bureau sent the form to Wilson at 145 Dawson Street in Dallas stamped "Rejected."

The entire next year of 1905 passed with no communication to the Bureau of Pensions from Private Wilson Shannon Baughman.

On Tuesday, April 10, 1906, still in Dallas, Wilson wrote to the Bureau..."please to send to my address some blanks for increase of pension. Blank applications being scarce in this city so I send to you for some and oblige. Yours Truly, Wilson S. Baughman." His address by then was General Delivery, Dallas.

On Saturday, April 21, 1906 the Bureau replied..."Complying with your request of the 10th received on the 13th...a blank application is herewith enclosed." (Author's note: So...mail delivery in three days from Dallas, Texas to Washington, D. C. Pretty darn good for 100 years ago.) Most offices worked a half day on Saturday in those years.

On Friday, May 4, 1906 Wilson had the applicaiton notarized before Dallas County notary M. M. Thompson. It was indeed witnessed by his son F. E. Baughman (Wilson's son Frank) and an acquaintance, R. J. Moore, who had known Wilson for three months. Wilson's address was still General Delivery, Dallas.

On Wednesday, June 6, 1906, in the Plateau Building, 397 Main street, Dallas, Texas... Wilson was examined by Doctors J. R. Bragg and Rufus White. He was 64 years of age, 5'8" tall, 135 lbs, fair complexion, eyes light brown, hair white, occupation nothing. Pulse rate sitting, standing, exercise 100-110-120, breathing rate 20-20-24, temperature 98.6. "General appearance feeble. Malarial Poisoning. Just had attack of chills and fever in April, liver some what tender over organ on pressure. Chronic Diarrhea. Has complaint of this trouble without intermission for past 3 years, averages from 2 to 3 stools per day, says he has blood more or less in every action, the rectum is congested and prolapsed. Heart action rapid but regular. Disease of eyes. Has corneal opacity of right eye covering almost entire area of cornea, vision lost, can't see any with right eye, left eye 20/200. Both eyes sensitive to light. Claimant has no vicious habits or other disabilities as far as we can see. In our opinion this claimant is so disabled from chronic diarrhea & impaired vision & general disability as to be incapacitated for performing any manual labor & is entitled to $30 per month."

The report of this exam was again handwritten. The Pension medical examining board in Dallas met every Wednesday morning at 10:00 a. m. in those years.

With unusual hurry this time..., despite the professional examining board's recommendation that Wilson should be receiving $30 per month instead of $17...on Tuesday July 17, 1906 Bureau of Pensions Medical Referee Sam Houston again signed a rejection of the claim for increase.

Just before Christmas, on Tuesday, December 4, 1906 Wilson was "readmitted to the Danville, Illinois Branch, National Home for Disabled Volunteer Soldiers."

And just as quickly, on Thursday, January 10, 1907 Wilson fired off another claim application for increase of pension. Despite his severe disability we can see the determination, perseverance, and devotion to "duty" that brought him through 3 years of Civil War battles and illness. The form was notarized by Joshua R. H. Potts, Notary Public for Cook County Illinois. However Potts was also Wilson's new attorney in the case with an address of 80 Dearborn Street, Chicago, Illinois. Phone: Central 5560. Wilson was assigned to Company E of the Danville soldiers home. His form was witnessed by two men who were likely friends in the home...Jacob Kohn and William Nelson. On that day their signatures were notably shaky and infirm.

On Monday, February 11,1907 Wilson appeared for examination before E. E. Clark M.D. in Danville, Illinois. Clark had been a practicing physician for 15 years, but had known Wilson only ½ hour. His report..."Chills every 3 or 4 days followed by fever. Severe lumbar pain at irregular intervals. Chronic diarrhea for 3 years and for last year 3 or 4 attacks a month keeping him in a weakened condition. Right eye has bad pterygion and both eyes are developing cataracts. Right vision 8/100. Left eye 3/100. The above conditions totally disable said applicant from any kind of work."

Oddly, in view of three very specific sworn medical testimonies showing virtually total disability...Bureau of Pensions Medical Referee Sam Houston again quickly rejected the claim for increase on Wednesday, February 27, 1907..."The evidence does not warrant medical examination as it fails to show that the pensioner's disabilities alone exist in such degree to warrant the next higher rate." Looking at the evidence...it makes one wonder if the "Medical Referee" was getting a bonus to turn down claims.

On Friday, May 29, 1908 there appeared a notice from the Danville Branch, National Home for D. V. S. to the Commissioner of Pensions informing him that Wilson S. Baughman, pensioned at $17 per month, had been discharged. It did not say where he went. On October 29, 1908 attorney Joshua R. H. Potts requested of the Bureau "Please furnish the condition of the claim mentioned below and state what evidence, if any, is needed to complete same. Wilson S. Baughman, Co A ,73rd Ind Inft, Increase, General law."

In the year 1909, though, we find where Wilson had moved. On Wednesday, April 22 he signed another claim for pension increase from 608 Adams Street, Montgomery, Alabama, the home of son William E. "Will" Baughman. On Monday, May 4th, V. Warner, Commissioner of Pensions sent an order for examination to Dr. R. S. Chapman of Montgomery, Alabama. The exam was scheduled for Wednesday, June 2, 1909. The board of examiners in Montgomery met at 1:00 p.m. on the first Wednesday of each month.

On that day Wilson sent a brief letter to the Commissioner of Pensions in Washington..."Sir, I appeared at 21 ½ Dexter Ave here today to be examined by the board under the notice sent me by your office, and although I waited until 2:30 p.m., not one member of the board was present up to that time. Very Respectfully, Wilson S. Baughman." This letter was not in Wilson's handwriting. On June 14th, Acting Commissioner replied that the "failure of the board to meet and make examination is being investigated...the matter will receive further attention."

On Wednesday July 8, 1909, Wilson finally was examined by the board of T. J. Stough M.D., B.S. Chapman M.D., and J.M. Anderson M.D. Wilson was 67, height 5'71/2", weight down again to 125, complexion dark, eyes brown, hair gray. After a long period of not working at all, he again listed his occupation as carpenter...obviously still trying to work when he could. Compared to the mountain of past recorded evidence of severe medical problems, this exam report seemed to down play the truly major factors of Malarial Poisoning and chronic diarrhea. These illnesses both can have good and bad periods, and perhaps the doctors just caught them in a time of remission...or were they just angry that Wilson had reported their exam meeting failure to the Bureau of Pensions? The doctors did note "cannot do anything but discern light with left eye, and has to wear glasses as well as use a powerful lens to read ordinary print with right eye. Cannot hear except in contact with left ear, and hears at a distance of 10 inches with right. Can hear ordinary voice at about 2 1/2 or 3 inches."

On Wednesday, September 30, 1909 the Bureau of Pensions ordered an eye exam by Dr. H. S. Persons, 21 S. Perry Street, Montgomery, listed as an expert in eye diseases.

Wilson was examined by Dr. Persons on Tuesday, October 6, 1909. His age that day was 68, height 5'8", weight still an "emaciated" 125, complexion now light again, eyes now gray, hair gray. He listed himself, again, as a carpenter, obviously still trying to work when he could. The report had considerable detail, but Dr. Persons wasted none of his time in drawing conclusions about Wilson's near total sight loss. He found Chronic Conjunctivitis (a diagnosis coming into use then instead of the term Sore Eyes) in the right eye, a growth covering the cornea to such an extent "that the applicant has only a small field of vision - & that to the extreme right. It is impossible to examine the internal eye structures owing to this. Vision 3/200 (instead of the normal 20/20) - not improved by glasses." In Wilson's left eye Dr. Persons also found Chronic Conjunctivitis, some scar tissue to inner half of cornea, and a cataract "more than half ripe which prevents any examination of the deeper structures. Vision 6/200."

Almost immediately, on Wednesday, October 27, 1909 Wilson's claim for pension increase was again rejected, this time by examiner J. D. McDermott..."Senile cataract excluded. Alleged chronic catarrh of head, bronchitis, affection of lungs, and impaired hearing not accepted." No mention of the reams of evidence for Malarial Poisoning and Chronic Diarrhea, which we now know was likely Amebic Dysentery.

On Wednesday, December 1, 1909...again not long before the Christmas season...Wilson traveled back to Danville, Illinois and was readmitted to the Danville Branch, National Home for Disable Volunteer Soldiers. The question lingers...if his disabilities qualified him for a place in a home for disabled soldiers, why did those same disabilities not qualify him for an adequate pension?

Just six months later, Wilson moved back to Indiana. On Friday, June 10, 1910 he reentered the Marion Branch, National Home for D. V. S. at Marion, Grant County, Indiana.

Obviously still determined and persevering despite illness, on Thursday, October 12, 1911 Wilson signed yet another notarized claim for pension increase. His address was Barracks #7, National Military Home, Marion, Grant County, Indiana. The document was notarized by Fred Drake, Clerk of the Circuit Court of Grant County in that year. In the claim Wilson appointed Grant County lawyer R. B. Sittrick as his attorney of record. The two witnesses, Theron D. Curtis and David W. Hazelrigg appear to have been fellow disabled soldiers from the old soldiers home. Their signatures were as shaky as his. Three weeks later, on Tuesday, November 7, 1911, C. F. Whitney, Medical Referee for the Bureau of Pensions issued an order for examination.

Just eight days later, on Wednesday, November 15, 1911 Wilson appeared before Grant County's Board of Pension examiners, Dr. G. W. Daniels, Sr, Dr. John C. Knight, and Dr. J. Patterson. The office was located in the Iroquois Block, room 212, Marion, Grant County, Indiana. The board met each Wednesday at 10:00 a.m. in those years. This report was typed, meticulously detailed. Wilson was then 69 years old, height 5'8", weight 129, light complexion, hazel eyes, gray hair, occupation farmer (Obviously this was listed only as his career). His pulse rate sitting, standing, exercise was 96-100-120, his breathing rate 20-24-36, temperature 98.

"Malarial Poisoning...This man is weak, emaciated and poorly nourished, with soft flabby muscles and a sallow parchment skin. He is nervous and tremulous, and Arterio Sclerosis is well marked. His tongue is broad and flabby and coated with brown fur. He alleges he had a chill two days ago, and has them on an average of once a week, and they are always followed by fever, and that he has had chills about that often ever since he came out of the army. The stomach is tender and tympanitic and walls thickened. The liver is very tender and enlarged. The Spleen is tender. The colon is tender and tympanitic throughout its entire course. He alleges Diarrhea ½ the time, and occasionally has periods of obstinate constipation. He has two internal piles, one is 3/4 of an inch in diameter, and the other is ½ inch in diameter, and are ulcerated. There is also two ulcers on the posterior part of the rectum, each ½ inch in diameter, and are discharging a purulent discharge. The sphincter is relaxed and vessels are engorged.

Disease of eyes...The right eye is practically blind; he just can distinguish light; this is caused by Cataract and encroachment on pupil of Pterygium which obliterates the sight of this eye. Left eye 5/100 (instead of the normal 20/20.) He has senile cataract of this eye.

Heart...apex beat in 5th space, just inside the nipple line. Impulse diffused. Action weak, rapid and regular. No murmurs. Alleges vertigo (dizziness). Has dyspnoe (shortness of breath) on exercise. There is cyanosis (blueness) of lips and odema (swelling) half way to the knees.

Lungs...33"-34"-35" Resonance and respiratory murmur clear and distinct over the whole of both lungs, except for bronchiae, where mucus rales are heard. He alleges a cough, with mucus expectorations.

This claimant is so disabled from Malarial Poisoning, Chronic Diarrhea and Disease of Eyes as to be incapacitated in a degree equivalent to the loss of a hand or foot for the purposes of manual labor, and is entitled to $24 a month."

Although long...we have included this medical report virtually in its entirety, as it so clearly confirms all of the symptoms which have been recorded by doctor after doctor, as well as neighbors and friends who knew Wilson well, for 22 years. Those symptoms also tied in directly to his numerous hospital stays during 1864, his last year in the Union Army. That the Pension Board of the War Department of the United States of America so often ignored or dismissed such sworn testimony is, needless to say, an awesome travesty of justice. But then, many, many years were to pass before President Ronald Reagan quipped..."the most frightening words one can hear are "Hi! I'm from the Government. And I'm here to help you!."

On Monday, December 7, 1911 Bureau of Pensions Medical Referee C. F. Whitney did...finally...approve Wilson's pension increase to $24 per month, back dating it to November 15, 1911. It took the War veteran 22 years of fighting injustice to get a pension he found sufficient to live "out of the Old Soldier's Homes" and on his own.

But in a twist of fate, by Monday, March 6, 1912 Wilson had moved yet again...entering the Mountain Branch, National home for D. V. S. in the mountains of Washington County, Tennessee, near Johnson City. This move seems simply to have been to obtain care for his severe disabilities, since he felt his increased pension was satisfactory for self sufficiency in normal health.

On May 11, 1912 the United States Congress enacted a new version of the Pension Act. Wilson had little hearing or sight by then, but he certainly had not lost his awareness of what was going on around him. It took him only 7 days to react to the news. On Thursday, May 18, 1912, at the age of 70, he fired off yet another claim for pension increase. It was affirmed by S. H. Cooper, a Notary Public in Johnson City and witnessed by

Victor M. Scull a fellow soldier in the home and John H. Miller of Johnson City.

But...by the time the order for examination was actually issued on Wednesday, October 23, 1912 Wilson had gone back to Montgomery, Alabama to stay with his son William E. "Will" Baughman who now lived at 515 Alabama Street, Montgomery.

In fact, on Friday, May 23, 1913 a letter from Wilson was sent from 515 Alabama Street, Montgomery asking about the disposition of his claim which had been made in Johnson City, Tennessee a year before. The letter was written and signed by someone else...likely Will Baughman's wife from the crispness of the handwriting.

ON June 11, the Bureau replied that "there should be filed medical evidence showing whether you were unfit for manual labor by reason of Malarial Poisoning, Chronic Diarrhea and resulting Disease of Rectum, and Disease of Eyes, independent of any other disability on May 20, 1912, the date of filing your application."

On Monday, June 16, 1913 Wilson was examined by Dr. S. E. Centerfit at his office, 19 1/2 S. Perry Street, Montgomery. His report was concise, but fully supported the finding of the previous Board of Examiners in Marion, Indiana, November 1911. Wilson sent it to the Bureau with an accompanying letter on that day.

On June 28, 1913, the Bureau of Pensions asked for proof of Wilson's date of birth. This...after being mustered into the army, listing a date of birth which was fully accepted... and being discharged from the same army with the same birth date notation.

On Monday, July 28, 1913, still living at 515 Alabama Street, Montgomery... now 71 years of age... Wilson sent a sworn General Affidavit referring to his enlistment and discharge certificates and his age at enlistment as proof. He signed the document with an "X, his mark."

On Wednesday, October 22, 1913 the Bureau sent Wilson an order to be examined again by Dr. H. S. Persons at 21 S. Perry Street, Montgomery.

On Thursday, November 27, 1913 Wilson underwent the examination. Dr. Persons noted his age as 72, although Wilson was actually 71. Height 5'7 3/4". Weight 125. Complexion fair (several other doctors said sallow). Eyes hazel. Hair almost white. Occupation farmer & mechanic. The exam and report seems hurriedly, sketchily, poorly done. The medical "expert" does find "severe Conjunctivitis in both eyes. In the left eye vision is not sufficient for practical use." Where several other doctors have found him "emaciated" at 125 pounds, Dr. Persons said "applicant, while now feeble from age, is about like the average man his age physically in weight, height considered. Nutrition is good. Spleen slightly enlarged. Liver is normal." Dr. Persons' exam report was an enormous, stunning contrast to the sworn medical evidence documented by the three doctor examining board in Marion, Indiana two years before. It was obviously, extremely, misleading. Was Dr. Persons simply an incompetent physician? Or, deep in America's South... did he just not like "Yankees." That sense of seething resentment about the Civil War lingered 100 years or more in small towns of Dixie. The fact, though, that soldiers from all sections of America fought together in trust and friendship during World war II eased such tension greatly. One thing about that November 1913 medical examination report is painfully clear. In spite of his "soft-pedaled" medical diagnoses, Dr. Persons well knew what Wilson's true medical condition actually was. The last sentence of his report read..."Applicant totally unfitted for work."

The Bureau of Pensions, however, grasped on to Dr. Persons' "soft-pedaled" diagnoses to refuse further claims for pension increase...completely ignoring the meticulous, far more accurate, sworn evidence provided by Drs. Daniels, Knight, Patterson and a number of others. That level of incompetence, and even purposeful bias, by government bureaucrats resulting in direct harm to the well-being of working Americans is still, too often, suffered 140 years later.

The Bureau "dragged its feet" until January 29, 1914 before notifying Wilson that his claim for increase was not approved..."...your claim under the disability clause of the act of May 11, 1912 is rejected on the ground that you have not been unable to perform manual labor by reason of malarial poisoning, chronic diarrhoea and resulting disease of rectum, and disease of eyes since the date of filing the claim May 20, 1912."

That statement was obviously, patently, false. In fact, the awful untruth of it could not have been missed by any caring person who, even casually, reviewed Wilson's forty-nine (49) year chain of evidence. The Bureau also told Wilson that he could apply again when he was 75...and that he had the right of appeal.

During that period, on Thursday, January 15, 1914, Wilson had himself discharged from the disabled soldiers home in the mountains of Washington County, Tennessee...remaining for a while with his son Will. In fact, as we suspected, some of Wilson's letters were being written by Will's wife. On Friday, February 6, 1914 she answered the Bureau's rejection notice..."Dear Sir, Mr. Baughman asked me to copy his letter for him in pen and ink, knowing that to be the requirements, but thinking it best for the letter to be in his own handwriting I send it just as he wrote it, with this note of explanation from me. He makes his home with me and I can corroborate his statements as regards his health. He is practically unable to do a thing, and many of his letters I have to write for him as it is impossible for him to use his right arm at all at times. Mrs. W. E. Baughman." She attached Wilson's handwritten letter...

"Feb 2nd 1914. To Commissioner of Pensions Washington D. C. Dear Sir, I rec your communication of recent date stating that your department had rejected my claim for increase of pension under the Disability Clause of the Act of May 11, 1912 as I couldn't rec anything under the age or service by reason that at that time I had rec all I could expect. But I thought that the Disability Clause could certainly fit my case for a pension increase up to the maximum rate of $30 a month which I am entitled to. (Authors note: $30 per month had indeed been recommended by two different doctors in their exams) I have not been treated justly by the doctor who examined me, they being Democrats. (Authors note: As we've noted, the lack of fairness seemed intensely true of Dr. Persons in Montgomery) And you can't get justice from them unless...?...be Catholic...?... if you are not that kind. That was the way it was in the National Military Homes. I have left the Home for good on that account. I have been afflicted by my disabilitys for a number of years. Am blind in one eye, deaf in one ear, and palsied in one arm. Have malaria quite often and bowel complaint all the time and other complaints that make me unable to perform manual labor according to the letter and spirit of the Law. Your decision that I was not unable to do manual labor since I applied on May 20, 1912, however before that date my record shows what was the trouble. You seem to be...?...about my case. Maybe if I was a good Catholic it might have been different. It seems that way in the Soldiers Homes. Well, I appeal my case before the Secretary of Interior for a rehearing, if not sustained then I will take it before Congress in a hearing. I know I'm entitled to $30 the maximum rate as the Law intended. I will leave it now to the Secretary of Interior so you can appeal it to him. I remain your obedient servant, Wilson S, Baughman. Late Co A, 73rd Ind Vol Inf. Claim No 775097. Address 515 Alabama Street, Montgomery, Ala."

(Author's note: 48 years after the Civil War ended, Wilson had suddenly used the infinitely courteous letter ending "Your Obediant Servant" which was used by his military officers in addressing letters and memos between themselves...often even Generals writing to lower ranked Colonels or Majors. It is also curious that Wilson mentions religious discord in the Soldiers Homes. Some of them may have been operated by Catholic agencies, as hospitals in America have been for decades.)

On Wednesday, March 11, 1914 Wilson was sent a two page, typewritten letter from the Commissioner of the Bureau of Pensions. It was simply a wordy confirmation of his previous rejection letter...telling him that he had the right of appeal, and reminding him he could apply again at age 75.

On April 10, 1914 Wilson sent another long letter of reply to the Commissioner of Pensions in Washington D. C...the last of his own letters in his file 27 years long. It is personally handwritten. It was obviously very difficult to accomplish, and likely took a long time. We can almost see him bent over within inches of the paper, able to see with just one eye. But, that day must have been a better one. His writing was surprisingly neat, firm, letters well formed, understandable. Much of it was a meticulous review of his medical disabilities, and a review of his case. "I now have an application on appeal to the Sec of the Interior," he said, "for a rehearing of my claim in hope he will do me justice for I am entitled to the maximum rate so stated in the Act of May 11, 1912. I hope you will present my case to him for consideration."

To give credit where a bit may be due, on Saturday, May 2, 1914 the Commissioner of Pensions did, in fact, refer Wilson's appeal to the Secretary of the Interior. However, he reviewed the case using medical evidence from Dr. Persons' very poor and misleading examination, with brief mention of Dr. Centerfit's only somewhat more accurate information. He did not refer in any way to the meticulous, precise, factual, exam report of the three doctor Board of Pension Examiners in Marion, Indiana.

Not surprisingly, very hurriedly, on Monday, May 11, 1914 Bo Sweeney, Assistant Secretary to the Secretary of the Interior of the United States of America replied directly to Wilson, rejecting his appeal. Though he mentioned in passing the report of an additional doctor, it is clear that Sweeney also relied on the enormously scant and misleading report of Dr. H. S. Persons in Montgomery. Sweeney could not in any way, in good conscience, have studied Wilson's Civil War record, numerous hospitalizations in 1864, and the full record of his certified medical evidence and reached that conclusion. It is the last record of any communication to or from Wilson in his pension file.

It was on a Friday, October 13, 1916, that Private Wilson Shannon Baughman, Company A, 73rd Indiana Volunteer Infantry Regiment passed from this life...a life span of 74 years, 8 months, and 14 days. He had moved yet again from Montgomery and was living in East Palatka...likely near, but not with, his daughter Ida Jane Baughman Thigpin and her husband George G. Thigpin. Wilson's ex-wife Sarah Jane Corkings Baughman was living with their daughter Ida. The doctor who attended... name not listed on the certificate... had known Wilson for only the day of his passing.

"Wilson S. Baughman, aged 74 years," said the Palatka News, Page 8, Friday, October 20, 1916, "died on Friday of last week. The funeral, in charge of Mooney & Davis and conducted by Rev. S. Grady, was held on Saturday afternoon, the interment being in Oak Hill. Mr. Baughman was a hero of the Civil War and a member of the G. A. R. He is survived by a wife and several children, among them being Mrs. C. D. Sands of Puerto Rico, James B. of Milwaukee, Wis., Mrs G. G. Thigpin of East Palatka, E. C. B. Of Okeechobee, and Wm. E. Of Montgomery, Ala. These have united in a request to the Palatka News that friends who assisted in the funeral be publicly thanked for their many kindnesses."

Seldom in the annals of war has the life of a simple soldier been followed from birth to death in so much detail. But, the pension records of this soldier are clearly an awful expose. They surely bare immense failure on the part of our Nation's War Department bureaucrats following the Civil War to meet the needs...in honorable, forthright, caring ways... of thousands of soldier veterans who had been ordered into battle, injury, and life-long illness. It simply is not possible that one might accidently stumble on just the one, single, case among thousands that happened to be so disastrously handled. Without doubt, there are many, many more just like it, hidden in aged records of our Nation's Military Pension Department. Direful lack of care must surely have brought calamity into the lives of thousands like Private Wilson Shannon Baughman, men who had been hailed as heros when they returned home from America's Civil War.

Colonel Abel D. Streight…Later Brevet Brigadier General Circa 1862

Chapter Seventeen

Colonel Abel D. Streight and His 51st Indiana Regiment

This book would not be complete without an account of the life and achievements of Streight himself, as well as the history of his 51st Indiana Volunteer Infantry Regiment.

Union Colonel, and later Brevet Brigadier General, Abel D. Streight has remained virtually unknown in annals of America's Civil War, while General Nathan Bedford Forrest has been accorded amply deserved fame commensurate with that of President Abraham Lincoln, Confederate General Robert E. Lee, and Union General, later President of the United States, Ulysses S. Grant.

Yet, in his week long, perilous, running battles with Forrest, it is astonishing how similar to Forrest's military genius were Streight's own battle strategies. In fact, Colonel Abel D. Streight's combat skill, determination, and military tactics may well be one of the most fascinating little known stories of America's Civil War.

With a year having passed, his imprisonment at Libby, escape, and the gathering of records, the commander of Streight's Brigade acknowledged to his Union Generals:

"I am unable to report the exact number of casualties in the command but from the best information I have been able to obtain, there were 15 officers and about 130 enlisted men killed and wounded. It was a matter of astonishment to all that so much fighting should occur with so few casualties on our side. But we acted purely on the defensive, and took advantage of the nature of the country as best we could.

From actual personal observation where we had driven the enemy from the field, and from what my surgeons left with our wounded learned in relation to the loss of the enemy, I am convinced that we killed more of his men than we lost in both killed and wounded.

Previous to the surrender, we had captured and paroled about 200 prisoners, and had lost about the same number in consequence of the animals giving out. The men unable to keep up, broke down from exhaustion and were necessarily picked up by the enemy. But in no case was the enemy able to capture a single man in any skirmish or battle within my knowledge.

In reviewing the history of this ill-fated expedition, I am convinced that had we been furnished at Nashville with 800 good horses, instead of poor young mules, we would have been successful in spite of all other drawbacks. Or, if General Dodge had succeeded in detaining Forrest one day longer, we would have been successful even with our poor outfit.

In conclusion, I will bear testimony to the bravery and uncomplaining endurance of both officers and men of my command during those trying days and nights. To my staff I owe much for their good example and constant labors."

(Author's note: This surprisingly low count in Union casualties was, perhaps, the one thing that did not go wrong in the "ill-fated" running battles of Streight's Raid. It is certainly likely that a number of the Boys From Lake County and their fellow soldiers of the 73rd Indiana and others of Streight's Brigade owed their lives to the skill, determination, and battle strategies of Colonel Abel D. Streight. However, after years of studying the details of Streights Raid, this writer strongly suspects that in this report Streight yet underestimates the ferocious determination of Confederate General Nathan Bedford Forrest. If General Dodge had delayed Forrest just one more day... it seems clear that Forrest would simply have found and attacked Streight's command... just one day later.)

Abel D. Streight was born on Tuesday, June 17, 1828 at Wheeler, Steuben County, New York. His family was of English background, his father Asa born in Vermont. His mother Lydia, daughter of Phineas Spaulding, was from Spencer, Tioga County, New York where the couple were married. Young Abel had four sisters, Maria, Francis, Susan H., and Jane. He also had four brothers, James P., Benjamin F., Sylvester W., and Charles F.

The nine siblings grew up on a farm in Wheeler where their parents settled after marriage. Their father Asa, quite successful in the operation of his farm, was financially well off, well known, and respected in his community as meticulous, industrious, and honest. He taught his children the same habits of industry and economy. His children received what was then called a common-school education. Asa Streight operated his farm until the age of 70 and lived until he was 84.

An unusually astute young man, Abel, at the age of 17 paid his father $60 per year for the balance of his non-adult period so he could go to work on his own. He displayed talent for mechanics, learning the carpenters craft without instruction. Before the age of 19 he had taken a contract and successfully built a large mill. At this early age Abel also owned a sawmill bought with money he earned. This led to the ownership of a lumber business at Wheeler which Abel operated with success until he sold out and moved to Cincinnati, Ohio in 1858. In 1859 he moved again to Indianapolis, Indiana and began a publishing business. As Civil War loomed, Streight deeply believed that the North should go to war, if necessary, to preserve the Union of the United States. He used his writing and publishing skills to produce a brief book "The Crisis of 1861 in the Government of the United States" heralding his views on how the preservation of the Union should be assured.

Streight's business and financial success, publishing efforts, and political activity made him well known in Indiana government circles. In fact, Indiana Governor Oliver P. Morton sent him to Springfield, Illinois as his personal emissary to Abraham Lincoln. Hence, Streight was appointed a Colonel as he entered the Union Army on September 4, 1861, and authorized by Governor Morton to enroll the 51st Indiana Volunteer Infantry Regiment.

Somewhat disappointed in opportunities for combat in his first two years, Streight and his 51st Indiana Regiment, never-the-less, fought well and bravely at the battles of Shiloh; Perryville; Stones River; Streight's Brigade; against General Joseph "Fightin' Joe" Wheeler's Cavalry at Dalton and Shoal Creek near Florence, Alabama (where Streight commanded five Brigades); Columbia, Tennessee; Franklin, Tennessee; Nashville; and once again at Columbia. As a Brigade commander, Streight was promoted to Brevet Brigadier-General. The 51st Indiana Regiment was not mustered out of the Union Army until December of 1865, but General Streight, seeing the slowing of opportunities for combat near the end of the Civil War, resigned his commission and returned to the business world on March 13, 1865.

He immediately resumed his publishing business, while also operating a farm on the outskirts of Indianapolis. In the same year, 1865, Streight established a lumber business, specializing in Walnut and hardwoods. This led to an interest in the Indianapolis Chair Company...a large chair manufacturer. Streight also had extensive land holdings.

Streight had married Lovina McCarthy of Bath Township, Steuben County, New York on Sunday, January 14, 1849. The marriage produced one son, John, who became the owner of a lumber business in Nashville, Tennessee. Lovina Streight was an unusual woman. She actually sometimes accompanied her husband on his military campaigns, often ministering to the wounded during battle. She was captured three times and exchanged for prisoners. Known and loved by her husband's command as the "Mother of the 51st " Lovina's funeral was accorded full military honors upon her death in 1910.

Abel and Lovina built a house on Washington Street in Indianapolis in 1866. But by 1876 they were recorded as owning, and living, at a "fine country seat" two miles East of Indianapolis on the National Road. In those years Streight was described in "Sketches of Prominent Citizens" as a large, fine looking man, florid complexion, sandy hair, and looking as though he had something better than Libby Prison fare."

Abel D. Streight had been active in Republican politics for much of his adult life both in New York and in Indiana. Eleven Years after the Civil War's end he won election to the Indiana State Senate in 1876, serving a two year term. During that term he was considered one of the key leaders of his party. In 1880 he ran for the Republican nomination for Governor of Indiana. Though that effort failed, Streight was unanimously endorsed by newspapers, cited for his honesty, iron will, uncommon intelligence, and patriotism. In 1888 he was elected to a second term as Indiana State Senator.

Abel D. Streight passed from this life on Friday, May 27, 1892, three weeks before his 64th birthday. Upon his death he was buried at his place of residence, but in 1902 was re-interred at Indianapolis' Crown Hill Cemetery.

Chapter Eighteen

Causes and Effects
of America's Civil War

**From The Book,
"Reminiscences Of The Civil War", (Chapter I)
John B. Gordon, Maj. Gen. CSA**

There is no book in existence, I believe, in which the ordinary reader can find an analysis of the issues between the two sections, which fairly represents both the North and the South. Although it would require volumes to contain the great arguments, I shall attempt here to give a brief summary of the causes of our sectional controversy, and it will be my purpose to state the cases of the two sections so impartially that just-minded people on both sides will admit the statement to be judicially fair.

The causes of the war will be found at the foundation of our political fabric, in our complex organism, in the fundamental law, in the Constitution itself, in the conflicting constructions which it invited, and in the institution of slavery which it recognized and was intended to protect. If asked what was the real issue involved in our unparalleled conflict, the average American citizen will reply, "The negro"; and it is fair to say that had there been no slavery there would have been no war. But there would have been no slavery if the South's protests could have availed when it was first introduced; and now that it is gone, although its sudden and violent abolition entailed upon the South directly and incidentally a series of woes which no pen can describe, yet it is true that in no section would its reestablishment be more strongly and universally resisted. The South steadfastly maintains that responsibility for the presence of this political

Pandora's box in this Western world cannot be laid at her door. When the Constitution was adopted and the Union formed, slavery existed in practically all the States; and it is claimed by the Southern people that its disappearance from the Northern and its development in the Southern States is due to climatic conditions and industrial exigencies rather than to the existence or absence of great moral ideas.

Slavery was undoubtedly the immediate fomenting cause of the woeful American conflict. It was the great political factor around which the passions of the sections had long been gathered--the tallest pine in the political forest around whose top the fiercest lightnings were to blaze and whose trunk was destined to be shivered in the earthquake shocks of war. But slavery was far from being the sole cause of the prolonged conflict. Neither its destruction on the one hand, nor its defence on the other, was the energizing force that held the contending armies to four years of bloody work. I apprehend that if all living Union soldiers were summoned to the witness stand, every one of them would testify that it was the preservation of the American Union and not the destruction of Southern slavery that induced him to volunteer at the call of his country. As for the South, it is enough to say that perhaps eighty per cent of her armies were neither slave-holders, nor had the remotest interest in the institution. No other proof, however, is needed than the undeniable fact that at any period of the war, from its beginning to near its close, the South could have saved slavery by simply laying down its arms and returning to the Union.

We must, therefore, look beyond the institution of slavery for the fundamental issues which dominated and inspired all classes of the contending sections. It is not difficult to find them. The "Old Man Eloquent," William E. Gladstone, who was perhaps England's foremost statesman of the century, believed that the Government formed by our fathers was the noblest political fabric ever devised by the brain of man. This undoubtedly is true;

and yet before these inspired builders were dead, controversy arose as to the nature and powers of their free constitutional government. Indeed, in the very convention that framed the Constitution the clashing theories and bristling arguments of 1787 presaged the glistening bayonets of 1861. In the cabinet of the first President, the contests between Hamilton and Jefferson, representatives of conflicting constitutional constructions, were so persistent and fierce as to disturb the harmony of executive councils and tax the patience of Washington. The disciples of each of these political prophets numbered in their respective ranks the greatest statesmen and purest patriots. The followers of each continuously battled for these conflicting theories with a power and earnestness worthy of the founders of the Republic. Generation after generation, in Congress, on the hustings, and through the press, these irreconcilable doctrines were urged by constitutional expounders, until their arguments became ingrained into the very fibre of the brain and conscience of the sections. The long war of words between the leaders waxed at last into a war of guns between their followers.

During the entire life of the Republic the respective rights and powers of the States and general government had furnished a question for endless controversy. In process of time this controversy assumed a somewhat sectional phase. The dominating thought of the North and of the South may be summarized in a few sentences.

The South maintained with the depth of religious conviction that the union formed under the Constitution was a union of consent and not of force; that the original States were not the creatures but the creators of the Union; that these States had gained their independence, their freedom, and their sovereignty from the mother country, and had not surrendered these on entering the Union; that by the express terms of the Constitution all rights and powers not delegated were reserved to the States; and the South challenged the North to find one trace of authority in that Constitution for invading and coercing a sovereign State.

The North, on the other hand, maintained with the utmost confidence in the correctness of her position that the Union formed under the Constitution was intended to be perpetual; that sovereignty was a unit and could not be divided; that whether or not there was any express power granted in the Constitution for invading a State, the right of self-preservation was inherent in all governments; that the life of the Union was essential to the life of liberty; or, in the words of Webster, "liberty and union are one and inseparable."

To the charge of the North that secession was rebellion and treason, the South replied that the epithets of rebel and traitor did not deter her from the assertion of her independence, since these same epithets had been familiar to the ears of Washington and Hancock and Adams and Light Horse Harry Lee. In vindication of her right to secede, she appealed to the essential doctrine, "the right to govern rests on the consent of the governed," and to the right of independent action as among those reserved by the States. The South appealed to the acts and opinions of the Fathers and to the report of the Hartford Convention of New England States asserting the power of each State to decide as to the remedy for infraction of its rights; to the petitions presented and positions assumed by ex-President John Quincy Adams; to the contemporaneous declaration of the 8th of January assemblage in Ohio indicating that 200,000 Democrats in that State alone were ready to stand guard on the banks of the border river and resist invasion of Southern territory; and to the repeated declarations of Horace Greeley and the admission of President Lincoln himself that there was difficulty on the question of force, since ours ought to be a fraternal Government.

In answer to all these points, the North also cited the acts and opinions of the same Fathers, and urged that the purpose of those Fathers was to make a more perfect Union and a stronger government. The North offset the opinions of Greeley and others by the emphatic declaration of Stephen A. Douglas, the foremost of Western Democrats, and by the official opinion as to the power of the Government to collect revenues and enforce laws, given to President Buchanan by Jere Black, the able Democratic Attorney-General.

Thus the opposing arguments drawn from current opinions and from the actions and opinions of the Fathers were piled mountain high on both sides. Thus the mighty athletes of debate wrestled in the political arena, each profoundly convinced of the righteousness of his position; hurling at each other their ponderous arguments, which reverberated like angry thunderbolts through legislative halls, until the whole political atmosphere resounded with the tumult. Long before a single gun was fired public sentiment North and South had been lashed into a foaming sea of passion; and every timber in the framework of the Government was bending and ready to break from "the heaving ground-swell of the tremendous agitation." Gradually and naturally in this furnace of sectional debate, sectional ballots were crystallized into sectional bullets; and both sides came at last to the position formerly held by the great Troup of Georgia: "The argument is exhausted; we stand to our guns."

I submit that this brief and incomplete summary is sufficient to satisfy those who live after us that these great leaders of conflicting thought, and their followers who continued the debate in battle and blood, while in some sense partisans, were in a far juster sense patriots.

The opinions of Lee and Grant, from each of whom I briefly quote, will illustrate in a measure the convictions of their armies. Every Confederate appreciates the magnanimity exhibited by General Grant at Appomattox; and it has been my pleasure for nearly forty years to speak in public and private of his great qualities.

In his personal memoirs, General Grant has left on record his estimate of the Southern cause. This estimate represents a strong phase of Northern sentiment, but it is a sentiment which is extremely difficult for a Southern man to comprehend. In speaking of his feelings as "sad and depressed," as he rode to meet General Lee and receive the surrender of the Southern armies at Appomattox, General Grant says: "I felt like anything rather than rejoicing at the downfall of a foe who had fought so long and valiantly, and who had suffered so much for a cause, though that cause was, I believe, one of the worst for which a people ever fought, and one for which there was the least excuse." He adds: "I do not question, however, the sincerity of the great mass of those who were opposed to us."

The words above quoted, showing General Grant's opinion of the Southern cause, are italicized by me and not by him. My object in emphasizing them is to invite special attention to their marked contrast with the opinions of General Robert E. Lee as to that same Southern cause.

This peerless Confederate soldier and representative American, than whom no age or country ever produced a loftier spirit or more clear-sighted, conscientious Christian gentleman, in referring, two days before the surrender, to the apparent hopelessness of our cause, used these immortal words: "We had, I was satisfied, sacred principles to maintain and rights to defend for which we were in duty bound to do our best, even if we perished in the endeavor."

There were those, a few years ago, who were especially devoted to the somewhat stereotyped phrase that in our Civil War one side (meaning the North) "was wholly and eternally right," while the other side (meaning the South) "was wholly and eternally wrong." I might cite those on the Southern side of the great controversy, equally sincere and fully as able, who would have been glad to persuade posterity that the North was "wholly and eternally wrong"; that her people waged war upon sister States who sought peacefully to set up a homogeneous government, and meditated no wrong or warfare upon the remaining sister States. These Southern leaders steadfastly maintained that the Southern people, in the exercise of the freedom and sovereign rights purchased by Revolutionary blood, were asserting a second independence according to the teachings and example of their fathers.

But what good is to come to the country from partisan utterances on either side? My own well-considered and long-entertained opinion, my settled and profound conviction, the correctness of which the future will vindicate, is this: that the one thing which is "wholly and eternally wrong" is the effort of so-called statesmen to inject one-sided and jaundiced sentiments into the youth of the country in either section. Such sentiments are neither consistent with the truth of history, nor conducive to the future welfare and unity of the Republic. The assumption on either side of all the righteousness and all the truth would produce a belittling arrogance, and an offensive intolerance of the opposing section; or, if either section could be persuaded that it was "wholly and eternally wrong," it would inevitably destroy the self-respect and manhood of its people.

A far broader, more truthful, and statesmanlike view was presented by the Hon. A. E. Stevenson, of Illinois, then Vice-President of the United States, in his opening remarks as presiding officer at the dedication of the National Park at Chickamauga. In perfect accord with the sentiment of the occasion and the spirit which led to the establishment of this park as a bond of national brotherhood, Mr. Stevenson said: "Here, in the dread tribunal of last resort, valor contended against valor. Here brave men struggled and died for the right as God gave them to see the right."

Mr. Stevenson was right -- " wholly and eternally right." Truth, justice, and patriotism unite in proclaiming that both sides fought and suffered for liberty as bequeathed by the Fathers-- the one for liberty in the union of the States, the other for liberty in the independence of the States.

While the object of these papers is to record my personal reminiscences and to perpetuate incidents illustrative of the character of the American soldier, whether he fought on the one side or the other, I am also moved to write by what I conceive to be a still higher aim; and that is to point out, if I can, the common ground on which all may stand; where justification of one section does not require or imply condemnation of the other--the broad, high, sunlit middle ground where fact meets fact, argument confronts argument, and truth is balanced against truth.

Chapter Nineteen

Secession? The North Said...Yes!

**Speech of Hon. Joseph Wheeler, of Alabama.
Richmond, Va., Dispatch, July 31, 1894**

**Opposition of Southern Colonists to Slavery.
Their Devotion to the Union.**

(Author's note: The Honorable Joseph Wheeler of Alabama was the same Confederate Civil War General Joseph "Fightin' Joe" Wheeler. After the War Wheeler served many years in the Congress of the United States representing his home District in the area of Pond Springs, Alabama. Following are key facts he imparted in this speech.)

On Friday, July 13th, 1894, the House of Representatives, being in Committee of the Whole on Appropriations and Expenditures, and having under consideration the bill to remove the charge of desertion standing against Patrick Kelleher, late private, Company C, Thirty-eighth Illinois Volunteers, Mr. Wheeler, of Alabama, as a member of the Committee on Military Affairs, made a speech which attracted widespread attention. The discussion, which became animated, led up to the causes of the late war and its immense expenditures. Mr. Wheeler brought out some startling historical facts. He said:

I did not intend or desire to enter into any discussion about the War, but in reply to the question of the distinguished gentleman from New York, General Curtis, I will say that these expenditures were caused by events which I deplored. The armies causing these immense expenditures were raised for reasons with which I was not in sympathy, and I regretted very much that they were raised. (Laughter and applause). I never

261

thought them necessary, because I believed then, as I believe now, that our appeals should have been heeded when we went on our knees at the Peace Congress, in Philadelphia, to beg for arbitration and peace, and to beg that some guarantee should be given that the Constitution of the country should be regarded.

Chief-Justice Chase told our Southern people, in his great speech of February 6, 1861, that neither he nor any of the leaders of the Republican party, could guarantee to the South that the party coming into power would obey the clause of the Constitution which pledged protection of the property of the people of the South. Mr. Chase said:

"The result of the national canvass (election) which recently terminated in the election of Mr. Lincoln (1860) has been spoken of by some as the effect of a sudden impulse or of some irregular excitement of the popular mind; and it has been somewhat confidently asserted that, upon reflection and consideration, the hastily-formed opinions which brought about the election will be changed. I cannot take this view of the result of the presidential election. I believe, and the belief amounts to absolute conviction, that the election must be regarded as a triumph of principles cherished in the hearts of the people of the (North). We have elected him (Mr. Lincoln). After many years of earnest advocacy and of severe trial we have achieved the triumph of that principle. By a fair and unquestioned majority we have secured that triumph. Do you think we, who represent this majority, will throw it away? Do you think the people will sustain us if we undertake to throw it away? I must speak to you plainly, gentlemen of the South. It is not in my heart to deceive you. I, therefore, tell you explicitly that if we of the North and West would consent to throw away all that has been gained in the recent triumph of our principles, the people would not sustain us, and so the consent would avail you nothing.

Mr. Chase, in that speech, with great force, gave the South to understand that the Northern States would not, and ought not, to comply with the obligations of the Federal Constitution. He said if the leaders attempted an enforcement of that part of the Constitution which the South demanded, the people of the North could not sustain them, and they would be powerless. But he said we may do this: We admit the contract, we admit the constitutional contract, and we may regard it similar to cases in chancery where circumstances have arisen that make a party unable to comply with his contract, and, therefore, the court decrees pecuniary compensation. There were many reasons which brought on the conditions which culminated in the war, which necessitated the vast expenditure of money which is exhibited in the table. The doctrine of States Rights, protective tariff, internal improvements, and in fact all the questions upon which the Democratic party differed with their political opponents, entered into the question.

I call attention to historical facts, which refute allegations that the responsibility of the (Civil) War rested altogether upon Southern people.

When the people of the South settled on the shores of Maryland, Virginia, the Carolinas, and Georgia, they had no intention of encouraging or even tolerating the institution of slavery. The thrifty New England seamen, in their voyages to the Indies and other countries, saw its practical operation, and solely with the view of profit in the transportation and sale of the African, they, with characteristic energy, urged upon all the Colonies the great advantages which would result from utilizing this character of labor. Their friends in the North readily acceded to their importunities, but not so with those of the South.

Oglethorpe and his colonists were possibly the most determined in resisting the importation, sale and use of African slaves; and for twenty years they were successful in the enforcement of the law which prohibited the landing of slaves in Georgia. Finally, together with the other Southern States, they succumbed, and the New England ship owners amassed fortunes by plying the business of buying negroes in Africa, transporting them to the United States, and selling them for the most part to Southern people. The evil of this traffic soon became apparent to the people of the South, and when the Constitution was framed in 1787, the South demanded that the fundamental law of our land should inhibit this traffic of importing human beings from Africa.

The South was resisted by the New England slave-traders, and as a compromise, it was agreed that the trade should be restricted, and after the year 1800, entirely prohibited, but, by the persistency of New England, the provision was finally extended to the year 1808.

It has been charged that the opposition of Southern slave-holders, which was manifested in the convention to the continued importation of slaves, was attributable to their desire to maintain the value of the slave property they already possessed, but contemporaneous writing clearly shows that the mass of these people were actuated by no such selfish motives. Very soon the people of the North found that their climate was not adapted to slave labor, and as the Constitution prohibited the continuance of the profitable business of catching or buying negroes in Africa and selling them to the people of the South, they ceased to have any interest in this class of property.

The Southern people loved the Union with a devotion which had no precedent in the history of the world. It was a work very largely of their creation. Their blood and treasures were freely given to secure its independence. The South gave to that sacred cause the voice and eloquence of Patrick Henry, to arouse the people to action; the pen of Jefferson, to write the Declaration that we were a free and independent people; the sword of Washington, to win the battles which made us one of the nations of the earth; and it also furnished Chief Justice Marshall, to proclaim the principles upon which American jurisprudence and civil liberty are founded. They were Southern with Washington who crossed the Alleghenies, one hundred and forty-one years ago, to defend the pioneers who were braving the dangers of the western forest. They were Southern men who, under Captain Gorman, hastened to the defense of Massachusetts at the first sound of battle at Concord and Lexington. In the war of 1812 the South gave her undivided support to the flag, and largely contributed to the success of our arms. The last battle of that war was fought by a Southern general, with Southern men, on Southern soil. In the Indian wars the South always furnished her full share of soldiers, and in the Mexican war the killed and wounded from the Southern States in proportion to population was about three times that of the States of the North.

In the (Civil) War of 1861-'65 the South furnished 640,000 to the Federal army, a larger number than it furnished to the Confederate army.

This was the only period during which there was any division of sentiment on this point among the Southern people, for since 1865 they have been as devoted to the flag and the Union as the people of any part of our land. The people of the South did not wish to give up the benefits of a government to the establishment of which they had so largely contributed.

They were loyal and law-abiding, and refused to follow the example of the participants in the Shay rebellion in New York, the whiskey rebellion in Pennsylvania, the Dorr rebellion in Rhode Island, and the Hartford convention rebellion in Connecticut; but they reluctantly succumbed to the conviction that the party about to take control would have no respect for their rights. For more than half a century they had been taught by their Northern brethren that when the people of a State found that it was not to their advantage to remain in the Union it was not only their privilege but their duty to peacefully withdraw from it.

Ninety years ago the people of Massachusetts expressed themselves in favor of the principle of secession by the enactment of the following resolution in the Massachusetts Legislature:

"That the annexation of Louisiana to the Union transcends the constitutional power of the Government of the United States. It formed a new Confederacy, to which the States united by the former compact are not bound to adhere.

It is clearly shown by the history of the times that the people of New England were very pronounced in their expressions that the Constitution recognized the unquestioned right of a State to secede from the Union. At the celebration of the fiftieth anniversary of the inauguration of Washington, April 30, 1839, ex-President John Quincy Adams delivered an address which was received with great approval by the people. In that speech Mr. Adams said:

"But the indissoluble union between the several States of this confederated nation is, after all, not in the right but in the heart. If the day should ever come (may Heaven avert it!) when the affections of the people of these States shall be alienated from each other; when the fraternal spirit shall give way to cold indifference, or collision of interest shall fester into hatred, the bands of political asseveration will not long hold together parties no longer attracted by the magnetism of conciliated interests and kindly sympathies; and far better will it be for the people of the disunited States to part in friendship from each other than to be held together by constraint. Then will be the time for reverting to the precedents which occurred at the formation and adoption of the Constitution, to form again a more perfect union by dissolving that which could no longer bind, and to leave the separated parts to be reunited by the law of political gravitation to the center."

It is very evident that Mr. Adams and the people of New England generally regarded these views as the correct interpretation of the original compact (Constitution) which bound the people together. I will call attention to the fact that three years later, January 24, 1842, he presented a petition to Congress from citizens of Haverhill, Mass. I read from Congressional Globe, volume XI, page 977:

MONDAY, January 24th.--In the House. Mr. Adams presented the petition of sundry citizens of Haverhill, in the State of Massachusetts, praying that Congress will immediately adopt measures favorably to dissolve the union of these States. First. Because no union can be agreeable and permanent which does not present prospects for reciprocal benefit; second, because a vast proportion of the revenues of one section of the Union is annually drained to sustain the views and course of another section, without any adequate return; third, because, judging from the history of past nations, that union, if persisted in, in the present state of things, will certainly overwhelm the whole nation in destruction.

This sentiment in favor of secession continually gained strength, and five years later the Legislature of Massachusetts passed another secession resolution. I read from "Acts and resolutions passed by the Legislature of Massachusetts in the year 1844," page 319:

1. Resolved, That the power to unite an independent foreign State with the United States is not among the powers delegated to the General Government by the Constitution of the United States.

2. Resolved, That the project of the annexation of Texas, unless arrested on the threshold, may drive these States into a dissolution of the Union.

3. Resolved, That his Excellency, the Governor, be requested to transmit a copy of the foregoing resolves to each of the Senators and Members of the House of Representatives of this Commonwealth in the Congress of the United States.

4. Resolved, That his Excellency, the Governor, be requested to transmit a copy of the same resolves to the Executive of the United States and of the several States.

Approved by the Governor, March 15, 1844.

A year later, February 22, 1845, the Legislature of Massachusetts celebrated Washington's birthday by passing still another secession resolution.

I read from the same volume, pages 598 and 599:

Resolved, That Massachusetts has never delegated the power to admit into the Union, States or Territories without or beyond the original territory of the States and Territories belonging to the Union at the adoption of the Constitution of the United States.

Resolved, and as the powers of legislation granted in the Constitution of the United States to Congress do not embrace the case of the admission of a foreign State or foreign Territory by legislation into the Union, such an act of admission would have no binding force whatever on the people of Massachusetts.

Resolved, That his Excellency, the Governor, be requested to transmit copies of the preceding report and resolves to the President of the United States, the several Senators and Representatives in Congress from this Commonwealth, and the Governors of the several States.

Approved by the Governor, February 22, 1845.

I beg to call special attention to the second resolution, and also to that part of the third resolution which directed the Governor to transmit copies of the resolution, etc. All this was a part of the history of our country when Mr. Lincoln was elected by the solid vote of the States of the North, opposed by the solid vote of the States of the South. A large part of the northern press contended that the States of the South had a full right to secede if the people desired to withdraw from the Union, and it was common to see in the northern press the words, "Erring sisters go in peace."

The Northern Press Advocates Secession

Mr. Lincoln's election was fully known on the evening of November 8, 1860, and the next morning, November 9th, Mr. Greeley's New York Tribune contained the following:

GOING TO GO.

If the (Southern) States shall become satisfied that they can do better out of the Union than in it, we insist on letting them go in peace. The right to secede may be a revolutionary one, but it exists, nevertheless.

And again, in the same issue of his widely-circulated and influential paper, Mr. Greeley said:

We must ever resist the asserted right of any State to remain in the Union and nullify or defy the laws thereof. To withdraw from the Union is quite another matter; and whenever a considerable section of our Union shall deliberately resolve to go out, we shall resist all coercive measures designed to keep it in. We hope never to live in a republic whereof one section is pinned to the residue by bayonets. Let them have both sides of the question fully presented; let them reflect, deliberate, then vote; and let the action of secession be the echo of an unmistakable popular fiat. A judgment thus rendered, a demand for separation so backed, would either be acquiesced in without the effusion of blood, or those who rushed upon carnage to defy and defeat it would place themselves clearly in the wrong.

The New York *Tribune* of November 16, 1860, again announced their views to the Southern people in an article headed "Secession In Practice," in which the paper used the following words:

Still we say, in all earnestness and good faith, whenever a whole section of this republic, whether a half, a third, or only a fourth, shall truly desire and demand a separation from the residue, we shall earnestly favor such separation. If the fifteen (Southern) States, or even the eight cotton States alone, shall quietly, decisively say to the rest: "We prefer to be henceforth separated from you," we shall insist that they be permitted to go in peace. War is a hideous necessity, at best, and a civil conflict, a war of estranged and embittered fellow-countrymen, is the most hideous of all wars. Whenever the people of the cotton States shall have definitely and decisively made up their minds to separate from the rest of us, we shall urge that the proper steps be taken to give full effect to their decision.

Three days afterward, on the 19th, the same paper uses these words:

Now, we believe and maintain that the Union is to be preserved only so long as it is beneficial and satisfactory to all parties concerned.

We do not believe that any man, any neighborhood, town, county, or even State, may break up the Union in any transient gust of passion; we fully comprehend that secession is an extreme, an ultimate resort--not a constitutional, but a revolutionary remedy. But we insist that this Union shall not be held together by force whenever it shall have ceased to cohere by the mutual attraction of its parts; and whenever the (Southern) States or the cotton States only shall unitedly and coolly say to the rest, "We want to get out of the Union," we shall urge that their request be acceded to.

The New York *Herald* of Friday, November 23, 1860, said:

The Disunion Question,
A Conservative Reaction in the South

We publish this morning a significant letter from Governor Letcher, of Virginia, on the subject of the present disunion excitement in the South; Southern constitutional rights, Northern-State acts of nullification, and the position of Virginia in this crisis. To this end would it not be well for the conservative Union men of the city of New York to make a demonstration, a northern movement or conciliation, concession and harmony? Coercion, in any event, is out of the question. A union held together by the bayonet would be nothing better than a military despotism. Conciliation and harmony, through mutual concessions, in a reconstruction of the fundamental law, between the North and the South, will restore and perpetuate the union contemplated by the fathers. So now that the conservative men of the South are moving, let the Union men of the North second their endeavors, and let New York, as in the compromise of 1850, lead the way.

And on the following day, November 24th, the *Tribune* says:

Federal Coercion

Some of the Washington correspondents telegraph that Mr. Buchanan is attempting to map out a middle course in which to steer his bark during the tempest which now howls about him. He is to condemn the asserted right of secession, but to assert in the same breath that he is opposed to keeping a State in the Union by what he calls Federal coercion. Now, we have no desire to prevent secession by coercion, but we hold this position to be utterly unsupported by law or reason. I will also quote an article from the New York *Daily Tribune*, Friday, November 30, 1860:

Are We Going to Fight?

But if the cotton States, generally, unite with her in seceding, we insist that they cannot be prevented, and that the attempt must not be made. Five millions of people, of whom at least half a million are able and willing to shoulder muskets, can never be subdued while fighting around and over their own hearthstones. If they could be, they would no longer be equal members of the Union, but conquered dependencies. We propose to wrest this potent engine from the disunionists by saying frankly to the (Southern) States:

If you choose to leave the Union, leave it, but let us have no quarrel about it. If you think it a curse to you and an unfair advantage to us, repudiate it, and see if you are not mistaken. If you are better by yourselves, go, and God speed you. For our part, we have done very well with you, and are quite willing to keep along with you, but if the association is irksome to you, we have too

much self-respect to insist on its continuance. We have lived by our industry thus far, and hope to do so still, even though you leave us.

We repeat, that only the sheen of northern bayonets can bind the South wholly to the evils of secession, but that may do it. Let us be patient, neither speaking daggers nor using them, standing to our principles, but not to our arms, and all will yet be well.

Each of these statements will command general assent. The only question likely to arise relates to the practical measures by which the" moderation and forbearance" can be displayed. And while the South Carolina Convention was in session, and before any State had seceded, and when it was doubted by many whether such action would be taken, Mr. Greeley said:

If it (the Declaration of Independence) justifies the secession from the British Empire of three million colonists in 1776, we do not see why it would not justify the secession of five millions of Southerners from the Federal Union in 1861. If we are mistaken on this point, why does not some one attempt to show wherein and why? For our own part, while we deny the right of slave-holders to hold slaves against the will of the latter, we cannot see how twenty millions of people can rightfully hold ten, or even five, in a detested union with them by military force. In the same issue of Mr. Greeley's paper we read the following:

If seven or eight contiguous States shall present themselves authentically at Washington, saying: We hate the Federal Union; we have withdrawn from it; we will give you the choice between acquiescing in our secession and arranging amicably all incidental questions on the one hand, and attempting to subdue us on the other, we could not stand up for coercion, for subjugation, for we do not think it would be just. We hold the right of self-government even when invoked in behalf of those who deny it to others. So much for the question of principle.

This conservative view of the question which Mr. Greeley gave to the world with such emphasis, and in which he expressed his opinion of the principle involved, was reiterated for days, weeks and months, with the characteristic persistence of that able leader. Mr. Greeley also said:

Any attempt to compel them by force to remain would be contrary to the principles enunciated in the immortal Declaration of Independence, contrary to the fundamental ideas on which human liberty is based.

These articles continued to appear in the northern press for months after the election of Mr. Lincoln, and until after most of the Southern States had seceded. They continued until after the people of the South had adopted a constitution, and organized their new Confederate Government; after they had raised and equipped an army, appointed ambassadors to foreign courts, and convened a congress; after they had taken possession of three fourths of the arsenals and forts within their territory, enrolled her as one of the nations of the earth. After all this, Mr. Greeley's paper continued to indorse the action of all Southern people as fully as it was possible for language to enable it to do so.

We have repeatedly said, and we once more insist, that the great principle embodied by Jefferson in the Declaration of American Independence, that governments derive their just powers from consent of the governed, is sound and just; and that if the cotton States, or the Gulf States only choose to form an independent nation, they have a clear, moral right to do so. Whenever it shall be clear that the great body of Southern people have become conclusively alienated from the Union, and anxious to escape from it, we will do our best to forward their views."

Mr. Greeley was earnestly and ably supported in his views by the most prominent men and able editors of Republican papers all over the North.

I cite the following from the *Commercial* which was certainly the leading Republican paper of Ohio. After Mr. Lincoln was inaugurated, the *Commercial* said:

We are not in favor of blockading the Southern coast. We are not in favor of retaking by force the property of the United States now in possession of the seceders. We would recognize the existence of a government formed of all the (Southern) States, and attempt to cultivate amicable relations with it.

In addition to all this, the commander of the Federal army, General Winfield Scott, was very emphatic in endorsing the views of the New York *Tribune* and other papers, to the effect that secession was the proper course for the Southern people to pursue, and his oft-repeated expression, "Wayward sisters, part in peace," seemed to meet the full approval of the great body of the people of the North. In obedience to all this advice, the Southern States did secede, and almost immediately the vast Federal armies were raised, battles were fought, money expended, and this, let me tell my friend from New York, was the cause of the vast appropriations regarding which he asked an explanation.

These appropriations were made to carry on the most stupendous war recorded in modern history. From April 15; 1861, to the close of the war, there were called into the service of the United States 2,865,028 soldiers. Besides this we have had evidence placed before Congress of numerous organizations called into service by the Governors or other officials of border States, which would probably number 500,000 men. That these men were brave is proved by the terrible casualties of the battles which they fought. The struggle from May 5 to May 12, 1864; at the Wilderness and Spotsylvania, which should really be called one battle, was a good index of the sanguinary character of the conflict. The losses of Grant's army in that conflict, as reported in Scribner's statistical record, was 9,774 killed, 41,150 wounded, and 13,254 missing. It gives an idea of the magnitude of this conflict to recall that General Grant's loss in killed and wounded in this battle was greater than the loss in killed and wounded in all the battles of all the wars in this country prior to 1861.

The loss in all the battles of the seven years of the Revolution was 2,200 killed, and 6,500 wounded. The loss in the army of 1812 was 1,877 killed and 3,737 wounded. The loss in the war with Mexico was 1,049 killed and 7,929 wounded; in all, only 19,227 men. Now, if we add all the losses of the Indian wars, including the French and Indian war, the entire loss would be less than half the killed and wounded in this great battle.

As another evidence of the gallantry of the officers and soldiers, I will mention that during that war forty-six generals of the United States army and seventy-six generals of the Confederate army were killed at the head of their commands in battle.

I have given an explanation of this matter to the best of my ability, and from the standpoint of one whose feelings were and are in entire sympathy with the Southern people, but who since the close of that war has been as devoted to the Union of the States and the prosperity, welfare, and glory of our country as the most distinguished soldier who fought in the Federal army from 1861 to 1865.

Bibliography

The Boys From Lake County

Helen Keller Public Library, Tuscumbia, AL, Judy Murphy, Head Librarian.

The War of the Rebellion, A Compilation of the Official Records of the Union and Confederate Armies. Begun 1865. Published 1899.

Rome Courier, Rome, Georgia.

Rome Library, Rome, Georgia

The Capture of Fort Donelson, Maj. Gen Lew Wallace, U.S.V.

National Archives of the United States of America, Washington.

Historical Times Encyclopedia of the Civil War, Edited by Patricia L. Faust

A Review of Streight's Raid, Rucker Agee, President Alabama Historical Society

The Prisoner of War and How Treated, Lt. A.C. Roach, 51st Indiana Volunteer Infantry, 1865

The Railroad City Publishing House, Col. Abel D. Streight, Proprietor, North-East Corner Washington and Meridian Streets, Indianapolis, Indiana, 1865

State of Alabama, Department of Archives & History, Montgomery, Alabama

Confederate Wizards of the Saddle, Bennett H. Young, 1914.

Libby Prison, Richmond, Virginia. Official Publication #12, Richmond Civil War Centennial Committee, 1961-1965, no copyright claimed, compiled by R. W. Wiatt, Jr.

Walls That Talk. Published by R. E. Lee Camp, No. I. C. V., 1884.

University of West Florida Library, Special Collections Department, Pensacola, Florida

Life of Lieutenant-General Nathan Bedford Forrest, John Allen Wyeth, 1899, 1904, 1908.

General Forrest, Capt. J. Harvey Mathes, 1902.

The Artillery of Nathan Bedford Forrest's Cavalry, John Watson Morton, 1909.

Emma Sansom, An Alabama Heroine, Thomas M. Owen, 1904.

Battles and Sketches of the Army of Tennessee, Ridley L. Bromfield. 1906

The Capture of Streight, Major M. H. Clift, 1906

Bill Arp So Called, Fifth Paper, Battle of Rome, Charles H. Smith (Bill Arp) 1866

Bill Arp's Peace Papers, Fifth Paper, Battle of Rome, Charles H. Smith (Bill Arp) 1873.

Extracts From Report of the Committee of the Senate, Testimony taken at Birmingham, Alabama 1883, Margaret Ketcham Ward.

Memorial Record of Alabama, Military History of the State, General Joseph Wheeler, 1893.

7th Regiment Illinois Volunteer Infantry, Chapter IX Corinth - Town Creek, D. Leib Ambrose, 1868.

A History of Rome and Floyd County, Part III, Chapter IV, Streight's Raiders Captured By Forrest, George Battey Magruder, Jr. 1922.

The Battle of Atlanta and Other Campaigns, Campaign up the Tennessee River Valley, Major-General Grenville M. Dodge, 1911

Recollections, Chapter XIII, Pursuit of the Streight's Raiders, Thomas D. Duncan, 1922.

Lieut. Gen. N. B. Forrest, General Thomas Jordan & J. P. Pryor, 1868.

History of Lake County, The Reverend Timothy H. Ball, Baptist Minister, 1872.

History of Lake County, Volume XI, The Lake County Historical Society, 1934.

Richard C. Schmal, Historian, Lowell, Lake County, Indiana

Miriam K. Baughman, Family Genealogy, West Canton, Ohio

Civil War in Indiana, Web Site. www.civilwarindiana.com

Civil War Preservation Trust

Richmond Dispatch, Richmond, Virginia, July 1894

Confederate Correspondence, Orders, and Returns Relating to Operations in Kentucky, Southwestern Virginia, Tennessee, Northern and Central Georgia, Mississippi, Alabama, and West Florida From March 16 June 30, 1865.

Earl C. Baughman, Family Genealogy, St. Petersburg, Florida

Cover Art, "Union Standard Bearer" Don Troiana, www.historicalartprints.com

Book Layout, Trent's Prints, Pace, Florida

Printed in the United States
66549LVS00004B/229-249

9 780979 044342